Buster

A Canadian Patriot and Imperialist
The Life and Times of Brigadier James Sutherland Brown

by Atholl Sutherland Brown

Foreword by Stephen J. Harris

Buster

A Canadian Patriot and Imperialist

Buster

A Canadian Patriot and Imperialist

The Life and Times of Brigadier James Sutherland Brown

---

by Atholl Sutherland Brown

Foreward by Stephen J. Harris

2004

Co-published by the Laurier Centre for Military Strategic
and Disarmament Studies, Wilfrid Laurier University,
Waterloo, Ontario, N2L 3C5
www.canadianmilitaryhistory.com

Note for Librarians: a cataloguing record for this book that includes Dewey Decimal
Classification and US Library of Congress numbers is available from the Library and Archives
of Canada. The complete cataloguing record can be obtained from their online database at:
www.collectionscanada.ca/amicus/index-e.html
ISBN 1-4120-2522-2
Cover portrait by Ina Uhthoff, ca 1938.
Frontispiece: Colonel James Sutherland Brown, DSO in 1916.
Author photograph William Rodney.
Cover design by author and Brian Grant.
Printed in Victoria, BC, Canada

Includes Bibliographical references and Index.
1. Canada, 2. Canada - Military history, 3. Canada - Armed Forces, 4. Great War - 1914-1918,
5. Defence of Canada, 6. Unemployment Relief Camps, 7. Biography, I. Laurier Centre of
Military Strategic and Disarmament Studies, II Title.

TRAFFORD

Offices in Canada, USA, Ireland, UK and Spain
This book was published *on-demand* in cooperation with Trafford Publishing. On-demand
publishing is a unique process and service of making a book available for retail sale to the
public taking advantage of on-demand manufacturing and Internet marketing. On-demand
publishing includes promotions, retail sales, manufacturing, order fulfilment, accounting and
collecting royalties on behalf of the author.
Book sales for North America and international:
Trafford Publishing, 6E–2333 Government St.,
Victoria, BC V8T 4P4 CANADA
phone 250 383 6864 (toll-free 1 888 232 4444)
fax 250 383 6804; email to orders@trafford.com
Book sales in Europe:
Trafford Publishing (UK) Ltd., Enterprise House, Wistaston Road Business Centre,
Wistaston Road, Crewe, Cheshire CW2 7RP UNITED KINGDOM
phone 01270 251 396 (local rate 0845 230 9601)
facsimile 01270 254 983; orders.uk@trafford.com
Order online at:
www.trafford.com/robots/04-0350.html

10 9 8 7 6 5 4

The splendour falls on castle walls

And snowy summits old in story:

The long light shakes across the lakes,

And the wild cataract leaps in glory:

Blow, bugle, blow, set the wild echoes flying,

Blow, bugle; answer, echoes, dying, dying, dying.

Nocturne
Lord Alfred Tennyson

By the Same Author

Silently into the Midst of Things, 177 Squadron Royal Air Force in Burma 1943-1945: History and Narratives

British Columbia's Geological Surveys, 1895 – 1995, A Century of Science and Dedication

Technical

Geology of the Queen Charlotte Islands
BC Geological Survey Bulletin 54

Porphyry Deposits of the Canadian Cordillera
Editor and a Principal Author
Canadian Institute of Mining and Metallurgy Special Vol 15

Lithoprobe: Southern Vancouver Island
(with C.J. Yorath and N.W.D. Massey)
Geological Survey of Canada Bulletin 498

Foreword

By Dr. Stephen J. Harris
Chief Historian of DND and author of *Canadian Brass*

I first encountered James Sutherland ("Buster") Brown during the summer between high school and university. It was 1965, and I was reading Volume 1 of James Eayrs' *In Defence of Canada – From the Great War to the Great Depression.*

Both Jameses impressed. Eayrs wrote well, of course, but it was the story he told that enthralled: who, back then, could have believed that Canada once had a military plan to invade the United States.

The author of the plan was no less fascinating. Eayrs portrayed him as sort of out of touch with reality, perhaps slightly mad, yet for someone my age at that time there was something romantically noble about Brown's devotion to safeguarding Canada's dignity and independence. Little wonder, then, that as the tide of anti-Americanism grew a few years later during the Vietnam era, brigades of "Buster Brown" protesters operated at its fringes. Something about his patriotism had clearly resonated.

I next met Brown in Charles Taylor's *Six Journeys.* Taylor also dealt with Defence Scheme No. 1, but this was a different Brown: not an eccentric or a fool, but a man legitimized as reflecting an "authentic Canadian tradition" – loyalist tory, with a social conscience, an abiding distrust of the United States, and no love for technology. Above all, an empire man.

A few years later, Brown became an important figure in *Canadian Brass.* Unable to agree with Eayrs, I argued that when he crafted Defence Scheme No. 1 he was only doing the job any professional soldier in his position had to do: accept that Canada's one contiguous neighbour might one day not be friendly, do the necessary sums, and plan for 'homeland' defence accordingly.

I argued that Brown did not assume a *casus belli* based on the Canadian – American relationship or even American Manifest Destiny in North America. Rather, he foresaw a clash between the United States and the British Empire, a clash in which Canada would inevitably become a principal battleground – precisely the same scenario British staff officers in Canada had worried about before 1914. Canada's only hope, Brown deduced, was to buy time by making a quick (and unexpected) foray into the United States and then fighting a defensive battle on American soil until help arrived from, Britain, India, and the rest of the empire.

My Brown was clearly not Eayrs' Brown, but I changed nothing in Taylor's portrait because all I had to worry about was Brown, the peacetime staff officer – whose colleagues accepted the need for what he wrote down. What follows is more rounded, more complete, and written from within. Atholl Sutherland Brown presents his father as a more complex man than the rest of us found: Grit in the beginning, not Tory: raised Presbyterian: and while of Loyalist stock, not doggedly anti-American. A professional soldier who could lead as well as write military plans, and who appears to have won the affection of the majority of those who served with him. Not a technocrat, to be sure, but a man consumed with the dignity of human life – a far more sympathetic character than Andy McNaughton, the man who put paid to Buster's military career.

Canada has changed since I first read about James Sutherland Brown, and the existence of Defence Scheme No. 1 is no longer a revelation. I'm unsure therefore, whether this story of his life will resonate the way Eayrs' did forty years ago, no matter how good the telling. But for his part Charles Taylor was right. Even if the Sutherland Brown presented here differs from the archtype described in *Six Journeys*, he still represents an "authentic" Canadian tradition worth reading about – and knowing.

Table of Contents

Foreword   vii

Buster - A Canadian Patriot and Imperialist   1

1   Out of Scotland   5

2   Hatched   13

3   Regimental Officer   25

4   Camberley   39

5   In The Great War,
Canada's Apprenticeship, 1914-1916   45

6   In the Great War,
Canada's Triumph, 1917-1918   69

7   Capital Ideas   93

8   Imperial Defence   123

9   Work Point   131

10   Hard Times   155

11   Old Sweats and Aide-de-Camp, 1933 -1951   173

Epilogue   191

Reference Notes   193

Acknowledgments & Primary Sources   199

Bibliography   201

Glossary   205

Appendix A - Staff Positions of a Canadian Division,
1914-1918   207

Appendix B - Rank, Appointments, Qualifications and
Awards Held by James Sutherland Brown   208

Appendix C - Report to the Secretary of DND on
Unemployment Relief, 24 May, 1933   210

Appendix D - Memorandum Re Retirement of
Brigadier J. Sutherland Brown, CMG, DSO   214

Index   219

List of Photographs

Cover: front cover portrait by Ina Uhthoff, ca 1938

Frontispiece: Colonel James Sutherland Brown, DSO in 1916 · · · · · · · · · · · ii

1-1   New Simcoe Armories built in 1913. · · · · · · · · · · · · · · · · · 11

2-1   Bugle band of the 39th Norfolk Rifles about 1897, James on right. · · · 14

2-2   Norfolk Rifles on parade at Niagara-on-the-Lake in 1896. · · · · · · · · 16

2-3   1st Lt. James Sutherland Brown of the Norfolk Rifles in
        about 1902. · 17

2-4   Colonel William Dillon Otter at Niagara-on-the-Lake in 1904. · · · · · · 22

3-1   Lt. James Sutherland Brown, Royal Canadian Regiment,
        about 1906. · 26

3-2   RCR Officers at Halifax in 1909. · · · · · · · · · · · · · · · · · · · 28

3-3   Clare Corsan, James' future wife, sailing on Lake Simcoe
        about 1913. · 31

3-4   RCR Officers at Sydney, NS, during coal strike, winter 1910-11. · · · · 32

5-1   Lt. General Sir Sam Hughes about 1915. · · · · · · · · · · · · · · · · 48

5-2   Major James (Buster) Sutherland Brown with Lt. Col.
        James MacBrien, Salisbury Plain, 1914. · · · · · · · · · · · · · · · · 52

5-3   Wagons of 1st Canadian Mounted Rifles near Stonehenge, 1914. · · · · 53

5-4   Lt. General Alderson and his 1st Canadian Division Staff,
        winter 1915-16. · 58

5-5   Buster's and Clare's Wedding party in Southampton, June 1916. · · · · 63

5-6   Tanks going forward, PoWs coming back. · · · · · · · · · · · · · · · 64

6-1   Prime Minister Borden reviewing the 1st Brigade before
        Vimy Ridge. · 70

6-2   Transporting shells to the front before the Battle of Vimy Ridge. · · · · 72

6-3   Transport van bogged down, 1917. · · · · · · · · · · · · · · · · · · 72

6-4   Ammunition dump at the end of light rail transport, 1917. · · · · · · · 75

6-5   Maj. Gen. A.C. Macdonell and staff at forward
        observation post, 1918. · 79

6-6   Maj. Gen. Macdonell and senior staff, Buster centre right, 1918. · · · · · 80

6-7   The Prince of Wales reviewing the 4th Division at Demain,
        October 1918. · 87

6-8   Gens. Currie and Macdonell at the German frontier
        November 1918. · 89

6-9   General Currie taking the salute of 1st Division, Buster third left. · · · · 90

7-1   Baba Blackwell on guard, about 1927. · · · · · · · · · · · · · · · · · 94

7-2   Buster, Director of Organization, with colleagues waiting
        for an early demobilization train in North Toronto, April 1919. · · · · · 96

7-3   Buster and Andy McNaughton (?) at Camp Borden
       with CAF, 1922. ·100

7-4   Canadian 'spies' in New York, 1923. · · · · · · · · · · · · · · · · ·106

7-5   Buster and family at camp at Petawawa, 1926 · · · · · · · · · · · · ·115

8-1   Imperial Defence College class, London, in 1928, Buster centre left. ·124

8-2   Clare in court dress, 1928. ·128

9-1   Buster encounters children's party at Work Point Barracks, 1932. · · ·132

9-2   PPCLI troops rest during manoeuvres, 1930. · · · · · · · · · · · · · ·135

9-3   Church Parade, 16th Canadian Scottish, Duncan, 1930,
       Buster saluting. ·140

9-4   Buster at cavalry camp, Vernon, 1931. · · · · · · · · · · · · · · · · ·142

9-5   HMS Dauntless discovered and attacked on Combined
       Operations training, 1930. ·144

9-6   Leyland lorry tried out during field manoeuvres, 1931. · · · · · · · · ·146

9-7   Buster with Cmdr. Leonard Murray greeting Prince Svasti
       of Siam in Victoria, 1931. ·150

10-1   General McNaughton, CGS 1929-36. · · · · · · · · · · · · · · · · · ·158

10-2   DND Unemployment Relief Camp, Michel BC, 1934. · · · · · · · · · ·165

11-1   Buster at Army and Navy Veterans Association, about 1945. · · · · · ·179

11-2   Buster and Clare at Christmas Ball at Government House
       with His Hon. and Mrs. Eric Hamber, 1939. · · · · · · · · · · · · · ·180

11-3   Buster, retired, with General Ashton and
       16th Scottish Colonels, 1934. ·182

11-4   Army supply tender, Brigadier Sutherland Brown, about 1943. · · · ·186

11-5   Buster and Clare welcome their youngest son home, 1945. · · · · · · ·188

List of Figures and Maps

Figure 1 - Sutherland Brown Coat of Arms and Crest · · · · · · · · · · · · · ·19

Map 1 - Western Front in the Great War. ·60

Map 2 - West Coast Region in the 1930s. ·134

Map 3 - Victoria in the 1930s. ·176

Buster - A Canadian Patriot and Imperialist

Introduction

When I was young I didn't know my father was a hero. As a child I loved him scarcely less than my mother. As a youth I respected him but rather feared him because of my own fecklessness and his strong sense of discipline. As a man I started to glimpse his heroism but not until middle age, when he was gone, did I properly comprehend.

> "Heroes show very human traits, including vulnerability, and have basic human needs. They experience reversals of fortunes. They face dilemmas requiring the suppression of personal desires in the service of some larger good. And the nobility with which they bear their suffering and come to grips with their setbacks is ultimately a crucial dimension of their heroic nature."[1]

Charles Taylor in his book, *Six Journeys: A Canadian Pattern*, recognizes the personalities of his subjects (including Brigadier James Sutherland Brown) as being heroic.[2] He quotes George Woodcock in the heading of his introduction as follows; "Canadians do not like heroes so they do not have them. They do not have great men in the accepted sense of the word." Taylor in his introduction goes on to say: "More than most people, Canadians are prejudiced in favour of the ordinary: it is a function of our history, our climate and our geography. In a harsh land, we still honour all those pioneering virtues which impose restraint and engender mediocrity. Despite this reluctance to acknowledge greatness in our midst, it is nevertheless clear we have produced some remarkable people whose qualities verge on heroic. Their society seldom heeds them. Sometimes it opposes them, although the opposition is almost underhand. It is not so much a case of destroying these disturbing visionaries, as making them irrelevant. When Sutherland Brown began to embarrass his political and military masters, they avoided an open confrontation, dispatched him with a flurry of memos. Perhaps this technique is particularly Canadian in its furtiveness..."

I am the third son of my father, James Sutherland Brown, and have felt for some time that he deserves a biographical study to put him in perspective with his times and the events of an important part of Canada's history. Previous studies such as Charles Taylor's did not deal adequately with his origins, wartime history nor his life after his resignation from the Canadian Army. This work tries to correct that. Such an enterprise, however, is burdened with difficulties. "Family biography is always a risky enterprise. Those who write about their previously [relatively little] known fathers usually attract more psychological analysis than literary criticism. Affection is said to outweigh judgement. Motives - from hope of expiating youthful sins to an attempt to establish a dynasty - are examined in more detail than the book they are assumed to have provoked. The son can only escape the allegation of dubious intention if the father is so intrinsically interesting that, filial piety aside, he deserves a biography. Even then it must be written with affectionate objectivity and relate its subject to the history of the time. Ideally it should tell the story of an age as well as a man"[3]

My father, James Sutherland Brown, led an interesting life as a professional soldier which made him well known to a limited segment of the Canadian public. Later, as Buster Brown, he became known to a larger segment which had little idea of his history or beliefs but which, rightly or wrongly, made him an icon of anti-Americanism. He grew up in fairly affluent circumstances in Southern Ontario but steered his own course in life until in late career when he came into conflict with his immediate superior, formerly a friend, and some of the latter's colleagues or, unkindly, lackeys. He has been the principal subject of several books, theses or articles and two CBC docudramas, *The Attack of the Killer Mouse*, and *The Great Unfinished Task of Colonel J. Sutherland Brown* that focused mainly on these conflicts and the reasons for them. The controversies have also been central to a number of other books and articles about the history of the defence of Canada. In all these works attention scarcely turned to his roots, early development, his 'crossing of the floor', distinguished service in the Great War, most aspects of his last command or how he bore himself after his eclipse. In fact, he has really not been seen as a many facetted man, let alone a hero, but instead lampooned as a cardboard cut out of Colonel Blimp. The complexity of his nature, his grasp of history and his profession, his ability to engender enthusiasm and support of his troops, senior and particularly junior ranks, or the origins of his attitudes received either scant attention or were interpreted wrongly.

That he was a Canadian patriot and an Imperialist is scarcely in doubt as not only did he see himself as such but so did his friends and detractors.[4] Patriot currently has a slightly unpleasant nuance, although real or true, Canadian does not. In current terminology he could be said to have been a true Canadian who believed the British Empire was a force for good in the world. He was a firm believer in Pax Britannica.

There is voluminous material on James Sutherland Brown's life and career, but he left a dearth of personal material about his origins, family or personal feelings. Unfortunately his loving wife, Clare, had his diaries burnt after his death worrying that they might be an embarrassment as much as for the problem of storing them in reduced accommodation. Her own Scottish family is fully documented from its emigration from Northern Ireland in 1821. Buster's background and early life were to me, the youngest son, a thin mist of rumour, myth and fact. His great-great grandfather emigrated from the Loch Fyne area of Scotland to Massachusetts in approximately 1750. Fortunately in the mid to late 19th century the family was fairly prominent in Simcoe, Ontario, and consequently well reported upon in the local newspapers. Still this leaves much to be desired regarding personal and family information, and requires some conjecture to fill out the canvas.

Sources of information on my father's life and times are numerous but dominated by his personal papers that reside in the Archives of Queen's University at Kingston. Other sources include papers from the Department of National Defence acquired through Access to Information, microfilm of newspapers including the *Simcoe Reformer, Sydney Record* and the *Victoria Daily Colonist*. The references in the bibliography all provide useful information but particularly Stephen J. Harris' *Canadian Brass*; Charles Taylor's *Six Journeys, a Canadian Pattern*, Richard H. Gimblett's *Buster Brown: the Man and his Clash with Andy McNaughton*. Richard A. Preston's *Buster Brown was not Alone: American Plans for the Invasion of Canada, 1919-1939*; James Eayrs' *In Defence of Canada*, Volume 1. Curiously James Sutherland Brown is not mentioned in John Swettenham's *Andy McNaughton*, a biography of his nemesis. Shirley Render's *The Inside story of Double Cross: James Richardson and Canadian Airways* reveals another side of McNaughton not noted in Swettenham's biography. This side is further revealed by Jack Granatstein in his book *The Generals* in regard to military qualities.

Material is endless for background to the Great War and the Canadian campaigns, and many new books are still being published. Among the latter are John Keegan's *The First World War*, Denis Winter's *Haig's Command*, Tony Ashworth's *Trench Warfare, 1914-1918, the Live and Let Live System*, Philip Warner's *World War One, A Chronological Narrative*, Morton and Granatstein's, *Marching to Armageddon*; John Swettenham's, *To Seize the Victory*, and for atmosphere, a novel by Sebasian Faulk called *Birdsong*. The view of Canadian soldiers in the trenches is portrayed vividly by *The Journal of Private Fraser* and the *Letters of Agar Adamson*. The official Canadian history of the World War was not published until 1962, *The Canadian Expeditionary Force*, by G.W.L. Nicholson. About the same age is A.J.P. Taylor's cynical and revisionist, *The First World War, an Illustrated History*.

Unfortunately for this biography, no contemporaries or significant subordinates are alive to interview and even my eldest brother, who would have had useful information, is now dead. Malcolm and I were significant informants to Charles Taylor so there is some circularity in quoting him but he conducted much research and had his own insights. I did, however, arrange and attend Taylor's interview with General Pearkes and have my own memories of it. There are, of course, other relevant personal memories, family photographs and memorabilia for my guidance. The large photographs used in this book are intended to amplify the text by lending an air of reality to the contemporary environment of the day. They show incidental intelligence of an increasingly remote past: the individual dress, the vehicles and horses, the buildings. Some things remain remarkably the same while others have changed significantly. They also reveal many elements of the personality and character of the the players in this story which small photos wouldn't.

1   Out of Scotland

My father's family origins are not well documented. No family portraits or bible have come down through my father to my generation in contrast to such material from my mother's family. My paternal grandfather was a third son which might explain this. Amongst my father's personal papers that were not destroyed is a hand written skeletal family tree, from father to son for five generations, with dates of birth, death and residence but without spouses or siblings. This holograph was written on the back of a letter from Burke's Peerage Limited, dated March 1938 requesting data for the company's preparation of a volume, Burke's Companionage, a work listing recipients of British Orders to which, as a Companion of St. Michael and St. George, James Sutherland Brown belonged. Another source of information is the text accompanying the Coat of Arms he was granted in 1929. Hence my father had much information that was not adequately communicated to my generation. Detailed factual information about his family in the late 19th century was gathered from the pages of the principal local weekly newspaper, the *Norfolk Reformer*, later called the *Simcoe Reformer*.[1] Census data from 1851 and vital statistics obtained at the Archives of the Eva Brooks Donly Museum in Simcoe also provide confirmatory data with slight inconsistencies partly related to mistakes in interpreting hand writing. Thus for the last three generations my father's list has been proven accurate except for purposeful errors about one of his siblings (*see later*).

The family probably originated in the village of Kilfinan in the Loch Fyne area of western Scotland. Kilfinan is an attractive small village set on the side of green hills, which roll down to the sheltered blue inlet of Loch Fyne. The village today consists of an old church and graveyard, a pleasant gabled white stone country inn, a few houses and two great estates. Presumably before the Highland Clearances it might have been larger. The Browns are a sept of Clan Lamont but there are few legible headstones with that name in the graveyard. However, there are many for Lamonts, and there is a private crypt under the church dedicated to them. Some headstones date to the 16th century. Curiously, the McNaughton family were said to come from the same area.[2]

The progenitor of the family was McArthur Brown of unknown birth date. Family legend has it that he was involved in the Jacobite uprising of 1745 led by Charles Stuart, the Young Pretender, but his emigration may just as well have been caused by the Highland Clearances, or possibly by both. McArthur Brown left for America about 1750 and settled in Massachusetts. Loch Fyne, then as now, must have been an attractive area in which to live, so something, either ambition, fear of reprisal, or the Clearances must have driven him to depart. Curiously, many Scottish Jacobites who emigrated to America twenty-five years before the American Revolution, after it, moved to Canada to be under the Georgian Crown rather than remain in the Republic. McArthur Brown was one of these so therefore would be a United Empire Loyalist by definition. He died in Canada in 1798.

His son Chauncey Brown was born in 1772, presumably in Massachusetts, but must have moved with his family when he was a child and lived most of his life in York (Toronto). Not much is known about him except that he died in 1832. His son, Augustus McArthur Brown was born in York in 1810. He apparently moved to Simcoe fairly early in his life and became a successful merchant in the area as was noted in a repetitive feature of the *Reformer*, Fifty Years Ago.[3] The census of 1851 lists he and his wife Henrietta as residents of Simcoe. Curiously his birth place is listed as England but his religion as Church of Scotland. Family members are not listed in Simcoe in the censuses of 1861 or 1871 so they must have moved out of Simcoe, possibly to the USA. The nature of Augustus Brown's business is not described. Possibly he retained some interest in it and in Simcoe for two of his sons moved back there or to the nearby village of Jarvis, 15 kilometres to the east, where they ran a business that traded into the USA. In his old age Augustus McArthur Brown lived in the town of Fulton near Oswego in New York State. His second wife, Juliet, who was the mother of his third son, Frank Augustus Brown, died there in 1888. After her death Augustus McArthur Brown was a frequent visitor to Simcoe to stay with Frank Augustus and his family which included the young James Sutherland Brown. His last visit was in September 1887, less than a year before he died and when James was just six.

Frank Augustus Brown was born in Simcoe in 1848. He was not listed as a resident in the census of 1861. In the more detailed census of 1901 Frank Augustus Brown is listed as moving to Simcoe in 1870 when he would have been 22. He was shown as a US citizen who was naturalized in 1888. In the census of 1881 Frank Augustus and his wife are listed but the census must have been recorded just before James was born.

The nature of McArthur Brown's business is not clear from any source. It also is not clear whether the same business continued after moving to New York State or whether Frank Augustus with one of his brothers, Chauncey as partner, took it over. The latter is likely and probably gave Frank a flying start in life. By 1883 Frank was a substantial person in the town and said by the *Simcoe Reformer* to be a 'capital citizen'.[4] He was also a City Councillor between 1889 and 1893. Frank Augustus was the principal merchant in Simcoe and Norfolk County dealing in farm produce and stock, but particularly in eggs for export to the USA. In 1889 he shipped 248 000 dozen eggs to the US market, chiefly Buffalo and New York City.[5] In fact, he was the second largest shipper of eggs in Canada.[6] His business was greatly harmed by the passage of the McKinley Bill in the United States House in October 1890 because it levied high import duties on Canadian products. That Frank was a perceptive and aggressive businessman is confirmed by his action in getting two railway cars full of eggs across the border hours before the McKinley Bill became law, saving nearly a thousand dollars in duties, a considerable sum in 1890. His business recovered quickly partly by finding new and unlikely markets such as England and partly by applying new technology. He proved to be in the vanguard of his times in the latter. He was among the first to use refrigeration and other processes for preserving eggs and the first to have a residential phone in Simcoe.[7] He was quoted as an authority on the export of farm produce.[8] He was a frequent visitor to Buffalo and New York City before and after the McKinley Bill to promote his business. His brother, Chauncey, was originally his partner in Simcoe but moved to Johnsville, NY, where he was probably Frank's agent.[9] In 1900 he formed a new partnership with a Mr. E. Edmonds to bolster his business.[10] However, not much was heard of Mr. Edmonds subsequently so the partnership must have languished.

Frank Augustus Brown was also a horse fancier and owner of prize carriage horses, some of which were used in his business where he employed three pairs on the road continuously.[11] His horses not only won prizes in the County Fairs but Frank went on to judge at such fairs. He also shipped prize horses to the USA.[12] Apart from his enthusiasm for horses, his intensity at his work and his involvement in civic affairs, Frank appears to have engaged in few sports or hobbies. He did not shoot, fish or play golf which all of his colleagues appeared to enjoy.

Frank Augustus Brown in 1879 married Mary Ann Horne, called Annie, the daughter of John Horne and Margaret McIntosh of Scotch Line, Woodhouse, a village 20 kilometres to the north. John Horne was a pioneer settler, farmer, a Presbyterian elder and a Temperance advocate. For their time the Hornes lived to advanced ages, she to 89.

Frank and Annie had four children: James Sutherland born on 27 June 1881, Margaret (Maggie) L. on 28 August, 1884, Julia M. on 23 March 1887 and John (Jack) H. on 26 December 1888. Maggie was tragically burned to death when she was only seventeen.[13] She was cleaning gloves with gasoline in the evening when it ignited from a nearby lamp and her night clothes caught on fire. She ran down the stairs where her mother wrapped her in a blanket but it was too late. Maggie died a day later and her mothers hands were badly burned. Maggie was said to be of "amiable and lovable disposition and of many endowments. Her musical ability was of a high order." She was the principal soloist at a number of local concerts. Her death had a traumatic effect on the whole family.

Frank Augustus Brown clearly was civically minded, a clever and hard working businessman and a devoted family man. He was involved to a considerable degree in the town's affairs for he was a City Councillor for four years and not uncommonly quoted in the Reformer as an advocate of progressive civic measures such as a new waterworks. These activities seemed to have been prompted by others who knew his capabilities, but he appears to have done them mostly as a duty rather than from ambition. He really did not take a prominent role in municipal, provincial or national politics because he was busy with his firm and committed to his family. He certainly had his chances to enter politics; the Hon. James Sutherland, MP, variously Chief Liberal Whip and a Minister in the Laurier government, was a close friend, mentor and godfather to his elder son. Frank was also a good friend of Hal B. Donly, publisher and editor of the *Reformer*. It would seem he could have had an easy route to a political career had he wished.

Simcoe may have been a United Empire Loyalist town but it was dominated by Methodists and their allies (not Anglicans) and by Grits (not Tories). Frank and his family were Presbyterians as were his ancestors but obviously not strong ones like his father-in-law. Like most of the prominent Grit citizens he was also a Mason, although again he did not appear to hold high office in the order. In addition, he was a member of the Ancient Order of United Workmen, hardly compatible with Toryism. In fact, Frank Augustus Brown was a Grit, Liberal, or Reformer, whichever name one chooses, if by choice not a very active or vocal one. Gimblett has a whole section of his thesis on the Loyalist tradition which states it is linked to Toryism and seemed to have no knowledge of Frank's and the youthful James' Grit allegiance. Similarly F.A. Brown, though part of a United Empire Loyalist family, seems very unlikely to have been anti-American considering his business dealings, his temporary American citizenship and his many family connections in the USA. This produces a paradox regarding his son James, given the usual custom of the times that sons followed their fathers in religion, politics and trade; James certainly was not indoctrinated into Toryism or anti-Americanism at home.

Frank Augustus appears to have been a caring man for he took in Annie's sister, Elen, when she was seriously ill when only in her thirties and the family looked after her until she died. He also sent his wife away for three months to live with another sister, Isabelle, on Georgian Bay to recover her own health. It would appear that Annie was not socially minded, she was never reported in the Reformer as being a hostess of parties, perhaps because of her strict Presbyterian upbringing, she did not approve of them. Nor was she said to partake in a social mode of the times; that of frequent overnight visits to nearby family or friends. The Frank Augustus Brown family appears to have been a closely knit and largely self sufficient unit.

Undoubtedly Simcoe, its environment and history, as well as his family, influenced James' development and attitudes. The town, the county seat of Norfolk, now called the regional municipality of Hallimand-Norfolk, is situated on the Lynn River 10 kilometres north of Lake Erie and eighty kilometres east of London. It was named after James Graves Simcoe, first Lieutenant Governor of Upper Canada, who camped on the site in 1795 after visiting Long Point and laying out Port Dover. He granted milling rights to Aaron Culver, a Loyalist settler whose mill became the centre of the small community. It is located in rich agricultural terrain. The town grew slowly and soundly but was plundered and destroyed by American soldiers during the War of 1812 after which it was soon rebuilt. The town and area was settled by UE Loyalists, dominantly white Protestants that were mainly Methodists and Baptists. Not surprisingly it was in some measure anti-American as, in addition to the calamity of 1812, it was threatened by Fenian raids which overran the nearby town of Ridgeway in May of 1866. Nevertheless, the area carried on a strong trade with the USA and many Simcoe residents had family connections with New York and other northern States. Indeed, briefly in the 1890s there was a strong movement for Annexation in the area led by the Norfolk Reformer which called it Political Union.

Norfolk County had a population of some 9000 inhabitants in 1840 and grew to about 86 000 in 1901. Since then, like many agricultural communities, it has lost population to the urban centres of Ontario. The town itself had only 14 000 people according to the 1981 census. In the 19th century the community was split in political and cultural affiliations between a Liberal, Methodist, prohibitionist, pro-free trade, American sympathizing majority and a Loyalist, Tory, Anglican, Canadian Imperialist minority, although the lines were not so clearly drawn as the bald statement implies. In effect, there was a reverse 'Family Compact' for the town was dominated to a considerable degree by a group of relatively wealthy Reformers.

Simcoe, according to the Toronto Globe in April 1889, was "one of the brightest and most attractive of Canadian towns. The superior class of building... the profusion of shade trees, well kept lawns and the general air of taste are the outward signs that tell the visitor that he is in a community prosperous and intelligent... . The Council [including F. A. Brown] is composed of a progressive class of men who have expended money and energy in building up and beautifying the town, and are abreast of the times in all modern appliances". The town by then had electric light, street lighting, modern fire engines, a telephone system, modern public water system and paved streets in the business district. It was well served by railways for there were three with two separate stations. The surrounding countryside was well wooded, gently rolling and picturesque. The land was productive for tree fruits and berries, grains, poultry and stock and later tobacco. There were mills for grain and wool. In addition, there were many small manufacturing industries including a foundry, strove works, sash and door factory, pump factory, saw mill, cooperage, cannery and two carriage works. Including the Erie shore, the area had become something of a tourist centre. There were also abundant cultural facilities: good schools including a teacher training institute, a large public library, and a commodious Opera House. Sporting facilities were also excellent with a race track and tennis courts concentrated at the large and attractive Agricultural Fair Grounds. A golf course was constructed before the start of the 20th century. Indeed Simcoe was not unlike Leacock's Mariposa. However, Simcoe was a UE Loyalist town that from its experiences of American incursions in 1812 and 1866 was wary of, if not hostile to its southern neighbours. As a result Simcoe provided an enthusiastic base for one of the better Canadian Militia regiments. The town had a drill hall for the County regiment, the 39th Norfolk Rifles, which played a prominent role in the town affairs, provided potential defence, support for military and civilian rifle associations, militia soldiering with spring boards to permanent military careers and an appreciated proficient band. The town and County were proud of the 39th.

Of the two weekly papers published in Simcoe, the *Norfolk Reformer*, was the oldest, and the longest lived. Owned, published and edited by the Donly family, the *Reformer* was started in1858 and remained remarkably stable and unchanging during the 19th and 20th centuries. Its banner stated 'The Price of Freedom is Eternal Vigilance.' Considering it was a small provincial journal it was remarkably broad in its coverage of na-

Photo 1 - 1. New Simcoe Armories built in 1913 and used by the 39th Regiment, Norfolk Rifles.

tional and international, as well as local affairs. Although it asserted it belonged to no party, the paper exhibited pronounced bias on Canadian affairs and, in fact, politically was strongly Liberal, ecclesiastically Methodist, pro-free trade and rabidly against Sir John A. MacDonald and the CPR. It was not notably pro-UE Loyalist nor was it anti-American, except in reaction to Fenian raids or threats and regular American talk of annexation. Curiously, in the 1890s it started to strongly advocate union with the USA. Another weekly, *The British Canadian*, was also published in Simcoe during the same period and, as one might expect, it was conservative and pro-UE Loyalist.

Although James Sutherland Brown was largely the product of his genetics and family nurture he was also influenced by the environment of his home town. His paternal and maternal parent's families tended to be hard working, intelligent and long lived. Both families had been flexible and far-sighted enough to emigrate to Canada and to continue to search for a desirable place to live. In Simcoe, his family found a secure and happy base for themselves and thus also, one from which to launch their children's lives and careers. The town provided a calm and attractive atmosphere with good schools and superior cultural and sporting facilities.

It was a good place in which to grow up. As a family the bleakest event which deeply affected them all was Maggie's tragic early death.

2 Hatched

James Sutherland Brown was born to Annie and Frank Augustus Brown on June the 28th 1881. Within a few months the family moved to a substantial home on Brock Street (now called Kent Street), which was where James lived until he left home. The family grew rapidly with the birth of Maggie, Julia and Jack, all born by the end of 1888. These were the years that Frank's career blossomed and the household must have been a happy as well as prosperous one because the house was full of children who were talented and well adjusted.

James advanced through the Simcoe Public Schools with superior if not superlative performance. Maggie was invariably head of her class while James was usually near the top and was normally on the honour roll. He undoubtedly had many non-academic diversions such as riding, fishing *etc.*, although it is hard to see him 'goofing off' as he was always so self-disciplined and his attendance record at school was excellent. According to Taylor, based probably on information from my brother Malcolm, "James (then called Jimmy)... devised elaborate games in which British forces and Canadian militia, led by himself, were given tasks of repelling American invaders [rather than playing] cowboys and Indians.[1] There were still memories of the destruction of Simcoe in 1812 and the last serious incursion of Fenians that occurred at nearby Ridgeway not 25 years before. James was only fourteen in 1895 when he entered high school and that Fall he was allowed to join the 39th Norfolk Rifles as a boy bugler, the start of his life's focus and his career. James attended Drill Camps at Niagara-on-the Lake with the Norfolk Rifles yearly from 1896, for three years as a bugler (Photo 2-1 and 2-2) and afterwards as a boy soldier. Clearly, because of his youth, this must have had his father's approval. The 39th was a fixture in Norfolk County and was strongly supported by its principal citizens among whom Frank was numbered.

When it came to examinations to enter McPherson High School in 1895, James was in the upper part of the class and was on the honour list all the way through that school until matriculation. After high school James entered the Model School in September 1899 and received his teacher's certificate in December 1901.

Photo 2 - 1. Bugle Band of 39th Rifles at Camp Niagara-on-the-Lake in about 1897. Bugler James Sutherland Brown on the right. Sutherland Papers, Queen's University Archive.

These were the Boer War years and many local men from the 39th volunteered to join the Canadian Contingent. James was made a corporal in
the Regiment in 1889, while scarcely 18, and he too wished to volunteer
but was just too young. It is stated by Taylor he attempted to join anyway
but his mother talked him out of it to finish his education and the war was
soon over.[2] James' mother had other marked influences on her son. She
was brought up at nearby Scotch Line, later the village of Scotland, which
was a strongly Scottish enclave. Annie, given her youth in this village,
could even have spoken with a Scottish burr as her parents did. Annie, or
her mother, taught James the little Gaelic he knew and awakened in him
the Scottish heritage that was largely dormant in Frank.

During his school years James was good but not outstanding in
sports, being noted in the paper as winning the odd foot race. With his father's intense interest in horses it would be strange if James had not been
an early rider and an enthusiastic equestrian. Certainly, he showed a life
long interest and skill with horses; owning his own charger while at the
Staff College, riding near the front during the war while carrying out his
line duties, strongly supporting militia cavalry in the 1930s (Figure 9-4)
and also, through much of his life, being a punter at the race tracks especially while he was a bachelor. Undoubtedly, when he was a youth he
had the use of his father's horses. There were few riding competitions in
Simcoe when he was a youth. It is tempting to think of him in the stables
grooming Frank's prize horses but probably he started with a pitchfork
and a shovel. Later, during holidays he probably helped to collect eggs on
carriage rounds and, later still, drove teams on the same quest. Frank
must have expected James to join him in the business but it became clear
in 1900 that this was unlikely. James' ambition had become set on an
army career; failing that, teaching or the law. The Permanent Force (PF)
was out of his reach unless his father could, or would, support him. A
subaltern's pay was inadequate on which to live even if one did not have
anymore to purchase a commission. It seems his father chose not to forward James' military option and this caused a serious breach between
them. Consequently, in December Frank formed his new partnership
with Mr. Edmonds, which he would have been unlikely to do if James
had been willing to join him. With the PF out of his reach James turned to
teaching and also to study for a career in law but meanwhile remained an
enthusiastic officer in the Militia. His early career advanced substantially
on these three fronts in stuttering unison.

In the year after obtaining his teacher's certificate it is not clear
whether James was articled to a law firm, attaining a higher teaching certificate or was actually teaching somewhere, probably the latter. By his
own statement in an application form for an 'Appointment of Officers to

Photo 2 - 2. Norfolk Rifles on parade at Camp, Niagara-on-the-Lake in 1896. NAC Photo 016653.

Photo 2 - 3. First Lieutenant James Sutherland Brown about 1902 in uniform of the Norfolk Rifles. Eva Brook Donly Archive, Simcoe.

the Permanent Force, he spent some time studying law but only from December 1904 until September 1905 was he known to be articled in Simcoe[3].

After Maggie's tragic death, James' younger sister Julia and brother, Jack, occupied more important roles in the family. Soon Julia was noted on the visiting circuit, attended the Model School and became a teacher. Jack followed much in James' footsteps by joining and later being commissioned in the 39th. The future rupture in relations between the brothers was the result of Jack's not following James to war. Jack joined the

Bank of Hamilton and in 1909 was moved to nearby Delhi. He continued to belong to the 39th as a Lieutenant and attended camps in Niagara. He advanced rapidly in the Bank and became prominent in Delhi's affairs, joining the Canadian Order of Foresters and becoming an officer in the Lodge in January, 1912. Later that year he was moved to Milverton, a small town just north of Stratford. He appears not to have been an officer in the 39th for a time but might have transferred to a different regiment. On 7 June, 1915, he married Daisy Hassenflug of Milverton. He was now married as well as in a protected profession but, nevertheless, he is listed next January as a Lieutenant in the 133rd Regiment[4]. This is the regiment formed in Simcoe as a replacement for the 39th which was not mobilized for overseas service. Col. Sam Hughes, Minister of Militia and Defence in the Conservative government, stigmatized it as a regiment of Liberals thus not worthy of going overseas. The 133rd was formed to avoid this obtuseness. Most of the old 39th joined it and volunteered to go overseas with this regiment, including the Bank of Hamilton's Manager in Simcoe. The 133rd did eventually go overseas in 1916 but as with most of the later-formed regiments, it was broken up to supply reserve troops and junior officers to other regiments after the carnage of the Somme. Jack was not among those who went overseas and it appears he resigned his commission. In the days of the 'White Feather' these were sufficient reasons for James not to speak to, or about, Jack for the rest of their lives. A contributing factor in James' rejection of his brother, given the mores of the day, was that Jack had married into a German Canadian family. James did not even list Jack in his skeletal family tree (*see later*).

Regardless of James' disappointment in his early quest for a permanent force career, the next few years were halcyon ones for James as he advanced in an independent life of teaching, soldiering and social congress. In December, 1902, he was hired to:

> "Take charge of the whole of St. William's School [near
> Port Rowan on Lake Erie] as the Junior department had
> been abolished. For the laborious work of teaching this
> [relatively] large school without assistance of any kind he
> is to receive $350 per year, which is just the amount
> formerly paid the retiring principal. The amount paid the
> assistant will be saved."[5]

Thereafter the *Reformer* published a flurry of reports about the progress of St. William's School and life on the Erie shore. James also read papers before the Teacher's Association in Simcoe, which were published in the Reformer. At this time his interest in history and love of books blossomed. He now could afford to indulge his tastes, so in 1904 he purchased a good five-volume edition of Mcauley's *History of England* as well as

Figure 1. Sutherland Brown Coat of Arms and Crest.

other substantial works. Also, his breach with his father was substantially healed for there were visits by Frank to Port Rowan as well as reciprocal visits home by James on weekends.

James' name requires some explanation. He was christened James Sutherland Brown by his parents to honour their great friend James Sutherland, MP, who was a prominent Minister in the Laurier Liberal Government and who became his Godfather. As a child he was usually called Jimmy; as a youth and a young man, Jim. In the Simcoe newspaper during this latter period, he was called, Capt. J.S. Brown or Teacher Jas. S. Brown, depending on whim or which was appropriate. The nickname 'Buster' did not stick to him until he was a member of the Royal Canadian Regiment (RCR) and especially after his stint in England at the Staff College in 1914. Buster was a common nickname of Browns in England as was 'Dusty' for Millers or 'Knobby' for Clarks. I never heard Clare call him anything but Buster. During his whole adult life his signature was consistently J. Sutherland Brown although many people, particularly the army bureaucracy, abbreviated it to J. S. Brown until he was a senior officer. Beginning in Chapter 3 he will be called Buster.

James feelings about family history, legitimacy and possibly about creating a dynasty led him in 1928-29 to create an authorized coat of arms (Figure 1) with the Lord Lyon in Scotland. This document is quite revealing of his character, desires and sense of history. The text iterates the background of his grandfathers and states his father was a third son. It describes the shield of the arms as follows: "Azure, a Maple Leaf between three Fleur-de-Lys Or, on a chief of the last three mullets Gules. Above the shield is placed a helmet befitting his degree with Mantling doubled Or and on a Wreath of his Liveries is set for Crest a black walnut tree proper and in an Escrol over the same this Motto Tireachadh." In plain language, the shield has a central gold maple leaf surrounded by three golden fleur-de-lys on an azure background. At the top of the shield are three red stars on a gold field. Above an appropriate helmet is an upright black walnut tree as a crest and above that a banner with the Gaelic word Tireachadh. My father was proud of his Coat of Arms and used it extensively, especially the crest, which featured in his book plate and was carved into several pieces of furniture that he had made. I can't remember his ever explaining the Coat of Arms to me any more than I can remember asking, with the exception of the crest. The black walnut was a symbol for Norfolk County, practically the only place it is native in Canada. He saw it also as a symbol for a colonizer as is the motto, combined with the idea of patriot. It is interesting that the symbols for Canada included three fleur-de-lys but only one maple leaf. The three stars commonly stand for a third son but might also have stood for an

American connection.

While he was in Port Rowan he was active socially, included in local parties, shooting trips to Long Point or ice fishing on Long Point Bay. In some of these events he was included with the establishment; politicians, school trustees, young lawyers and clergy. Some reports of these activities in the papers humorously describe the guests arriving on prancing horses, the game bags of fishing trips (five rods equal one perch) or even the weather. James was making his way socially and breaking out of his family's rather puritan environment. Soon after his arrival on the Lake Erie shore it becomes apparent that he is the correspondent and the author of the weekly letter about the area printed in the *Reformer*. Both his father and James were life long friends of the publishers, the Donlys. When he left the area the column printed a paean of praise in celebration of Port Rowan and thereafter the paper had a dearth of local comment. Writing poetry was something James carried into later life for he frequently composed poems to Clare on her birthday or at Christmas. These were carefully penned on cardboard, commonly that used to stiffen laundered shirts. She would glance at it, say thank you Buster, but scarcely read it.

During his time in Port Rowan his role in the 39th became more important. In 1899, when he was seventeen, he had been made a corporal and soon thereafter a sergeant in No.8 Company. He left high school that summer and in the Fall started teacher training at the Model School. Simultaneously, he advanced rapidly up the regimental ladder of rank. In February, 1901, he was gazetted a Lieutenant.[6] These promotions were achieved on merit not privilege. He attended a series of courses: at Wellsley Barracks, London, in 1900; at Stanley Barracks, Toronto, in 1902 for his Lieutenant's certificate; and again in 1903 for his Captain's certificate. In 1904, at Toronto, he qualified for his Field Officer's certificate and finally took the Long Course at Royal Military College (RMC) in order to qualify as a Permanent Force Officer.[7]

In September, 1902, as a relatively new Lieutenant (Photo 2-3) in the regiment, James was appointed acting Adjutant and issued orders for the camp in Niagara-on-the-Lake, published in the local newspapers. Normally this was done under the Commanding Officer's name. In November of the next year, he wrote an article of four broadsheet pages in successive issues of the Reformer on the history of the Canadian Militia, a subject he was to return to several times in later years.[8] He was then 22 years old with only teacher training behind him and with inadequate library resources. The section headings of the article were: Introduction, *The Militia Act*, Northwest Mounted Police, Royal Military College, New

Photo 2 - 4. Colonel William Dillon Otter of Riel Rebellion fame and later Major General Sir William Otter, the first Canadian CGS; pictured at the Militia camp Niagara-on-the-Lake in 1904. Col. Otter was something of a mentor to James as a young officer. NAC Photo C31370.

Infantry Training, Annual Military Camps, Soldiering - its peculiarities, benefits *etc.*, Pay, and Militarism in schools. In June he relinquished the Adjutant's appointment to take over No.6 Company which was centred on Port Rowan. Immediately he started a recruiting drive in the valley with the help of the PF drill Sergeant attached to the regiment.[9] In the following camp in front of the Minister of Militia, Sir Fredrick Borden, cousin of the future Prime Minister, and Col. William Dillon Otter (Photo 2-4) of Riel Rebellion fame, Capt. J.S. Brown's Company No.6 won the prize for the smartest in the Regiment.[10] The following months he attended a course at Stanley Barracks to obtain the certificate for Field Officer's rank. In the Fall, his Company won the competition in the 39th's Rifle Association meet, and he won second individual prize.[11] He was also secretary of the Association. Shortly thereafter he gave up teaching to study law.

The following year, 1905, was pivotal for James military career. In March he applied for an appointment in the Permanent Force and was recommended by Lt. Col. Atkinson of the 39th and approved by Col. Otter, DOC MD, No. 2.[12] In April he was appointed Vice-Chairman and Secretary of a Committee under Mayor Gunton for the Dominion Day celebration, of which the 39th was to take a major role dressed in their new khaki uniforms.[13] At camp that year, No. 6 Company again won the CO's prize given by Col. Atkinson for the smartest and most efficient company. Miss Julia Brown, now at the Model School, was among the guests at the Officer's Mess Tent. In August James application was acted upon and he was approved by the Minister in Military Council to attend the Long Course at RMC in September. According to the *Reformer*, which published his portrait, he graduated head of his class.[14] Next March it was arranged that James report to Stanley Barracks to complete his infantry training with the RCR. However, he had an inauspicious start for there was a foul up and delay in issuing his travel requisition (not the last time). He completed his infantry training with the RCR and his earlier courses and training were taken into consideration as equivalents for permanent status. Equally important, he was believed by Col. Otter to make an efficient officer of the PF.[15] It was recommended that he return to the 39th to retain command of his Company at Camp Niagara before reporting to the RCR. He was Gazetted to a Lieutenancy in that regiment effective 25 June, 1906.

James did not think about his move without some regret. He had a deep affection for the Rifles as well as 'Glorious Norfolk' County that remained with him throughout his life. He also had a great sense of loyalty which, incidentally, he expected of others. These attributes are revealed in numerous ways. He continued to subscribe to the *Simcoe Reformer* until at least 1929. He returned to the town infrequently but kept in touch with a number of Simcoe residents including the Donly family of the *Reformer*. In 1928, on one of his last visits, he stayed with the Donlys and they appealed to him to help get a military pension for a long time Medical Officer of the 39th who was old, ill and had insufficient funds to support himself. This James did and received a letter of thanks from Mrs. Donly.[16] More tellingly, when he was attending the Imperial Defence College in 1928, he re-established contact between the British Norfolk Regiment and its Canadian affiliate. As a result he was asked with short notice, which caused some disruption of his affairs, to lay a wreath at the Cenotaph of the 2nd Battalion of the Norfolk Regiment in England on 25 November, 1928. In addition, when the 39th's title was changed to the Norfolk Regiment of Canada, he responded to the Commanding Officer's request about suitable symbols for regimental badges and buttons.[17]

Clearly, during these years James Sutherland Brown developed into an intelligent, ambitious, and hard working young man full of initiative. He gave and expected loyalty from all his associates. He was as far from being a prig as he was from being intemperate and was known for his buoyant good humour and his froth-blowing ability. Nevertheless, he already exhibited a certain sternness, a lack of willingness to compromise and elements of personal recklessness that became integral parts of his character. At a comparatively young age he showed a flare for absorbing military knowledge and skills as well as capability in staff work and an ability to lead. He also demonstrated a love of history together with an ability to conduct research in this field that was remarkable, considering his lack of true university training. In addition, he had an ability to marshal facts, to write clearly and to organize things and people. General recognition of the latter skills seemed a good thing for James at the time. It advanced his career rapidly; however, it dogged him all his life for, with only a few exceptions, it led to constant staff appointments. Thus, in spite of his knowledge and recognized leadership skills, he had few opportunities to command fighting units, which General Lewis MacKenzie recently stated was the most satisfactory part of army life.[18] When Charles Taylor was writing *Six Journeys* and was staying with me in Victoria, I arranged an interview for him with Major General George Pearkes, VC. We had tea with the General and his wife, Blytha, in their garden. In the course of discussion the General said it was such a pity Buster had no opportunity to command which was the first time I realized what a disadvantage this was for his career.

3 Regimental Officer

James Sutherland Brown joined the Royal Canadian Regiment on 25 June, 1906, just before his 25th birthday (Photo 3-1). He had already served eleven years in the Militia as bugler, boy rifleman, a corporal at seventeen and a sergeant at eighteen. He was commissioned at age 19 and immediately appointed acting Adjutant. James became a company commander at 22 and his company, based away from headquarters at Port Rowan, quickly won regimental awards as the smartest and most efficient company. They also won rifle shoots regularly and James took part in the competitions and won prizes. He was a seasoned militia officer when he joined the RCR, who had already shown superior capability to lead and inspire militia soldiers as well as in administration. He had passed all the mandatory courses in fine style. If he ever flirted with the idea of joining the Royal Canadian Dragoons because of his love of horses it was fleeting. He was an infantry officer but one with a broad outlook.

The delay in his arrival in Toronto was the subject of a series of telegrams and letters that indicated he was needed. Indeed, almost as soon as James arrived at Stanley Barracks he was involved in one of the first extensive army evaluations of the Ross rifle Mk.1. The new rifle was issued to I Company about August, 1906, when the company OC had gone abroad on three months leave. James was actually in command of the company when they went to Long Branch range for their annual musketry exercise, all a bit unusual for a subaltern new to the regiment but it shows there was already great confidence in him. James decided to submit a report on the rifle and its deficiencies to Military District No. 2. He had all the officers, NCOs and men, about 50 in all, submit a report on their experience with the newly issued rifle. Every gun had a defect, some of which were common to all, others were peculiar to a particular rifle. James' report listed 10 defects which were basically the ones that during the coming war made the Ross Rifle loathed by the infantry at the front.[1] The principal faults as a military weapon were that many rounds hung fire or misfired, many rifles did not eject properly, the rifles jammed on rapid fire, the breech and retaining lug did not function properly, the rifle frequently discharged on closing the bolt. James gave the report to Lt. Col. Hemming, OC No. 2 Regimental Depot. Hemming was summoned

Photo 3 - 1. Lieutenant James Sutherland Brown, in full dress uniform of the Royal Canadian Regiment (RCR). From the Simcoe Reformer, 27 April 1916 but probably taken in 1906.

to Ottawa to give evidence, even though he had not fired the rifle. James surmised this may have been intentional.[2]

James remained in I company stationed in Toronto until April, 1907. Knowledge of his staff skills quickly caught up with him for he was dispatched to K company at Wolsley Barracks in London on 5 April, 1907, to act as Adjutant while the regular one was in England: an appointment that was also remarkable for such a newly commissioned officer. In July he was transferred back to Stanley Barracks and remained there for a year except for courses and camps. The Regiment, together with other units of the Permanent Force, had a yearly combined summer training course at Camp Petawawa. At the camp in, 1907, James was one of only five officers commended by Sir Percy Lake, the Chief of the General Staff (CGS), for outstanding work.[3] He was starting to get noticed by senior officers.

In early autumn, James was detailed to the Canadian School of Musketry at Rockliffe as Paymaster and Quarter Master as well as to take the course. Here again he was confronted by the merits and many failings of the Ross rifle. "As QM, I had an awful lot to do with the issue and continual exchange of rifles to students. There was a tendency to blame the rifle for bad shooting. It was difficult to say at this time how much was the fault of the person or the rifle [but the students did not like the gun]."[4] At this school James established once again that he was a marksman for he was rated 'Distinguished in Musketry' on his yearly evaluations ever after.

During these years with the Regiment, James started to establish lasting friendships with other junior officers, R.O. Alexander, G.G. Chysler, W.W.W. (Billy) Gibsone, Murray K. Greene, E.W. Pope, A.E. Willoughby, and O.A. Hoad, on exchange from the Australian Forces. In addition, many of the senior officers became his friend such as then Major A.H. Macdonell, DSO, and Major P.E. Thacker (Photo 3-2). The Officers Mess resembled a cross between a gentleman's club and a fraternity, except that their more serious purpose made them truly a 'band of brothers'.

However, life was not all work, so that James, in addition to spending leaves in Simcoe, was able as a gay bachelor in the old sense, to indulge his love of moderate gambling at the race courses and in the mess at bridge and poker. Also, if his life as a teacher in Port Rowan is a guide, he must have had a social life outside the mess. Some time in his years at Stanley Barracks, but probably not until about 1912 to 1913, he met Clare Temple Corsan, his future wife. Clare's photo album had images of all her close friends, both male and female. James does not appear in the album until the last pages where there are two photos of him, one on horseback. Clare was a recognized beauty seven years his junior but he courted her and later won her to his perpetual joy. She followed him to England and they were married in 1916. Late in her long life when she was in a nursing home I asked her, "Mom, why as a recognized beauty, did you not marry until so late in life?" twenty-eight being then considered spinsterly. She replied, "Perhaps I wanted too much, I wanted my husband to be handsome, loving, courtly and wealthy." I followed by saying, "Then why did you marry Pop for he was none of those things," although probably only the last was true. She responded only with a smile.

Clare was born in 1888 to Alma Ellen Browne of Kingston, Ontario, second wife of Thomas Corsan of Hamilton. The Corsans were a Scottish family originally from Ayr but resident in County Leitrim, Ireland, from which they emigrated to Canada. Thomas Corsan was the scion of a wealthy family who became impoverished by bad investments so that Clare grew up in Toronto in gentile poverty with just enough money to be sent to good schools. As soon as she matriculated she worked for a living

Photo 3 - 2. Officers of the RCR at Halifax, summer 1909. The CO, Lt. Col. R.L. Wadmore, seated in front of doorway, Major A.H. Macdonell to his left, Lt. James Sutherland Brown in front of down pipe.

but at the same time was a popular debutante. Clare was the first female teller in Toronto where she worked at the Bank of Montreal at Front and Yonge Streets. This did not inhibit her from having many of what she called 'Beaux' (Photo 3-3) and she lived a gay social life although far from a thoughtless butterfly. James felt himself extremely lucky to win her love and consequently they had a long and happy marriage.

In July, 1908, James was posted to Halifax, the Regimental HQ and home of six of the ten companies of the RCR. He was hardly there before the regiment took part in the Quebec Tercentenary which involved a parade and march past of a major part of the Canadian Militia on the Plains of Abraham in front of the Prince of Wales, later King George the Fifth.

This was the greatest military concentration yet seen in Canada with 13 551 troops, 2495 horses with 26 guns as well as 1786 sailors and marines of the Royal Navy, plus contingents of visiting US and French Navies who swept by in brilliant sunshine.

The Prince was accompanied by Field Marshal Lord Roberts, Chief of the Imperial General Staff (CIGS). The parade was commanded by the first truly Canadian Chief of the General Staff (CGS) and former Commanding Officer of the RCR, Major General William Dillon Otter (Photo 2-4). In the march past, the RCR with its superb band brought up the rear.

The Prince enquired, "What regiment is this?"

General Otter replied, "The Royal Canadian Regiment of the Permanent Force, Sire."

"But should they not have been in the van, General?"

Otter replied, "By right they should, Sire, but I ordered them to march past last."

For a moment the Prince look puzzled, then his face lightened with understanding. "I see, General, you kept the best wine for me until the end."[5]

In February, 1909, Lt. Brown wrote and passed exams for promotion to Captain and later in the year received the highest pay for subalterns, a princely $2.50 per day. The routine life of the regiment in Halifax, of training and instruction of the Militia, was soon interrupted for James as well as many of his brother officers and men as they became involved in one of the army's least favourite duties, 'aid to the civil powers'. Government intelligence was unusually alert and accurate as a major strike threatened violence in the coalfields of Cape Breton. The senior officers of the United

Mine Workers of America (UMWA) declared on 3 July, 1909, that if their ultimatum was not met by the Dominion Coal Company (DCC) that all mines in the coalfield would be struck on Tuesday, 5 July. The government judged in advance that it would be an ugly and violent strike and so it turned out to be. They ordered two companies of the RCR together with lesser numbers of Royal Canadian Artillery (RCA) and Royal Canadian Engineers (RCE) to stand by at 13:00 hours on 7 July, and at 01:00 on the 8th they were commanded to leave for Glace Bay, Cape Breton. The troops entrained at 13:40 that morning under the command of the RCR CO, Lt. Col. R.L. Wadmore with Major A.H. Macdonell as chief of staff.[6] Lt. J. Sutherland Brown was among the officers dispatched.

The strike had some cardinal aspects that generated bitterness and violence. Firstly, it was an inter-union dispute as much as a strike against the company. The UMWA was attempting to take control of the Nova Scotia coal miners from the Provincial Workman's Association (PWA). The latter resembled a guild more than an American union and, although it had a cosy relationship with company management, it had been successful in achieving good working conditions, wages and safety; very much better than the miners in Pennsylvania enjoyed. The President of the UMWA in Indianapolis, T.L. Lewis, father of J.L. Lewis, was trying to secure his reign as president by aggressive leadership. It was said by a US Senate Report at the time that his actions were followed by riot, blood and violence. There was also a suggestion of conspiracy with Pennsylvanian coal companies to capture Canadian markets.[7] Unbelievably, Glace Bay Mayor Douglas was in favour of the strike although his Council was not. The Mayor appointed a new group of constables from among the strikers while the company had its own police with the farcical result that members of the opposing constabulary started to arrest each other.[8] Where were Gilbert and Sullivan? Nevertheless, here was a recipe for riot and violence that exceeded the capability of either police force to control. The call out of the military was fully justified and very timely.

The strike from its beginning was only partially successful as less than half the miners went out and the others continued to work and cross the picket lines.[9] The number of strikers steadily decreased and mine production slowly rose to normal. But as the strike was increasingly seen as a failure, the violence escalated under the urging of the American UMWA provocateurs. Worker's houses were set on fire; explosions were set off, some of which threatened hundreds of miners; stonings, assaults; sniping and murder took place. By the time the strike petered out in March, 1910, 46 men were sentenced to jail for criminal acts.[10]

The strike against the DCC soon escalated by striking other compa-

Photo 3 - 3. Clare Corsan, James future wife, sailing on Lake Simcoe with some of her Beaux about 1913. Her hair is wrapped around her head like a busby.

nies and mines in Cape Breton. As a result another detachment of a hundred RCR troops was sent to Inverness.[11] The army's presence was critical in inhibiting riot as they guarded the numerous mines from destruction and patrolled the critical areas to prevent overt hostilities. Their role was particularly effective because they had established phone communications between HQ and all the outposts in the days when such ability was rare. "Wadmore's force was maintaining order in the face of constant danger. Exposed to indignity and insult, with orders not to retaliate... the force as a whole stood prepared for open hostilities... [which were] averted only by the troops' friendly and confident bearing".[12] Although the strike became increasingly ineffective the danger remained severe so winter quarters had to be constructed (Photo 3-4) and the troops moved out of the tent camp at Table Head. As the hazard decreased, troops were successively withdrawn from Cape Breton; first the RCA and the engineers and then some RCR. The remainder returned to Halifax March, 1910, except for Lt. James Sutherland Brown who stayed on at the request of the coal company.[13]

Photo 3 - 4. RCR officers in Sidney, NS, during the coal strikes, 1909-10. Lt. Col. Wadmore right centre, to his left Major A.H. Macdonell and then Lt. James Sutherland Brown.

During James' posting in Sydney he had established his superior capabilities in handling the difficult assignments of this duty not only with his senior officers but also with the mine management, miners and strikers alike. His trait of being able to establish relationships both above and below was one he repeatedly exhibited in his life and, with the latter, notably with the unemployed at the Relief Camps in British Columbia in the Thirties. He was able to sympathize with the disadvantaged and oppressed while recognizing the need for justice, law and order. His earthiness enabled him to joss with the strikers yet still maintain respect. This term of duty brought James into contact with American agitators of the UMWA and was probably one more element in the growing distaste he developed for the United States. His activities at Sydney and Glace Bay appear to have been greatly admired and appreciated by the mine management. The Dominion Coal Company merged with the Sydney Steel Company during the strike and a new Vice President and General Manager, M.J. Butler, was appointed in Sydney. Butler had been Deputy Minister of Railways in Ottawa before his appointment so had many connections in the capital. He specifically requested Lt. Brown stay on as a Special Constable in charge of police when the regiment left.[14] The Manager applied first to Lt. Col. Wadmore, then on through General Drury, District Officer Commanding (DOC) and finally to the Minister of Militia. The request was granted for only a limited period because Sutherland Brown had to return to study in preparation for exams to qualify for field rank. On a further request from Butler to the Deputy Minister of Militia, Col. Fiset, the former stated how valuable Lt. Brown had been and could he be spared for another two months or at least replaced by another officer.[15] The Deputy Minister replied that he could not order an officer to such duty and none would volunteer to replace Brown. This was probably the first time James came to the attention of General Drury and, more importantly the Minister and his Deputy.

James must have thought his role at Glace Bay was effective because much later in a letter to the Attorney General of British Columbia, R.H. Pooley, he recommended that from his experiences in Cape Breton that two of his senior officers be appointed Provincial Constables as he had been in Nova Scotia. He stated, "There would be no possible abuse and no cost to the [BC] government." This was suggested to solve some of the problems of 'aid to the civil powers', regarding possible riot in the unemployment relief camps in 1933.[16]

Soon after James' return to Halifax it was recommended by Lt. Col. Wadmore that Lt. Brown be appointed Adjutant of I company at No. 2 Depot, Stanley Barracks. In a letter to the Military Council the CO stated that James had "passed for the rank of Captain and is in possession of a

Musketry certificate, capable of instruction, in possession of a certificate of equitation and was physically fit." His appointment came through in July. He was also recommended for promotion to Captain in November 1910 and was gazetted so in March 1911. A new CO took over the Regiment in September, 1910, graced with the name of Lt. Col. Septimus Julius Augustus Denison, CMG. James would feel at home with another Augustus. Unfortunately, Lt. Col. Denison was soon promoted to DOC of MD No. 4 in Montreal so another CO, Lt. Col. A.O. Fages took over in January in 1913. Col. Fages also had a glorious second name, Octave.

In 1911, in addition to a month long combined PF camp at Petawawa in the summer, the regiment sent two teams to the Toronto Garrison's marching and firing competition for the St. Croix Cup after the RCR being absent for seven years. "Twenty three teams competed, but the Royal Canadian Regiment's entries commanded respectively by Capt. J.S. Brown and Lt. N.V. Sankey won first and second place by a substantial margin."[17]

Late in 1911, James had one of his many brushes with military bureaucracy and what he felt were unreasonable aspects of King's Regulations and Orders (KR&O). He was posted to RMC in January, 1912, to study and write exams for entrance to the Staff College at Camberley, England. He asked permission to take his servant, Private Quick, RCR, as batman and groom with him. This was said not to apply to schools of instruction 'of arms other than their own' and was not needed by other than cavalry and horse artillery officers. After being batted about between the Adjutant General and his underlings it was decided that, as the course had been lengthened to seven months, that it be permitted, assuming no expense to the public be incurred and that KR&O be revised accordingly.[18] He won this one but lost many others.

James was at RMC until July, 1912, studying for entrance to the Staff College. His studies and exams also included all the necessary requirements for promotion to the field rank of Major. The application of Capt. J.S. Brown to the Staff College was signed by Col. Septimus Denison, CO of the RCR, and Lt. Cols. Fages and Carpenter who certified that:

> 1. That the applicant's conduct is marked by steadiness, prudence, and he is temperate in his habits.
>
> 2. That he is active, energetic, and has force of character.
>
> 3. That he is zealous, active, intelligent, and discreet in the performance of his duties, and that he takes an interest in his profession.

4. His disposition and temper are such as to enable him to perform his duties with tact, discrimination and in a manner calculated to ensure cheerful obedience of orders conveyed by him.

5. He has no characteristics that render him unsuitable.

[Furthermore], that the candidate is in every respect a thoroughly intelligent and a good regimental officer. And that he is an officer I would select as an Adjutant, or to serve on my own staff. Captain Brown was also certified physically fit.[19]

It is possible that James met Clare Corsan at the RMC June Ball because she was present and he had not yet left but it is certain from a family photograph he was not her 'beau'. After his duties at RMC James returned to Infantry Depot No. 2 in Toronto soon enough to be involved in the summer PF camp at Petawawa. A series of incidents that were precursors to the Great War surfaced in these years such as the Agadir Crisis of 1911, in which the German cruiser, Bremen, berthed in Montreal quickly slipped out to sea to avoid possible internment. Then the Balkan War erupted. In October, 1912, Capt. James Sutherland Brown applied to the Militia Council through the GOC of No. 2 Division in Toronto to be sent as one of the English-speaking Attaches (observers) to the Balkan conflict. He was strongly recommended for this duty by the GOC but he was not selected by the Minister.[20] Instead, he remained at the Toronto Depot in charge of infantry training for the next year. His principal duties involved training Militia regiments. As an officer skilled in musketry and a prize-winning shot he also took part in another evaluation of the newly issued Ross rifle Mk.2 with screw elevated sights although the primary trials by the Regiment were in Halifax. The evaluations were exhaustive and the conclusion very unfavourable to the rifle because of its deficiencies in rapid fire, feed, firing on closing the bolt among other things. The negative report was not acted upon because of the Minister's, Col. Sam Hughes, bias in favour of the rifle. As a result, when the Canadian Expeditionary Force (CEF) went to France it was burdened with an unsuitable rifle until 1916, even though it proved greatly inferior to the Lee Enfield in the mud of Ypres and the Somme. Additionally, the report provided another black mark in the Minister's opinion against the Regiment which he remembered in 1914 by ordering them to Bermuda on garrison duty instead of with the First Contingent.

James returned to RMC to write further exams from 1 May to 23 June, 1913, for a position at the Staff College. He must have been greatly disappointed when in September of that year he received notice he had failed.

He had, in fact, done well in aggregate marks, considerably above a pass. However, he was never a linguist and failed the obligatory subject of French language. What happened then is unclear but by December he was notified he was off to Camberley for two years and sailed on 3 January of the fateful year of 1914.

James did not know it at the time but this was his farewell to the Regiment. Although he disguised it well he was quite an emotional man. All his service career, and afterwards until his death, he bore a great love for the Regiment, his brother officers and the troops, from his batman, Pte. Quick to the Regimental Sergeant Major. Little things like his tattoo of the regimental crest on his forearm exhibited his attachment. Whether this was drawn following high jinks after a mess party or in sober circumstances hardly matters. More importantly, his affection was shown in July, 1928, when he was struck off strength of the Regiment after having been a member of it, or nominally of its reinforcement satellite, the Nova Scotia Regiment, ever since he left it in 1913. His letter in 1928 to Lt. Col. E.A. Seely Smith, the current CO states:

"I have just received the Gazette, with mixed feelings, [noting] I have been struck off strength of the old Regiment... on promotion to Colonel.... I assure you my heart, my thoughts and my efforts have always been with the Regiment. Not only with the serving [personnel] but also with the vast number of ex-members whom I have constantly come into contact... personally or by letter.... I hope the [authorities] will continue to show me in the list of old soldiers entitled: 'Removed from the Regiment and still on the active list.' I assure you, the officers and men of the Regiment that wherever I am; my best wishes will be with you all and any small influence I have will always be at the command of the Regiment as also will be my best endeavours to advance its course.... I visited with pleasure and interest the depot of the Gloucestershire Regiment [an affiliated regiment] at Bristol last January and intend to see the Territorial Battalions in competition next month. Kindest regards [to all]."[21] This letter was circulated to all ranks in the Regiment and Seely Smith responded to James that "all members of the Regiment are heartily sorry to see your name taken off the Regimental list."

James carried through with his commitments. He revisited the Gloucesters and later proposed a rifle competition between the Gloucesters and the RCR for which he donated a silver cup as a perpetual trophy for the winners. He also responded to many requests regarding such things as battle honours for the Regiment and suggestions regarding future COs, Colonels-in-Chief and Honorary Colonels. He agreed with Seely Smith that Arthur, Duke of Connaught, should be asked to become the Colonel-in-Chief, which he accepted and proposed that General Otter should be asked to become Honorary Colonel but, unfortunately, he died before he could be asked. He also was asked confidentially by the CGS for his opinion about succession of Regimental COs so he continued to influence the course of the Regiment.

James Sutherland Brown's skills, personality and attitudes continued to develop during his years in the RCR. He entered the Regiment from a family that was politically Liberal with strong connections to the United States. He underwent a slow transformation to Toryism and developed a definite bias against Canada's neighbour believing it had a baleful influence on Canada and even presented a military threat. In addition to his strong allegiance to Canada he was now a convinced Imperialist. His military and administrative skills continued to develop and he had frequently been selected for difficult and critical roles. James had repeatedly brought companies under his command to high levels of efficiency in dress, drill, marksmanship and tactics. He was a great believer in realism in training schemes. James had impressed his superiors in the regiment and in higher commands with his superior capabilities and he had been selected to attend the Staff College. He was ready to play an effective role in whatever lay ahead.

4   Camberley

Buster did well at his exams to enter the Staff College at Camberley, Surrey, England but he failed French. He received notice of his marks and his failure in a letter from the CGS dated 12 September, 1913. Although entry to the College was known to be difficult, and while many tried but few succeeded, this must have been a crushing blow to Buster. Nevertheless, later in the year he was informed that he was to attend the College. He had just enough notice to put his affairs in order and spend Christmas leave in Simcoe before departure from Halifax on 3 January, 1914. Probably during this visit home was the last time he saw his father who died in January, 1915, and although Buster was recalled to Canada on the outbreak of war he did not get any leave during his short stay.

James Sutherland Brown arrived in early January at the handsome buildings and grounds of the College in Camberley, some 30 miles west of the centre of London. Here he was in his element with like-minded officers in a British milieu and a challenging academic and practical military environment. The atmosphere was intensely competitive but also highly collegial. The course was supposed to last two years with the first devoted primarily to acquiring knowledge and the second largely to its application in field exercises and staff tours. Graduates were entitled to attached the letters p.s.c. (passed staff college) to their names. A p.s.c. was a requisite for future advancement in the services to senior rank. The College enrolment totalled 105 students. Among them were four Canadians: J.H. MacBrien and F.S. Morrison of the Royal Canadian Dragoons, and A.H. Borden and Buster of the RCRs. British students included W.E. 'Tiny' Ironsides and John 'Jack' G. Dill, both of whom became Chief of the Imperial General Staff (CIGS) during WWII, and J.F.C. Fuller who later forcefully and abrasively articulated armoured corps strategy and tactics. These and many other survivors of the war became life long friends to Buster.

The former Commandant who had just left the College in October 1913, was Maj-General W.R. Robertson, a formidable character, whose father had been a simple village postmaster. He himself had advanced from the ranks to the influential position of Commandant, and later, during the middle of 1915, was selected as CIGS. According to him the product of the College was expected to "display keen foresight, great activity and devote the whole of their attention to duty and so be always prepared... to be able to give concise statements showing not only the position, strength and movement of all parts of his forces, but also information regarding such important matters as: the quantities of supplies, ammunition and stores available; the possibility of renewing them; the casualties that have been suffered; the fatigue and hardship that have been undergone: and, the amount of energy estimated to be still available."[1] Clearly, preparation to carry out such a role was going to be very demanding, involving intense study and exhaustive exercises that received close analytical scrutiny by the College staff.

Robertson had substantially changed the syllabus so that purely academic subjects such as language (Buster's weakness) and mathematics were dropped. What remained was highly practical:

- Military history and geography, [ancient and modern];
- Principles of Imperial Defence, defence of frontiers, plans of concentration, naval strategy and bases, defending ports, food supplies to the UK, British and foreign armies, landings on an enemy's coast, overseas expeditions;
- Systems of transport and supply, economic geography, commercial law;
- Medical and ordinance services as affecting commanders and staff officers;
- Staff tours.[2]

Just before Buster's class arrived, Robertson was succeeded by Brigadier General L. Kiggell who was an intelligent but not very forceful or innovative officer. During the war he became Chief of Staff to Field Marshal Haig. He is most often remembered for his statement of surprise when he first saw the mud of Passchendaele after the battle. Haig and his staff were not noted for getting close to the front but preferred the French headquarters style of life in a chateau at a distance. When Kiggell did see the morass he is reported to have cried and said, "Good God, did we really send our men to fight in that".[3]

During Buster's preparation for the Staff College he had already met in his entrance exams the type of exercise that was required at the College. The following are examples of some of questions and answers that had relevance to his future work:

- "Explain the organization that exists for the supply of ammunition for a field force of a certain size that includes 13 and 18 pound guns, cavalry and infantry; and detail the division between refuelling points and fighting units; diagram refuelling points in relation to the front and topography." This was a problem he faced continually during the war.

- "How the military forces of Canada are raised, organized and equipped, or should be". His essay, among other things, indicated the need of an Imperial General Staff but with Canadian officers as an integral part of the organization. This confirmed his bias for Canadian representation within an Imperial structure.
- A general paper on strategy in which Buster emphasized the need for superior organization along the elder Moltke's lines, including rapid and complete mobilization, a better system of transport and supply and the ability to launch a superior force at some critical location. Buster illustrated his points by examples drawn from Wellington's Peninsular campaigns in Iberia with maps reproduced from memory.
- "If Napoleon had won at Waterloo, what then"?

The latter question was in French. Many of his essays were marked 'very clear'; 'you have a good idea of the subject'; or 'good'; one was labelled 'utopian'.

All questions in his entrance exams, as well as those at the College, required comprehensive military and topographic knowledge as well as imagination and practical experience. In particular, he had to carry out an exercise in Canada in 1913 that required him to outline a defence of Red Force (eastern Canada) from an attack by Blue Force (USA) into southern Ontario.[4] The scenario Buster devised was a precursor to Defence Scheme No. 1 which, as Director of Intelligence and Operations, he was instructed to develop in the mid 1920s for the defence of Canada from an attack by the USA. This scheme has become a source of scorn and ridicule from some historians when it became generally known from perusal of the Sutherland Brown papers in the Queen's University Archives in the 1960s (*see later*). The fact that it was set as an exam paper in 1913 shows his superiors thought it had aspects of reality. The exercise was set on 1 August, 1913, not as just a topographic board assignment but was run as a field exercise until 17 August, with active manoeuvre by the militia and PF, and received abundant press coverage. Buster served during these exercises as Staff Officer or Brigade Major to Col. W.W. Burleigh.

Buster's scheme was to seize the initiative by control of the Great Lakes and the Saint Lawrence River system through expeditious mobilization and offensive action forwarded by the favourable geographic projection of the Niagara Peninsula into the Blue Heartland. Red Force was capable of quicker mobilization and concentration as a result of historic

Militia precedent and geography. Redland was able to exploit these advantages through early penetrative and disruptive advances into Blue heartland while anticipating aid from Britain through early intervention by the Royal Navy. The parallels to Defence Scheme No. 1 are obvious.

At Camberley Buster was set a series of exercises singly or as a member of a syndicate of two to five. The exercises included an example based on Petawawa with which he was familiar. It involved rapid deployment of signal units, crossing the Ottawa River in force by cavalry, employment of Divisional engineers and defence of an isolated bridgehead. Most of the many other exercises involved locations in the UK such as the defence of Green Hill, a cavalry scheme, an artillery scheme with a practical field camp on Salisbury Plain, with which, the following year, he would become very familiar. All his papers received extensive critical reviews with many favourable comments such as, "you bring out your points clearly, well worked out or well described and illustrated;" but others were fairly negative such as, "written orders must be precise". Clearly from the number of described exercises the students were intensively worked. They also had monumental reading lists. As Bond states, "It would be difficult to study the schemes set in the immediate pre-war years and remain unimpressed by either the sophistication of the exercises or the practical lessons they were designed to inculcate".[5] Unlike some earlier classes where the whole emphasis was on offence they also studied effective ways to retreat. And yet there was one important thing that was not anticipated in the widely sweeping exercises: the possibility of a long static stalemate of trench warfare; and, more importantly, methods to break out of it.

The College staff and students seemed to have their weekends off in typical British style during which they enjoyed an active social life. Included was much riding since they all had their own horses (chargers). Hence, point to point races and the like were frequently enjoyed. A close social fabric developed and, what in effect was the last summer of the Edwardian era was upon them, but there was little anticipation or apprehension of the future. The assassination of Arch Duke Ferdinand on 28 June was scarcely noticed and the staff gave its annual garden party only three days later.

> "[It was] an idyllic scene: present and past students strolling
> beneath the huge beech trees by the lake, watching tennis or
> cricket and listening to the band. How many of them
> realized Britain [and the world] was on the brink of war? As
> July wore on there were hints of an approaching crisis:
> horses were to be sold, and officers on leave were ordered to
> keep within distance of instant recall. [Later] during the last

exercise of the term [the students had difficulty focusing on the problem and instead were] contemplating a picnic party on a launch or what price they would be offered for their horses... . The term ended on 31 July without special orders... . On 4 August the tension was broken and [all] dashed off to junior staff positions and the College was closed. More than 150 p.s.c.s, or 49 percent of recent graduates, were never to return indicating a staff officers life was at great hazard unlike some popular images."[6]

With the outbreak of war Buster was immediately recalled by telegram to Canada.

5 In The Great War, Canada's Apprenticeship, 1914-1916

The Great War was anticipated by many and was prepared for by all the Great European Powers, nevertheless, when it developed it was still a surprise to most people. At first it was greeted by nationalistic and chauvinistic enthusiasm in all major countries including Canada. However, it turned out to be a tragic and bloody conflict that in John Keegan's or A.J.P. Taylor's opinion was largely accidental and unnecessary. Other historians including Philip Warner, believe the imperial desires of Germany and the general arms build up made the war inevitable. Certainly, the interaction of accidental incidents, established alliances, government posturings, menacing mobilizations and threats all seemed to lead irretrievably to the 'guns of August'.[1] As the European Powers joined or were dragged into the conflagration so too were their allies, dependencies, and in the UK's case its Dominions. What in Keegan's opinion might have been another small Balkan war escalated quickly into a world conflict with resulting decimation of young males in all states involved and virtual bankruptcy of most of the major players.

Whichever way the cause of WWI is interpreted, it was different from WWII and the potential WWIII between the NATO Allies and the Soviet Union. In 1914 the European Powers were arming heavily for conflict on sea and land but there was no preparation for a long war; no expansion of munitions factories and no stockpiling of armament for attrition, no expectation of deadlock and years of trench warfare. In contrast, in 1939, the Axis Powers, at least Nazi Germany and Imperial Japan, were preparing in every way for an all out war of territorial conquest and, because the Allied Powers diplomatic and military responses were slow and confused, led inevitably to war because of miscalculation by the aggressor governments of their chance of a quick victory. WWIII did not occur even though the potential combatants expended tremendous resources on armament and delivery systems in the second half of the century. Both sides realized the likely result would be complete mutual destruction.

In Canada, in 1914, concern was insignificant within the government or among the people that the events in Sarajevo presaged a great war. Parliament was in summer recess: the Governor-General, the Duke of

Connaught, the Prime Minister, Sir Robert Borden, and the ebullient Minister of Defence and Militia, Colonel Sam Hughes, were widely dispersed across Canada at the end of July.[2] There seemed little fear that Britain would be involved in a war, which by treaty it would if France or Belgium were attacked. Canada in those days would be automatically drawn in if Britain was involved but the scale of participation could have been determined by the government. The Colonial Secretary in London pointed out the commitment to the Governor-General on 29 July by cable. Consequently the Duke returned immediately to Ottawa from Banff as did Borden from Muskoka. Sam Hughes had already returned and started his disruptive independent activity which started with a unilaterally called meeting of the Militia Council, followed by promising mobilization of the Militia and by stating Canada would have 22 000 to 25 000 men ready to dispatch to Britain very soon.

France and Russia were allies by treaty. When Russia mobilized, Germany declared war on 1 August against the Tsarist state, and against France on 3 August. Britain hesitated briefly so Hughes, up to form, ranted at 'Perfidious Albion', but he and Canada had not long to wait. Germany served an ultimatum to Belgium demanding unimpeded transit through the country. Belgium requested French and British aid in compliance with existing treaties if it was attacked. On 4 August Germany invaded Belgium launching the Schlieffen Plan for the conquest of France by a counter-clockwise sweep through Belgium, Flanders and on to Paris. Britain then demanded the Germans withdraw by midnight and when this did not happen all the major European powers were joined in war.

In spite of the state of the armed forces in 1914, it is arguable that Canada was better prepared for WWI than for its successor. In August 1914 there may have been only 3000 regular troops but these were buttressed by a volunteer Militia of some 64 000 men and a pool of ex-militiamen because, in the culture of the day, the military were neither despised nor starved of resources as they were in the 1930s. Still, the forces in 1914 were relatively poorly prepared or equipped, with few qualified staff officers, little artillery, almost no vehicles, unsuitable uniforms and burdened with the Ross rifle. However, in 1914, even the continental armies, though great in manpower, were also relatively unsophisticated technologically. Nevertheless, Canada not only couldn't compare with European armies in numbers but neither could it in training, experience or organization. Canada had little recent history of war and the armed forces had only 12 officers who had been to Camberley, including Buster and his classmates.[3] Regardless of the lack of a trained army, on 1 August, Borden offered, and the Cabinet confirmed on 7 August, the despatch of an expeditionary force of one Division to Britain. Canadians were as exuberantly in favour of such a response as were most European nationals to their mobilizations. Canadians immediately rallied to the colours in great numbers. Most expected the war would be over by Christmas, no one expected four years of bloody stalemate in the mud and trenches of Flanders and the Somme.

Although Canada was a relatively new and uncohesive nation in 1914, nationalism was intense amongst the people of British origin, whether of Canadian or British birth. This was based essentially on loyalty to the Crown. This nationalism, as Corns and Hughes-Wilson reported:

> "sprang not just from Darwinian ideas of racial superiority and Nietzchean influences on educated thought but also from the unifying symbol of the 'British Empire'. British national consciousness was inextricably entwined with imperial glory, rights and responsibilities;... the Empire was a source of stability, self-belief in their superiority, pride, or stern duty. Half the globe coloured pink really meant something in a way we today find incomprehensible, if not downright embarrassing. We are [now] a different people... [and] it is almost impossible for us to realize just how strong a unifying feature the 'Empire' was. ... Imperial ties were a genuine force in 1914 and were sufficient to pull hundreds of thousands of new Canadians, Australians, New Zealanders and South Africans from the white colonial dominions back across the oceans to volunteer to fight - and die for 'the mother country'."[4]

However, it was during this war that Canadians, new and old, began thinking of themselves as something separate and special. This is widely attributed now to the catalysis of the victory of the Canadian Corps at Vimy Ridge where others had failed but the concept was solidified by the continuing operational success of the Corps. Canada had embraced a myth from Colonial days that the defence of the country was in the hands of its own rural Militia that could be called out by a *levee en masse*, rather than relying on the small British garrisons. All able bodied men would assemble, mostly with their own arms, to defend the country (the Sedentary Militia, no pun intended). These untrained, unorganized and unpaid defenders could be mustered by law at least once a year, more often if necessary. They were supported by a part time Active Militia composed of paid volunteers. The myth was enhanced during the War of 1812 when elements of it seemed to be substantiated by successes of the militia

Photo 5 - 1 . Lt. General Sir Sam Hughes, controversial Minister of Militia, 1911-1916. NAC Photo C 2458.

against better trained and organized troops of the Republic and again during the rebellions of 1837. Later, during the American Revolution, Sir John A. MacDonald, fearing an American invasion, presented a Bill to Parliament to increase the size of the Militia to 50 000 men who were to be equipped, trained and mobilized for a month each year. His government was defeated as a result of the Bill but seeds of better preparedness had been sown and the Active Militia developed forthwith. The Militia myth bore heavily on Canadian's psyche. It was a factor in 1914 in the rapid recruitment of Canadian-born militiamen and ordinary citizens. British-born, new Canadians, were driven to volunteer by loyalty to the Crown.

Mobilization of the First Canadian Contingent for the overseas war was greatly confused by the then Minister of Militia, Colonel Sam Hughes (Photo 5-1). Previously, in the Boer War as a Militia Colonel Hughes had made an offer to the British Government to raise a contingent for the war without going through the proper Canadian Government channels. Nevertheless, his offer was not exactly refused. Hughes resolutely expected that he would lead the force when it was raised but those in power put command in the hands of Col. W.D. Otter (Photo 2-4), a proven and efficient PF officer, and Hughes was shunted aside even though he went to South Africa to await the call. The incident was one of many that led to Borden's wariness of Sam Hughes after the former became Prime Minister. Nevertheless, when the Conservative government was elected in 1911, Hughes' political clout led to his being appointed Minister where he unilaterally caused confusion, confrontations, irritation and embarrassment until he was finally demoted in 1916; and even after. The South African incident also led to Hughes' increasing dislike of the PF.

Sam Hughes at the start of the Great War repeated aspects of his earlier role but magnified because he was in control. His interference in the mobilization for the First Contingent caused great confusion, needless turmoil and significantly increased costs. Canada had two well codified mobilization plans, one for raising six Divisions and a more modest one, designed in 1911, for a single Division with a cavalry brigade and auxiliary troops. Both plans called on the Military Districts, or the new Divisions that were replacing them, to carry out enlistment, documentation, outfitting and purchase of horses. The recruits would then move to existing camps, particularly Petawawa. Hughes unilaterally rejected both plans and established his own 'Call to Arms'. Two hundred and twenty-eight night letters were sent to the COs of Militia units to sign up likely men; normal channels were ignored and commands by-passed. Existing regiments and their names were to be abandoned and a new system of numbered battalions was introduced. At a single stroke, the organization and *esprit de corps* of existing regiments, dependant importantly on local involvement and pride, was destroyed with nothing initially to replace it. To complete the charade, a new camp, Valcartier, was to be cut out of the bush in the Cartier River valley adjacent to Quebec, the proposed port of embarkation. That the land was owned by friends of Hughes was apparently neither an embarrassment nor an impediment. Contractors were still clearing land when the first recruits arrived on 18 August. Lack of supplies and tents, uniforms of inferior cloth, and inadequate boots compounded the bedlam. The deficiencies of the Ross rifle, though widely known, was still an insiders secret. Many of the horses purchased were laughable so they were sold for a pittance or shot. Wagons of many patterns were ordered but all were unsuitable for the narrow roads and villages of Europe. Less confusion existed with the artillery, signals and engineers because they were recruited, mobilized and trained by existing units.

Thus, the First Canadian Contingent of the Canadian Expeditionary Force (CEF) was created overnight with great confusion, duplicated effort, wastage and bottlenecks.[5] It was said, as a complement by his friends, that only Hughes could have done it. He himself thought it was all a tremendous success and much better than using the normal channels.[6] Nevertheless, when the Second Contingent was raised, its mobilization was carried out by the 1911 scheme.

Yet something arose out of the early Fall mists of the Cartier valley: a body of men 32 660 strong (7000 more than prescribed). These potential soldiers were poorly equipped and virtually untrained but that changed with time. Although Col. Hughes was the Minister and not the Commander-in-Chief (CinC) he led all parade reviews on his charger including the last one, prior to embarkation on 27 September, in front of the Governor-General. At least Hughes was a good horseman.

Hughes' baleful effects weren't limited to mobilization. He despised the Permanent Force as only some Militiamen could, thinking Canada's defence should be solely the responsibility of its traditional rural citizen soldiers as in the myth. His abhorrence of the PF showed in several ways; he combined the Royal Canadian Dragoons with Lord Strathcona's Horse, only to separate them again soon after. Neither unit was to be part of the CEF in spite of their excellence and high training level but were slated to run camps in Canada. Likewise, the RCR was to be sent to garrison Bermuda to release a British unit for France but many believed it was also intended to humiliate the well-trained PF unit. He repeatedly interfered with command structure and appointed officers to regimental units and the camps chiefly on the basis of politics or cronyism. As a result he created an abundance of supernumerary officers of field rank at Valcartier who later sat in Britain rather than on duty with troops in France. Amongst his many actions some were positive ones such as approving the creation of a motorized machine gun brigade, a Canadian innovation which could be looked on as one of the first armoured units.[7] Curiously, he also chose some excellent senior officers although the reasons appear to have been convoluted. Firstly, he selected Major General E.A.H. Alderson, a Briton, to command the First Contingent (soon the First Canadian Division), although Hughes would have preferred to lead it himself.[8] He also chose Lt. Col. Arthur Currie to Command the 2nd Brigade as a result of strong recommendation by his son, Garnet Hughes. Furthermore, Sam Hughes probably accelerated the dispatch of the First

Contingent but the level of its organization, staffing, equipment and training was deplorable at the time of embarkation.

Buster had received orders on 24 August to return to Canada immediately and left within twenty-four hours aboard the S.S. Calgarian.[9] Buster left England in such a hurry he had to abandon most of his personal effects and hadn't time to sell his excellent horse, which he turned out to pasture on the correct assumption he would need it later. While he was at sea a number of requests were made for his services; the first by Lt. Col. Fages for him to return immediately to the RCR in Bermuda as the regiment was short of experienced officers. However, the Adjutant General replied he was needed for staff duties.[10] On his return, on 5 September, he was appointed Acting Director of Military Operations at Militia HQ nominally in Ottawa, but most of his time was spent in Montreal inspecting shipping and hiring transports for the 1st Contingent. During this period the CGS, General W. Gwatkin, recommended that he be appointed General Staff Officer third class (GSO 3) of the 2nd Division. Later the CGS amended this to GSO 3 at HQ Ottawa, both positions would have had higher rank as well as double the rate of pay he was getting. When it was sorted out, J.S. Brown, still a Captain, was appointed by the CGS to be Deputy Assistant and Quarter Master General (DA&QMG) of 1st Canadian Division on 25 September just days before the Contingent sailed (see Appendix A - Staff Positions of a Canadian Division, 1914-18). Buster was also recommended by the RCR for appointment as a Major on 14 September, but did not hear about it although it was gazetted on the 23rd while he was still in Canada. The welter of appointments and recommendations reflects something of the confusion at HQ at the time but Buster actually served virtually continuously from his return inspecting and approving ships to transport the Contingent until he himself embarked. He was responsible for assembling twenty-eight fine liners that carried the troops to England. If the fleet had a fault it was that too few of the ships could handle the heavy freight adequately: guns, vehicles and wagons. Although there was confusion in mobilization, encampment, training and embarkation, there was no disorder in chartering vessels despite it being in the hands of a relatively junior officer, who was at least properly trained in staff work and who experienced little interference. During the crossing Buster had his hands full getting to know the personnel, his new job and what was known of the organizational arrangements he would have to make in England to provide transport, supplies and munitions for the whole Division on Salisbury Plain.

The Contingent started disembarking on 17 October at Devonport, England, a small port adjacent to Plymouth, because the risk of submarine attack was considered too high on the normal route to Liverpool.

Photo 5 - 2. Major James (Buster) Sutherland Brown and Lt. Col. James H. MacBrien probably on Salisbury Plain, 1914.

This change resulted in extremely slow disembarkation; a week or more, and for example, five days for Arthur Currie and the Second Brigade. Because of his staff duties Buster was among the first ashore. Actually the staff and troops were surprised on their arrival to find the camp of bell tents mostly had been set up for them by Territorial troops but that was one of the few pleasant surprises (Photo 5 -2). There was no flooring for the tents, no hard standings for the horses, none of the extensive baggage at the port had been dealt with and the troops refused to carry their own heavy kit. Also, there was no provision for stores and no accommodation for HQ. It started to rain heavily soon after the Division's arrival and continued with little respite most of the autumn and winter, accumulating twice the long term average for the area. It made living conditions ex-

Photo 5 - 3. Wagons of a Canadian Mounted Rifle Company on Salisbury Plain with Stonehenge in the background. IWM, Q53573.

tremely uncomfortable. The plains and the camp grounds were overlain by a sticky layer of grey mud above the impermeable chalk. Perhaps this provided good preparation for Flanders. Hutments were supposed to be provided in lieu of tents but the first were not ready until 9 November and 11 000 troops were still under canvas at Christmas. Actually, it was later shown that living in the open air of the tents, even though wet and cold, was better for the troops' health than living in the ill-ventilated hutments where lung diseases became rampant. Regardless of the weather, intensive training under Lt. General Alderson started almost immediately on arrival with schemes for sections and platoon and working up to Brigades and eventually the whole Division. By early 1915, the Canadian Division was regarded by outside observers as being ready for the fray but still lacked that special knowledge gained only in battle.

Four camps were set up to accommodate the Canadian Division on Salisbury Plain. Buster was quartered appropriately in Bustard Camp, only three and a half miles northwest of Stonehenge (Photo 5-3). He apparently lodged with General Alderson in the relative comfort of the Ye Olde Bustard Inn, where the Division established its HQ. Buster hadn't met the General before their stint on Salisbury Plains but was on his staff there, and later as DA&QMG at Canadian Corps Headquarters. Within the realms of their positions they became friends. Buster stated in a letter of condolence to Lady Alderson, after the General's death in 1928, that the latter had been very kind to him, recommending him for the DSO which he received at the end of 1915 and also that Sir Edwin had offered personal advice to Buster suggesting, for example, that he should smile more often.[11]

General Alderson was 55 years old but fit and had the advantage of knowing Canadians well, as the Royal Canadian Dragoons and the 2nd Canadian Mounted Rifles were part of his command in South Africa. His acquaintance with Canadians was probably part of the reason for his selection as Divisional and later Corps Commander. The troops presented an early discipline problem on Salisbury Plain as they soon learned to abandon their wet and cheerless camps in the evenings for the neighbouring pubs and often returned drunk and disorderly. Alderson's solution was to establish 'wet canteens' in the camps which quickly brought the problem under control but brought angry protests from Temperance Groups in Canada, many of which were Sam Hughes' political supporters. Buster, either before Salisbury or after, became a strong advocate of these facilities where troops could relax under loose control without damaging discipline, morale, private property or public relations. The experience of the First Division troops and officers at Salisbury was unpleasant and led to its abandonment for the following Divisions of the

Canadian Expeditionary Force (CEF) for training and accommodation of reserves. The Second Division was encamped near Shornecliffe in Kent (*see* Map 1), which according to Fraser the troops actually enjoyed.[12]

Alderson also quickly recognized that the Canadian equipment was mostly substandard and initiated a program of replacement with British equipment. The catalogue of shoddy or inappropriate equipment was considerable, and much of it the result of favouritism shown to suppliers who were friends of the Minister or purchased without critical appraisal as a result of hasty decisions made in Ottawa under pressure to get the war effort rolling. Amongst the laughable products of the injudicious equipment purchase policy was the MacAdam trenching tool and shield which was patented by Minister Hughes' secretary, Miss Ena MacAdam. The idea was essentially copied from a similar tool seen during Swiss Army manoeuvres attended in 1913 by Hughes on a boondoggle with a group of Militia Colonels and their wives, probably including Miss Mac-Adam.[13] Twenty-five thousand of these were ordered yet they proved to be unable to stop a rifle shot, were heavy, cumbersome and useless as a spade. The troops scoffed at them.[14] They soon were sold for scrap.

Because of his position as DA&QMG Buster had a prominent role in pointing out the deficiencies of the equipment to Alderson which, from Buster's and the General's points of view, would have included the Ross rifle. This was also the opinion of the troops in the trenches.[15] In this regard Hughes would not hear of a change, and at the time the British were short of Lee Enfields, so the matter rested. Even in cases where the Canadian equipment was superior, such as with some motor vehicles, these too had to be replaced because of inadequate provision of spares of all types. Buster was appointed a member of a Court of Inquiry ordered by the War Office first to consider Canadian vehicles, then wagons and all other equipment (Photo 5-3). After the Court of Inquiry it was decided to replace most of the Canadian materiel. The program of replacement soon brought General Alderson into conflict with General Hughes and resulted in continuous hostility between them until both were replaced in 1916, first Alderson as a result of Hughes' initiative, and then Hughes by the Prime Minister. Happily for Buster he was below Hughes' line of sight so did not suffer. Actually Buster and Sam's son, Garnet, were fairly good friends although of different rank and they corresponded throughout their lives. When Garnet was GOC of the 5th Division, in March 1917, he wrote to Buster for advice on names for a DAQMG for the Division.[16] Years later Buster wrote to Garnet inquiring about schools in England for his sons.[17]

Alderson was also caught in the cross fire between the War Office and Canadian political authority. After keeping his masters in Ottawa informed by responding to their telegrams and by requesting decisions from them, he was ordered by the 'Imperial' War Office that he must not communicate with them directly.[18] This was the start of a slow and reluctant process by the British to learn that the Dominion Forces were not 'their' forces and also for Canada, with its emerging nationalism, to adapt to a new form of control of its forces within an Imperial system.

Buster led the Advance Party to France, on 2 February 1915, where he was in charge of billeting and arranging supplies for the Division. The party landed at Boulogne on 4 February and proceeded to the (British) Second Army HQ at Hazenbrouck where he was received by Sir Horace Smith-Dorien, the GOC. On the same day the Advance Party arrived in France, the 1st Division was reviewed by King George V on Salisbury Plains, fittingly in the rain. Then, once again, the Division proceeded to an inconveniently small port, Avonmouth, where it took days to embark for France. The convoy proceeded to St. Nazaire on the coast of the Bay of Biscay, again for fear of submarine attack. The troops were packed into many small vessels, and in transit they were subjected to a full force gale followed by a long disembarkation. The famous painting of the landing by war artist Edgar Bundy, which shows the Generals casually reviewing the pipes and drums of a Canadian Highland Regiment marching by, whilst the troops disembark, seems a little decorous considering what they suffered at sea. The Division proceeded to Hazenbrouck and Strazeele west of Ypres where Buster was in charge of the detraining from 12 to 17 February. The entire staff of the 1st Division during this early period on the Western Front is shown on Photo 5-4. The Division underwent brief trench warfare training in the line until 22 February, one-on-one with troops of British III Corps. The long ordeal of living in the muddy trenches during the stalemate on the Western Front had begun, which was punctuated regularly by bloody battles without significant breakthroughs. The battle sites at which Canadians fought are shown on Map 1, the Western Front during the Great War.

The pattern of Buster's life at the front was soon established. He proceeded to carry out his line duty as DA&QMG at Division HQ from Sailly-Sur-Lys on 22 February and remained there until 24 March, a period during which the battle of Neuve Chapelle took place (10th March to 13th). Buster's duties included both personnel services and supply and equipment during this time but mostly the latter: planning and executing embarkations outside the theatre of operations, billeting, supply of equipment and munitions, provision of transportation including remounts and veterinary services. He could not have carried out his duties properly without close personal observation of the front and good intelligence of operations when the Division was in the line, as well as gathering knowledge of the geographic situation of the whole environs. He was at or close to the front most of the time.

The Canadians were only on the fringe of this battle but even there they experienced an intensive cannonading for the first time. A break through was expected from the British attack which the 1st Canadian Division was expected to exploit. The first day of attack went well but the surprise gained was lost by poor communications resulting in a failure to follow up on the initial success. The Canadians were not called upon to advance. Regardless, it turned out to be a bloody fight for Haig's First Army of British and Indian troops.[19] Following the battle the Canadians were withdrawn into General HQ Army reserve five miles behind the front where they remained until they marched some thirty miles to the Cassel area of Flanders in preparation for an expected German attack on the Ypres Salient. On 14 April the Division motored to the front carried incongruously in double-decker London buses which presumably Buster had been able to engage. There, they relieved a French Division in the trenches before the Second Battle of Ypres.

This battle, which began on the 22 April, was the first in which the Germans deployed chlorine from cylinders instead of by shelling. This gas attack was expected by the Allies but the French and Algerian troops, who bore the brunt of the toxic green cloud as it rolled down the gentle slope to their trenches, abandoned their positions leaving a gap of four miles on the Canadian flank without defenders. Fortunately, the Germans did not properly exploit this advantage and the Canadians rallied and repeatedly counter-attacked to fill the gap that night.[20] This was the Canadians first real taste of battle and they helped block the path of enemy forces from rolling into Ypres, important as the only significant Belgian town still in Allied hands. The next day was relatively quiet and the commanders and staff used it to visit their units and appraise the situation, gun positions and topography. However, another attack followed the next day, the 24th, when the only protection the Canadians had from the second cloud of chlorine gas was water- or urine-soaked cotton bandages. The troops suffered greatly from the choking gas but they held. In the Canadian brigade commands there was some confusion about orders because of poor or absent communication. Brigadier R.E.W. Turner's 3rd Brigade fell back to a defensive position while Currie's 2nd Brigade held firm where they were but the commander retired to Army HQ to find out what was happening. Both were later criticized but the Canadians were credited with saving the day according to a War Office communique. The Division sustained it's first high casualty count, more than 6000 officers

Photo 5 - 4. Lt. Gen. E.A.H. Alderson, DSO, and his First Division Staff probably behind Ypres in the winter of 1915-16. Alderson front and centre with a whip, Brig. A.C. Macdonell, DSO, front row seated left, Major James Sutherland Brown seated right with a sword. Look at their faces, most are clearly characters. The British Army on the staff do not have their rank on the sleeves.

and men, but they prevented a breakthrough. In this early experience the Canadians showed a determination and skill in battle that was to become characteristic of them. The troops also demonstrated what they thought of the Ross rifle in combat for they threw them away and picked up 1452 Lee Enfields from their fallen British comrades.[21]

Commenting in 1926 on the battle to Colonel A.F. Duguid, first official Canadian historian of the CEF, Buster wrote:

> "At no time had we at Divisional HQ lost confidence or at no time were we looking over our shoulders with a view of retirement. I hold the view that, notwithstanding minor mistakes - some quite serious - the Division as a whole acquitted itself in a most efficient, noble and gallant manner; and the stand of the Canadian division on the left of the British line undoubtedly prevented a very serious disaster."

Buster did not think Edmonds, the official British historian,[22] did justice to the Canadian stand.

Buster remained in line duties after the Second Battle of Ypres until 5 May after which he and the Division retired to British III Corps reserve until 16 May. Then Buster was involved in a series of attachments to the Indian Corps and IV Corps as Alderson's staff was largely stripped from him briefly while he was in command of an informal corps called Alderson's Force. During his attachments Buster was involved in planning and supply for these Corps for the battles of Festubert from the 15th to 25th May and Givinchy on 15 June. Both battles were typical of 1915, stolid attacks with insufficient preparation which achieved small or no gains against defences in-depth and resulted in high casualties for the attackers in no-man's-land. As the bombardment by Canadian artillery markedly increased during these and later battles of 1915 in attempts to cut the masses of barbed wire in front of the German trenches, Buster faced serious problems of how to provide the great quantities of shells needed.

During the last of the year, and early 1916, Buster received promotion, awards and new appointments. He was confirmed in the rank of Major on 14 September, which had been his acting rank for a year. He was mentioned in General Alderson's despatches on 30 November 1915, and awarded the DSO on Alderson's recommendation on 1 January 1916. The citation for neither has been found. Buster received the award from the King at Buckingham Palace on 16 April that year.[23] He was appointed

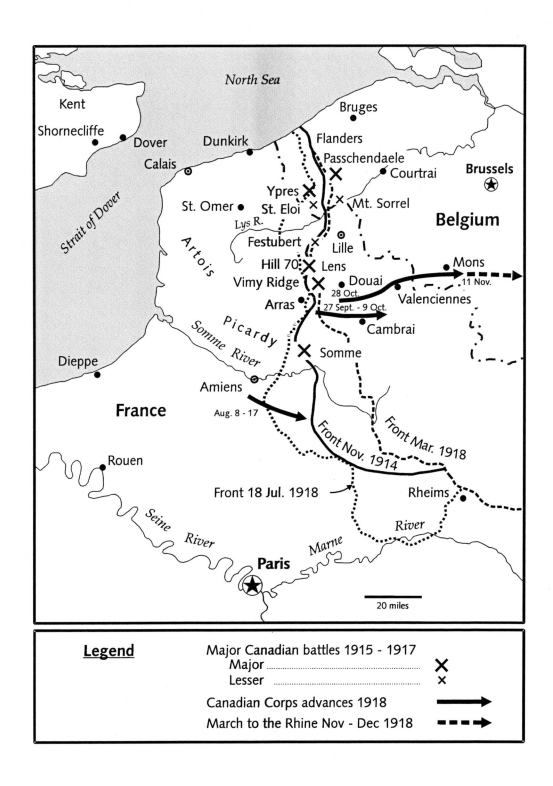

Map 1. The Western Front in the Great War.

AA&QMG of 1 Division on 16 January, 1916, and on 14 May, DA&QMG under Alderson at Corps HQ with the temporary rank of Lt. Colonel.

The latter part of 1915 was relatively quiet for the Canadians as they moved into the line in the Poegetert and Messine front, on 26 June, while battles raged elsewhere with the French and British. The shallow sodden Canadian trenches were awash during the following cold and rainy winter and casualties from trench foot and other diseases caused by the conditions were serious additions to battle casualties.

Nevertheless, the First Division developed a program of major raids such as the one at Petite Douve that were very successful; achieving damage, prisoners and good intelligence, including captured new German respirators while suffering few casualties themselves. These raids were reckoned to be model operations and kept morale high in spite of the conditions. There was little, 'live and let live on the Canadian's front'.[24]

The First Division was joined by the Second on 15 September to form the Canadian Corps. Machinations by Sir Sam about commands were largely counteracted so that promotion to the command of the Corps went to Lt. General Alderson; the Second Division to Maj. General R.E.W. Turner, VC and the First Division to Maj. General Arthur Currie. General Sir John French, GOC of the British Expeditionary Force, ordered the 1st Canadian Divisions to be armed with the short Lee Enfield, thus putting an end to the disadvantage the troops of that Division had faced in battle, even if not to the controversy. Sir Sam Hughes blamed both Alderson and Currie and he did not soon forget it, getting one fired and the other subjected to calumny in the protected precincts of Parliament. Turner was also in effect fired but landed on his feet as the GOC of Canadians in the UK. When the 2nd Canadian Division arrived at the front in September and the 3rd on Christmas Day 1915, they were both still armed with the Ross rifle.

In late March the Canadian Corps moved once more to the Ypres Salient to hold the line from St Eloi to the Menin Road. The Battle of St. Eloi that followed was another in which many things went wrong. The detonation of seven large British mines was miss-timed and the resulting craters were misidentified for several days by both British forces and Canadian 2nd Division. Aerial reconnaissance was not possible because of heavy ground mists, so gaps in the line were unrecognized. In addition, there was an important break down in communications, all of which contributed to serious Allied losses; classic Clausewitz 'fog of war'. Alderson was sacrificed and Hughes was able to get rid of him on 28 May although his replacement, Sir Julian Byng, was probably no more to his liking.

Buster was on Alderson's staff as DA&QMG, with the temporary rank of Lt. Colonel. When Alderson left, to Buster's sorrow, he continued with Byng whom he soon learned to like and respect. Buster retained this appointment until 19 September although he acted in the ungazetted role of AA&QMG to the Corps for much of the period. The Third Division was involved in its first real action in trying to repel the German attack of Mt. Sorrel from 2 to 13 June. The 3rd fell back but held. Then the new Corps commander chose Currie and the 1st Div to recover the ground following rehearsal of the attack and then a major and innovative sequence of bombardments. The counter-attack was a success because it recovered the high ground, but both sides suffered heavy casualties; the Canadians 8000 men, the Germans nearly six thousand. The battle confirmed, finally, the Ross rifle's inadequacy; the War office authorized an exchange of rifles and Ottawa consented during an absence of Sir Sam Hughes.[25]

For Buster, after these battles there followed an idyll; Clare Corsan had responded to his wishes and came to England to marry him. She left New York on 29 May 1916 and arrived in Falmouth on 7 June. She stayed with her half-sister, Mrs. R.F. Hoskyn in her Southampton home until their marriage on 27 June, 1916, in Highfield Anglican Church, Southampton. Buster was fortunate not only to have Clare accept his proposal but also that the battle of Mt. Sorrel was finished without any following hot action. Clare's firm friend, Mrs. Eric Osborne, was her Matron of Honour; her younger brother, Sgt. Edward Corsan, RCR, gave her away and Buster's long time colleague from the RCR, Capt. A.E. Willoughby, also secured special leave from the front to act as Best Man. The weather was ideal and the reception, attended by a score or so of Canadian friends, was held in the Hoskyn's attractive garden (Photo 5-5). Buster and Clare then had a short honeymoon, first in London at the Berkeley Hotel followed by a trip to Edinburgh. Clare had made arrangements for them at a hotel on Princes Street, which was fairly elegant but turned out to be a Temperance hostelry. Buster was less than pleased but it became a family joke. She did much better finding them a pleasant home at 74 Melbury Gardens, Wimbledon, which they rented until the end of the War.

They had an extremely happy marriage from the beginning. He wrote her love letters from the front that were both endearing and verging on erotic. After my father's death I returned from Princeton to help make arrangements. When I reviewed the contents of his large, dark mahogany desk I found some of these letters. I replaced them and soon left for my summer fieldwork, never to see them again. My memory of one of the letters is that after an unrevealing description of his activities at the front he concluded with a paragraph of deep affection and, in coded lan-

Photo 5 - 5. Buster and Clare's wedding party in her half-sister's garden, Southampton, 27 June 1916. From the left, Miss Janet Corsan, Clare's younger half-sister; Sgt. Ted Corsan, RCR, Clare's younger brother; Mrs Kate Hoskyn, Clare's older half-sister; Clare; Buster; Mrs Eric Osborne, matron of honour; Capt. A.E. Willoughby, RCR.

guage, a statement of the joys of joint climaxes.

Buster returned from his leave to France where he became heavily engaged in administrative arrangements first regarding the relief of the Canadian Corps by the Australians. His next responsibility was to organize the march of the Canadians fifty miles south to fill positions recently vacated by the Australians in the Somme. Such a move was equivalent to moving the population of a small town. He had to arrange food, water, basic munitions to accompany or be deposited along the route, which itself had to be secure. Bivouac areas and billets had to be found. The troops had to march but still much transport had to be arranged. The thousands of horses had also to be fed and watered and fuel supplied for the vehicles.

Photo 5 - 6. Tanks going forward, German PoWs, as supervised stretcher-bearers, wearing gas masks as they go to the rear. Photo not at the Battle of Courcelette, where tanks were first used as support for a Canadian attack, but probably in a battle in 1918. IWM CO 2977.

This move was the Canadian's prelude to the vast grinding co-ordinated Allied battles that started in July and continued through the autumn of 1916. After some skirmishes at the beginning of September, the three Canadian Divisions mounted a major attack towards the village of Courcellete on 15 September. This was the first battle in which Canadians were supposed to have tank support (Photo 5-6). Only five of the seven assigned tanks started, and four of these were quickly destroyed by enemy artillery. The German staff were not impressed by tanks and seem to have made no immediate attempt to have similar fighting vehicles made. They did not consult their common soldiers who reportedly greatly feared these monsters. At least Haig saw their value and ordered a thousand to be built.[26] Fighting in the village of Courcellete and beyond was fierce as the enemy arose from underground dugouts behind the 2nd and 3rd Division to its left. However, the Canadian's advance was slowed in the following days by heavy rain so the bloody battle bogged down with high casualties on both sides but without significant results. Both sides needed to reconsider tactics and design a better way to victory than attrition.

During these battles Buster was transferred to the Third Division in which his beloved RCR and the PPCLI served. He was made AA&QMG on 20 September and continued until he was invalided out of the line with a group of related serious diseases: diarrhoea, tonsillitis, conjunctivitis, and rheumatic fever. The latter normally develops from streptococcal bacterial infection and caused the tonsillitis and related symptoms. In the days before antibiotics, the infection could seldom be controlled and it spread to his joints and inflamed them, his eyes and finally to his heart. Buster was very seriously ill. He had been living for a month in a deep, dank dugout when he contracted these illnesses, rather than living in a comfortable billet further behind the lines. He was admitted to No. 1 New Zealand Stationary Hospital, Amiens, on 5 October, and then evacuated on 17 October to the Royal Free Hospital, in London, where he recovered slowly. He was finally discharged to sick leave at the end of the year. The sequela from this affliction came back repeatedly in later life, once seriously in 1922 and again in his retirement. It almost certainly shortened his life. Buster attributed his infection to association at the front with many sickly, coughing veterans of the Gallipoli campaign in his dugout.

About the same time Buster contracted his serious infections, trouble of a different source was brewing for Sir Sam Hughes. He had been exposed in the letting of contracts to friends who, without substantial equity involved, got large contracts to make shell fuses. The resulting scandal generated a government inquiry in which Sir Sam managed to avoid serious repercussions. Nevertheless, the Prime Minister was becoming increasingly upset with his Minister of Militia. Subsequently, the PM questioned members of Hughes' power base, the Orange Lodge, to find that he was not all powerful politically and also investigated Hughes' claim that 'his boys', the troops, would not stand for his dismissal, which was the reverse of the truth. Two more major confrontations occurred between Sir Sam and Sir Robert in late 1916. Firstly, Hughes created a so-called Sub-Militia Council of his senior cronies in Britain against the strict orders of the PM. Hughes also fired the Head of Medical Services overseas and appointed a friend who immediately started a witch hunt within the Service. This provoked the Prime Minister who, to general approval of all but Hughes' sycophantic friends, removed Sir Sam from the Ministry of Militia on 9 November 1916.[27] Buster later commented on these events in a letter to Col. A.Z. Palmer, Assistant Adjutant General (AAG) at HQ in Ottawa, in which he called Hughes, "the Great Interferer".[28] Buster had cause to be upset by Sir Sam as, being on the QMG side of the staff, he was continually dealing with the results of the Minister's erratic procurement decisions. Borden in his memoirs stated that:

> "In my experience [Hughes'] moods might be divided into three categories; during about half the time he was an able, reasonable and useful colleague, working with excellent judgement and indefatigable energy; for a certain other portion of his time he was extremely excitable, impatient of control and almost impossible to work with; and during the remainder his conduct and speech were so eccentric as to justify the conclusion that his mind was unbalanced."[29]

After the dispatch of Hughes, Borden took a more prominent role in military affairs including reviewing the troops in France before the battle of Vimy Ridge (Photo 6-1).

James Sutherland Brown had been among the first of the Canadian Contingent to land in France and he remained there on line duty almost continuously from 4 February, 1915, until he was invalided to the UK in October, 1916. All this time he had been serving as an active senior staff officer, either with Alderson at the First Division or the Canadian Corps, with Currie at the First, or L.J. Lippset at the Third. He had been Mentioned in Dispatches for gallant and distinguished service in the field by the Field Marshal and CinC, Sir John French. He had received the DSO on General Alderson's recommendation on 14 January, 1915, and the privilege of adding p.s.c. after his name. All his commanders had praised his efficiency and dedication in dispatches, by awards or to his face; they trusted him to do the job and had befriended him. Still, he remained a temporary Lt. Colonel on the staff without major advancement or command, possibly because well-trained Canadian staff officers were rare and sorely needed in the Corps to offset the many Britishers in Canadian HQs (Photo 5-4).[30] This was particularly true on the Q side of the staff where there were practically no senior Canadian officers in the Corps but Buster. Understandably, the successful commanding officers of battalions and brigades were the ones who received attention and significant advancement and, as is usually the case with those behind the scene, good routine staff work passed unrecognized.[31] The Canadian staffs, unlike most of the French and some of the British, shared the hard living and danger with the troops to a considerable degree. General Robertson, the CGIS, stated that the staff should not make themselves comfortable until the troops could do the same.[32] Buster was as noted for this approach as he was for his ability to josh with troops and hobnob with the 'toffs'.

Few of Buster's records of this period are personal so we have little idea what he thought about the carnage or the abysmal conditions on the Western Front. It is most likely he felt much as Currie and Macdonell, who hated both but were determined to fight to the end, limiting casualties as they could, until victory was achieved by the Allies. He treasured the general valour of the troops and young officers. He would have agreed with Lawrence Binyon's poem, *For the Fallen*.

"They went with songs to the battle, they were young,
Straight of limb, true of eye, steady, and aglow.
They were staunch to the end against odds uncounted,
They fell with their faces to the foe."

Buster's war service, divided naturally into before and after his major illness, *i.e.* 1914 to 1916 and 1917-1918, mirrored Canada's role on the Western Front. By the end of 1916 Canada had completed its apprenticeship and its soldiers were no longer amateurs in modern war. Coincidentally, the country passed a node on the path by which the Dominion became a nation. From 1917 forward, its army was professional and known on both sides of the trenches as capable, courageous, motivated and well led. They were considered by the enemy as elite troops although they were just starting to regard themselves as something special. Like elite troops everywhere there was little of the 'live and let live' philosophy among the troops, which was rampant late in the war in some French, German and British troops.[33] A nation of about eight million or so by the end of the war had created an army of some 600 000, mostly volunteers, who formed both an effective as well as a substantial force. In relation to the control of this force the Prime Minister had let the British government and Imperial General Staff know that it was a Canadian force which submitted willingly to Imperial command but that it was distinct from the British Army. In effect, he forced the British Prime Minister to appoint him to the War Cabinet. Nevertheless, most of the British Generals, their staffs and the British press did not adequately acknowledge this Canadian sovereignty. Although Buster was an Imperialist and an Anglophile it is apparent he believed that the excellent fighting qualities and discipline of Canadians, together with their achievements, gained partly through superior leadership, organization and planning, set them apart. He was very pro-Canadian as well as an Imperialist, not an unusual characteristic among officers and men of the CEF.

6 In the Great War, Canada's Triumph, 1917-1918

Buster's slow recovery from serious infections was complete enough for him to be discharged from hospital at the end of 1916, but further rest and recuperation were prescribed by the doctors so that he did not return to France until the beginning of March, 1917. Throughout the winter the Canadian Corps undertook no major operations except trench raids, which were launched in greater numbers and ferocity. These were considered models for other Allied forces to emulate. Otherwise, this period was a time of training, recovery, and strengthening defences, while its Divisions were in the line just south of Arras in the Somme. It could be said with some justification that Buster didn't miss much.

When Buster returned on 4 March he reported to Corps HQ under Lt. Gen. Sir Julian Byng and was employed briefly in planning for the Corp's coming assault on Vimy Ridge as part of the British III Army's attack, called the Battle of Arras, from the Scarpe River south. Buster was then ordered on 14 March to return to the 1st Division under Maj. Gen. A.W. Currie as AA&QMG where he felt much at home since he was well known to all the Division Staff. He immediately became involved in the final planning, preparation and practice of the Division for the coming offensive. He was also responsible for maintaining the War Diary for the Division HQ. A major part of his challenge was assembling large dumps of supplies and munitions, particularly shells, for the devised major barrage. This involved laying light railways and improving roads, especially lateral ones, since practically none existed. Much of the work was at night to avoid observation. The dumps eventually contained some 42 500 tons of shells with a further 2500 tons to be brought forward per day once the engagement started (Photo 6-2, 3 & 4).[1] The engineers had to prepare four miles of protective tunneling to the front lines so the assault troop movements could not be observed from the heights of the ridge occupied by the Germans. The large number of horses involved in supply had themselves to be provided with much forage, and pipe lines, pumps and large new reservoirs for their water. The signalers were required to provide miles of wires deeply buried so as to maintain communications during counter battery shelling. However, a vitally important prepara1n for a successful assault went beyond sand table exercises to realistic training at

Photo 6 - 1. The Canadian Prime Minister, Sir Robert Borden, reviewing the First Brigade near the front in March 1917 before the Battle of Vimy Ridge. With him is Brigadier General Macdonell, Bob Rogers, and probably Lt. Col. J. Sutherland Brown who had just returned from sick leave. IWM CO 1046.

full scale on marked out terrain, and extensive briefings that included subordinate leaders and NCOs.[2]

Bombardment started on 20 March but about half the batteries deployed remained silent to disguise the scale of the attack. Nevertheless, its impact was devastating, destroying trenches and shallow defensive works, cutting the barbed wire as well as severely limiting supply, especially food to the enemy. The preparations were practically complete by 1 April. Rain, however, continued to pour down. To achieve some tactical surprise, the bombardment slacked off on 8 April, and the customary intense final barrage was dispensed with. The weather gods then half smiled on the attackers for the rain stopped and the temperature dropped sharply so the mud of no man's land froze permitting easier movement of the heavily-ladened troops up the difficult traverse to the low limestone ridge (*see* Map 1).

Vimy Ridge

On Easter Day, 9 April, 1917, the Canadian attack began at 05:30 hours on a four Division front with the 1st on the right at the south to the 4th at the north. The First had the longest advance to their objective, some two and a half miles up the gentle slope of their southern part of the ridge and down the steeper eastern slope. The thunderous rolling bombardment was provided by 983 guns and mortars, supported by 150 machine-guns sweeping ahead in no man's land. The four lines of objectives were taken successively, the first by 06:15 hours; the last, which was down the reverse slope to Farbus Wood, by 14:30. Only the 4th Division was delayed in reaching its objectives. Casualties for a major offensive were light and totalled some 7700, of which 3000 were fatal. More than 3500 prisoners were captured. The weather was cold with snow flurries and sleet but this helped the assault troops as it was in the face of the defenders. A renewed attack on the German northern strong point called the Pimple, was launched on 11 April by the 4th Division together with a British Division and the hill was taken with difficulty on 12 April. Thus was captured the whole of the strategically important ridge. Unfortunately, once again neither cavalry nor the fledgling Tank Corps were in proper position or strength to exploit the advantage by debouching onto the plain beyond. This was the case in spite of requests by Byng to Haig.

Kegan wrote of the battle: "The success of the Canadians was sensational. In a single bound the awful bare, broken slopes of Vimy Ridge, on which the French had bled to death in thousands in 1915, was taken, the summit gained and, down the precipitous eastern reverse slope, the whole of the Douai plain, crammed with German artillery and reserves, laid open to the victors' gaze. There was nothing to prevent us breaking through [except the inflexibility of the overall plan]."[3]

On 14 April Buster moved the Division HQ well forward to the Labyrinthe Tunnel at Ecurie and began preparing on the 19th for a further advance to Arleux and Fresnoy.[4]

As well as being a major accomplishment in the Great War, the Battle of Vimy Ridge has a special place in Canadian history. It is widely thought to be seminal in developing Canadian pride of nationhood. For the first time the Canadian Corps of four Divisions was employed together in mounting a major assault; they captured all their objectives and held them against counter attacks; accomplishments that the French Army was unable to do. The planning, training and execution of the battle were exceptional, as indeed was the courage and elan exhibited by the troops. The tactics were novel from the application of the artillery, to the

Photo 6 - 2. Realities of supply; horses loaded with shells at a forward dump to be carried on flooded roads to the 20th Battery, Canadian Field Artillery, April 1917 during the Battle of Vimy Ridge. NAC, PA-001229.

Photo 6 - 3. Realities of supply; transport van bogged down in mud being unloaded of shells before recovering it; probably near Vimy Ridge.

use of the machine-guns, the infantry advance by platoon as well as in the broad understanding of the terrain and objectives by leaders down to NCOs. Considering the daunting challenge and the subsequent achievement the casualties were light. Understandably, the German High Command immediately launched an inquiry and the Army Commander and his Chief of Staff both lost their posts.

Among Buster's duties when he came back to the Division was the preparation of HQ War Diaries. These documents signed by him were really a complete appraisal of the Divisions situation. Items regularly included were casualty lists for men and horses and changes in staff. Appendices usually included a list of units and intelligence reports; the situation regarding billets and baths; salvage; position of railhead and dumps; state of ammunition and supplies; fuel, and water; burials; evacuation of wounded; YMCA services; battle stragglers, posts, traffic control, and sports organization.[5]

Buster also paid attention to his personal concerns. He started a letter to the Assistant Adjutant General in Ottawa, Lt. Col. A.Z. Palmer, on April 8, the day before the Battle, which was obviously not completed until later. In it he said, "We fought a great battle from the 9th April up to two days ago. The Division captured the southern objective on the Vimy Ridge and in the three subsequent shows captured Willerval, Arleau-en-Gohelle and Fresnoy [successively further east from Farbus] with comparatively small losses to ourselves [but] heavy losses to the Boche." This was an informal letter of transmittal to Palmer conveying an official one concerning serious errors regarding Buster's qualifications in a recently published Militia List. The errors included dates of his promotion in the RCR to Major, and to his temporary rank of Lt. Col. on the staff, the omission of his p.s.c. and certificate of equitation etc. He felt the errors could negatively affect his promotion. The official letter was counter-signed by General Currie. It shows a characteristic of Buster that even in the melee of the offensive he was calmly concerned with his army status and disdainful of administrative laxness.[6]

In May the Allies generally were suffering bloody battles of attrition without significant advance except for the 1st Canadian Division's capture of Fresnoy on the fifth. The Division then went into corps reserve for the rest of the month. Meanwhile, mutinies broke out in the French Army stemming from the troops' perception that their commanders were incompetent, remote and lacking in concern for the excessive casualties resulting from their bloody and unsuccessful engagements. These mutinies had no central leadership, no Trotsky, to foment and direct them. Haig wished to start a new offensive in Flanders not only to relieve the severe pressure on the French and disguise their problems, but also to neutralize the U-boat bases in Belgium. First, there were matters to take care of in Artois, an offensive just north of Vimy Ridge to take Hill 70 and the town of Lens. The 1st Canadian Division, however, was relieved at the front on 5 May, and went into reserve. The Division HQ also pulled back to Acq at the junction of the light railways and moved into the Chateau D'Acq. This immediately came under repeated attack by the German air force which caused difficulties and casualties at HQ.

A concern for the health of the men and efficiency of the Corps led to a conference in June of Division AA&QMG's. Participants included Buster for the 1st, Lt. Cols. Harry Boak of the RCA for the 2nd, Billy Gibsone of the RCR for the 3rd, and Edward deB Panet of the Royal 22nd, represented by Major Riffenstein for the 4th. All were old friends of Buster's. Together they established a large central bath and laundry facility for the Corps to ensure cleanliness, combat lice, and thus aid morale.[7]

Command Changes

June was a crucial month in the life of Arthur Currie. On 1 June he was knighted (KCMG) in the field by King George V, acknowledging his effective leadership and the Division's marked success. His headquarters at the Chateau was bombed on the night of the 3rd and Currie luckily was only grazed by a fragment although he was only about 10 yards from a blast. Unluckily, two of his staff were killed and 15 wounded. One of the staff, Napier Price, who slept next to Buster was completely covered in dirt but the latter, according to Currie, was only rudely awakened.[8] On 6 June, Sir Arthur was promoted GOC of the Canadian Corps, succeeding Byng who, in turn, replaced Lt. Gen. Allenby as GOC of British Third Army. Currie was the first non-regular officer in the Canadian Corps or the British Army to reach such a high command.

Currie was a large man with a pear-shaped trunk exaggerated by the cut of his uniform tunic and the high position with which he wore his Sam Browne belt. This was the cause of some comic shots at the General but they couldn't detract from recognition of his superior leadership qualities then or now. He had been voracious in study of military history, tactics and strategy. He believed in careful preparation, "train hard -fight easy." He demanded a good staff, consulted them continuously and commonly acted on their advice. Recently, Denis Winter wrote, "Currie remains the most successful allied general and one of the least well known.... . His capture of the Drocourt-Queant Switch in the autumn of 1918 remains the British Army's [sic] greatest achievement of the Western

Photo 6 - 4. Realities of supply: forward end of the light railways at an ammunition loading station. Note horse artillery going forward on horizon, October 1917. NAC photo PA-002122.

Front."⁹

The 1ˢᵗ Division was then taken over by Maj. Gen. A.C. Macdonell who had a curious reputation, lovingly called 'Batty Mac' by the troops for his nonchalance in the face of danger but Archie or Black Mac by his colleagues.¹⁰ He looked fierce with his cap squarely on his head, the brim down to his eyes and his bristling white moustache (Photo 6-1, 4 & 5). He did not tolerate fools or slackers but otherwise was a gentle and understanding commander. He was also immensely supportive of his troops and officers. Macdonell, like Currie, believed in a forward style of observation and command (Photo 6-5). Also, like Currie, he wasn't shy about using expletives. His appointment was insisted upon by Currie over the objections of the PM and others who wanted it to go to Garnet Hughes, 'the son of Sam', in part to mollify the latter.¹¹ Macdonell had long known Buster and was his friend and mentor both during and after the war. One of his sons, J.M., was on his staff as Aide-de-Camp. The other, Ian, had been a pilot in the Royal Flying Corps (RFC) but was shot down and killed in 1916 on the Somme front. Buster named his second son, born in 1919, Ian Macdonell Sutherland Brown after the pilot, and the General himself became the Godfather. Ian Sutherland Brown, the namesake, too, was killed as a pilot flying in the RCAF in 1941.

Hill 70

The Canadians remained in reserve until early June and then only took part in a number of large raids until 7 July when they replaced British I Corps opposite the ruined coal town of Lens, which was Haig's objective. Currie thought Hill 70, north of the town, would be a more strategic objective, as it had a commanding position and would be easier to hold. He convinced the Army commander, General Horne, and then the Germans with a cleverly planned attack. Intensive preparations started in the rain in early August until the delayed assault on the 15ᵗʰ at 04:25hrs. The Division took its objective by their expected time and once again suffered only light casualties. The weather improved as the Division consolidated its position and held on through a score of fierce counter attacks mounted to regain the advantage of a strategic position. Haig then visited the Division on 27 August to express his satisfaction and pride in their work on this front but he had another agenda for them forthcoming in Flanders. Meanwhile, the Division held sports meets in the short break before they moved into a British sector. Here, Buster soon found out, after the hand-over of dumps from the British, that there were great deficiencies, especially in ammunition, which necessitated quick and major administrative and supply activities.¹² The effectiveness of the Division depended on good staff work, audit of stores and quick remedy of deficiencies.

In September Buster moved HQ once again, this time to Barlin on 6 September. Moving HQ meant arranging transport, provisions and billets for 20 to 30 officers an equivalent number of NCOs and men. Following the move Buster inspected the 107th Canadian Pioneer Battalion on 13 September, 1917, and then went on leave for two weeks just before his first son, Malcolm, was born. Buster's best man and long time companion from the RCR, Capt. A.E. Willoughby, became Malcolm's Godfather.

When Buster came back to the front so did the rain. The Division prepared for a wet and cold winter but before the Corps could settle in it was ordered to move again to Flanders in the Ypres salient to help with Haig's northern offensive. Buster arranged for the Division to march there in three stages and, with the Deputy Assistant Adjutant General (DAAG), inspected billets and arranged supplies. With an autumn offensive brewing, the Division was now almost exactly where it had been two years before in the swampy lowlands and muddy morass of Flanders. Before this it was visitor's week as in quick succession, the Duke of Connaught, the IIIrd Army GOC, Byng, the Ist Army GOC, General Sir H.S. Horne, and the Corps commander came for inspections and medal presentations. They were not there for a nastier side of the war when a Quarter Master Sergeant was shot for desertion on 21 October.[13]

Passchendaele

Starting on 29 October, the 3rd and 4th Divisions in fairly good weather assaulted the German positions, which were hardened pill boxes standing like low islands in the sea of mud and deep water-filled craters. This was called the Third Battle of Ypres but commonly Passchendaele by Canadians. The attacks exhausted these Divisions, which suffered high casualties and were then replaced at the beginning of November by the 1st and 2nd. The weather remained good but the ground was still a morass. Fierce hand-to-hand fighting took place in the soggy, pockmarked, blood-spattered and cadaver-rich terrain. The Divisions, however, pressed home their attacks and on 10 November captured the pathetic remains of the village of Passchendaele and hung on until the counter-attacks petered out. Currie had opposed mounting this offensive as strongly as he could. He predicted the Canadians would suffer 16 000 casualties. They suffered 15 654.[14] This was the end of the battle and it was here that General Kiggell made his revealing statement, "Good God did we send men to fight in that." Haig treated this Canadian success as an important victory in the war of words. Congratulations on the Corps' work flowed in. The most telling, as it came from a fighting soldier, was an earlier comment by an Australian, "If the Canadians can hold on there they are wonderful troops."[15]

Division HQ moved several times and for a while there was dry weather and a quiet front. In late December the HQ moved to Auchel and stayed there for a month. While there, on 22 December, Buster was touring the Division units with Capt. Hill, GSO 3; Lt. Macdonell, ADC; and driver, Sgt. Mothersill. When they left the small town of Bethune they experienced a bombardment during which three shells struck close by. Hill was wounded badly in the hip and had to be evacuated; Macdonell was hit in the arm; Mothersill in the head; but Buster once again was lucky and escaped injury.[16] Soon after this he went on leave and saw his son for the first time.

At the start of 1918 the front continued to be quiet but the air war continued. Brig. General G.S. Shepherd DSO, MC of the RFC's 1st Army Group was shot down near the HQ at Auchel and buried with honour by Division troops. He was the highest ranking air force officer to be killed in the war.[17] On January 23rd, HQ moved to Bacquemont, and soon after Buster was visited by Col. J.K. Millan of the US Army to learn about the Canadian systems of arranging dumps, railheads and light railway.[18] It was still quiet on 14 February when the original officers who came to France in 1915 with the 1st Canadian Division met at the Officers Club at Camblain L'Abbe for dinner. Of the 130 original officers some 56 attended with HRH the Duke of Connaught, as guest of honour and Generals, Macdonell, Farmar, Hodgins, and Radcliffe present. The Old Red Patch* officers thought they had some achievements to celebrate, Buster as much as any. Nor were the NCOs and men forgotten. On 18 February Buster and Lt. Col., the Reverend Canon Scott of Macdonell's staff (Photo 6-6) addressed 230 married soldiers, original members of the Division, telling them they had made it the finest of all Divisions on the Allied front because of their steadfastness, courage and skill. They then entrained for three months leave in Canada.[19] In addition, Buster was in charge of three officers from each Division who were ordered to Paris from 24 to 28 February, to inspect both the lines of communication and leave facilities for the troops. The latter were excellent but they commented that the scores of thousands of prostitutes in Paris presented a serious health hazard.

A large German bomber, a Gotha, landed undamaged near the HQ

---

*Starting in 1917 the Canadian Divisions wore coloured shoulder patches and almost immediately the 1st, which wore a two inch red square, started to call themselves the 'Old Red Patch'.

Photo 6 - 5. Maj. Gen. A.C. Macdonell with binoculars during forward observation with his staff; Lt. Col. J.L.R. Parsons with maps and Lt. Col. F.H. Hertzberg looking at the camera, February 1918. NAC, PA-002451.

on 12 March and the crew of two officers and two NCOs were arrested by Military Police. This was the last event of the winter quiet.

It could not be recognized at the time but Vimy Ridge was the start of the end of the stalemate. There, the Canadians made a significant advance but one which was not exploited. Likewise, the capture of Hill 70 (Lens) was not able to be exploited. These battles were followed, for the Canadians, by the last tragic one of the stalemate in the sea of mud at Passchendaele where again there was limited advance (*see* Map 1). Thereafter, a war of movement started, initiated by a last desperate German offensive, which achieved great advances but without creating a real breakthrough. The attack had been expected but the location of its main thrust

Photo 6 - 6. Major-General A.C. Macdonell, GOC 1st Division, and his senior staff in April 1918: Seated left to right: Lt. Col. J.L.R. Parsons (GSO1), Brig. Gen. H.C. Thacker (CRA), the GOC, Lt. Col. J. Sutherland Brown (AAQMG), Lt. Col. H.P. Wright. Standing: Lt. Col. F.H. Hertzberg, Hon. Lt. Col. the Rev. Canon F. G. Scott; Lt. J.M. Macdonell, (ADC); NAC, PA-002619.

was not. The British 1st Army front was expected to receive the weight but it fell mainly on the 3rd and 5th Armies.

German Spring Offensive

The situation for all combatants in the Great War was changing. Russia had been defeated and withdrew in ignominy after the Bolsheviks took control, and signed the *Treaty of Brest-Litovsk* in March. However, this loss in Allied power was beginning to be more than balanced by the US Army's arrival in increasing numbers. Contemporarily, peace feelers were put forward by the Central Powers and considered seriously by politicians of some Allied governments. War weariness affected all major nations but, more importantly for Germany, it was not only reaching the end of its manpower and economic reserves but also the Allied naval blockade was biting hard as it prohibited importation of substitute materials. With these facts in mind the German General Staff planned a last, potentially devastating, blow to win the war. The offensive was designed to penetrate at the junction of the British and French Armies but then fall mainly on the former. Although the attack was anticipated it still caught the British poorly prepared and greatly extended because they had just taken over many miles of trenches from the French. When the attack began on 21 March 1918, it fell on the British 3rd and 5th Armies between the Rivers Scarpe and Oise. For the Canadians all leave was cancelled but most of the Divisions were not significantly involved because Currie resisted Haig's desire to have the Corps broken up, as were the ANZAC Divisions, and then applied piecemeal as reinforcements for the British Army. Most of the Canadian Corps occupied defensive positions along a wide front near Arras. However, the 2nd Division was ordered into GHQ reserve and Buster organized the 1st Division's move south to the Third Army in heavily overloaded buses.[20] Their orders were confused but they ended up as reserve for Horne's First Army with a HQ at Fosseux. Here they were bombed on 6 April but the Division moved later that day to Villiers au Bois and Ecouvres to relieve British 4th Division. In the next few days HQ was repeatedly shelled. Currie's stubborn insistence that the Corps be reassembled was successful, and in the middle of April the 1st Division returned and the three divisions held nine miles of front. The first Division's HQ returned to Chateau D'Acq but started arrangements for a possible retreat, Buster initiated preparations for destruction of ammunition and supply dumps. This became unnecessary although HQ came under fire again. The 2nd Division didn't rejoin the Corps until July.

The German offensive under General Eric Ludendorff scored great tactical victories and drove parts of the French and British Armies back 40 miles, capturing 80 000 prisoners and hundreds of guns. However, the attack was not decisive because it didn't break through the Allied fighting retreat. The Germans advanced to the Marne River by the end of May but then their impetus died. The Central Powers were exhausted. By June the northern front was quiet and the French advanced steadily in the south. As a result of the early summer quiet, while they were in reserve, the Canadians recuperated, rested and trained for open warfare. Also, they had the leisure to become preoccupied with sports for a short while. The 1st Division had a sports day on 17 June in which 20 000 including French civilians were present. RAF 64 Squadron kept the skies clear of German raiders. This event was followed on Dominion Day, 1 July, by a general holiday and Corps Sports day on grounds the First Division had prepared at Tincques near Arras. Fifty thousand troops participated or watched while the Duke of Connaught, Sir Robert Borden and the GOCs of the 1st and 3rd Armies, and General Pershing, CinC of the American Expeditionary Forces, attended. First Division provided the Guard of Honour and the massed Pipe Bands of the Corps entertained the troops between events. The RAF again kept the skies clear. The Championship was won by the 1st Division on aggregate points with 101, the Second and Fourth tied for second with 58 points, Corps troops amassed 56 and the Third Division had a presentable 43.[21] This interlude elevated the spirits of the whole Corps' which continued high as they moved to the front ten days later. A few may even have suspected that this was to be the start of the end of the grim war. The Allies were now able to prosecute their own campaign of movement which for the Canadian Corps was called the Hundred Days or the advance to Mons (see Map 1).

Haig was able to convince Marshal Foch, who had been made Generalisimo or Supreme Commander in March 1918, that his plan to have the British Armies launch an attack through the sodden terrain of Flanders was a mistake. Haig's partially prepared alternative, comprising a fairly concentrated assault from Amiens, was preferable. The British Fourth Army on the left in the north, with the ANZAC and Canadian Corps in the critical centre adjacent to the First French Army on the right in the south, would clear the environs of Amiens. There, the firm land would enable the British and Commonwealth forces to use tanks to advantage. Preparatory troop movements occurred at night and the battle units and their equipment were concealed by day in woods. This, together with omission of a preparatory bombardment, created a real surprise for the enemy.

Amiens and the start of the Hundred Days

As part of this scheme of attack along the Somme from Amiens the Canadian Corps moved to the front on 11 July with the HQ at Etrum.

While there the new Minister of Militia, Maj. Gen. S.C. Mewburn, CMG, visited the First Division on 16 July; such an event was often a prelude to an attack although the Canadians did not know of it yet. On 24 and 25 July following, Buster with the DA&QMG and the Artillery Staff Captain, carried out a reconnaissance for ammunition dump sites and determined the status of supply. It was clear that ammunition supplies were marginal at best and action had to be taken. On 26 July he reconnoitred for a suitable site for Division baths. A week later Buster visited all administrative units to reinforce the need for secrecy in regard to coming operations. Only the GOC, GSO1, AA&QMG (Buster), Brig. General Thacker, the CRA (Commanding Royal Artillery, still used in Canadian Corps) and three Brigade Commanders (Brig. Generals Griesbach, Loomis and Tuxford) knew the planned deployment of the Division.[22]

Buster made the administrative arrangements for the secret move of the Division from Artois to the Somme by strategic train and approach march between 1 and 7 August. There was little room for error as the schedule was so tight. The Australians and Canadians attacked at 04:20 hours the next morning. Again, the 1st Canadian Division occupied the critical site in the centre. The tanks led to good effect at the beginning of the attack by crushing the web of wire and destroying machine gun nests but then the three brigades outran the tanks and leapfrogged ahead to cover 8 miles and capture 3000 prisoners that day. The RAF kept the skies clear and probably for the first time provided continuous observation and wireless reports of the battle's progress, which greatly aided command and control. Wise states that more than any previous battle of the war Amiens was to feature planned co-operation between the air and ground forces.[23] This day, 8 August, was what Ludendorff called the German Army's Black Day. The next day the Division forged ahead again and passed through the 4th Division to occupy the village of Beaufort. That afternoon Buster and the DA&QMG were up front reconnoitring the captured ground, selecting dump sites and arranging access for supply columns. These were critical duties in preparing for an offensive. In the evening, with the GOC and GSO 1, he toured the battlefield and visited each of the three Brigades. The battle essentially ended on 11 August; nevertheless, the Division HQ was shelled and bombed from the air on the 13th and again on the 15th. On 17 August HQ advanced to Le Quesnel as the first rain in three weeks fell. The Division was relieved by the French on the 19th for an eight day rest.[24]

The Battle of Amiens had been won. General Ludendorff and the German General Staff were demoralized and for the first time admitted to themselves premonitions of the Central Powers defeat. Ludendorff said, "the war must be ended."[25]

Drocourt-Queant Line and over the Canal du Nord

On the 22 August the Division came briefly under the Australian Corps. Here Buster met General Rawlinson, IVth Army GOC, who spoke to him in no uncertain terms of the good work of the Division and Byng later said the Canadians at Amiens fought the finest operation of the war. The Canadian Corps had met and defeated elements of 15 German Divisions, destroyed four, captured more than 7000 prisoners and 200 guns. However, they themselves suffered nearly 12 000 casualties of all sorts, a heavy price but necessary in attacking such a dug in force across flat terrain.[26] Buster then made the elaborate arrangements, needed at short notice, to move the Division on 25 August back to Artois by train and march. Hence the Division was not part of the start the next day of the Battle of the Scarpe, 1918 (Second Arras). There the 2nd and 3rd Divisions surprised the enemy by an attack at 03:00hrs that they carried beyond Monchy-le-Preux. On 30 August the 1st Division passed through the 2nd Division to attack at 04:20hrs, overran their objectives and beat back a counterattack. They suffered only light casualties. The next day the 2nd Brigade attacked at 05:00hrs and captured the working trenches of the Vis en Artois Switch and 15 machine guns. The next objective was the formidable Drocourt-Queant (D-Q) line. Buster carried out a recce for advanced dumps on 1 September, and the 1st Division started another attack on the right at 05:00hrs on 2 September. They broke through and captured five towns including Cragnicourt. That evening the GOC, his aide, Capt. Mitchell, and Buster rode the battlefield before the expected counter attack. The Division had captured 81 officers, 3938 troops, 80 guns and 55 machine guns, in these operations.[27] Furthermore, all the enemy gains from their spring offensive had been recovered.

The next objective for the Division was to cross the unfinished but partially flooded Canal du Nord, another formidable task. From 18 to 26 September Buster was at a new HQ at Warlus planning and organizing the movement of many units, as well as reconnoitring for dumps and acquiring tons of fodder for the hard working horses. Currie and his staff had planned a difficult manoeuvre involving an advance across the dry southern end of the Canal, funnelling the Corps through this gap to fan out northward behind the flooded terrain and on to Cambrai. It was a bold plan. It required engineers to devise ramps and bridges under fire followed by precise movements of the infantry. The 1st and 4th Canadian Divisions were to carry across the Canal whereupon the First was to wheel north to advance to their objective of Sains-les-Marquion in the centre and then 5000 yards beyond to Haynecourt and the Arras-Cambrai road. They had accomplished the greatest advance of the day even though ammunition became a problem. That night the GOC, GSO1, Buster and the General's aide rode over the battlefield and visited all Brigade HQs and some Battalions. Ammunition continued to be a problem as supply could only just keep up with need. The Division captured thousands of prisoners as it advanced. It was relieved on 3 October by the 11th British Division. The 2nd and 3rd Canadian Divisions then passed through to attack Thun-St.-Martin, six miles northwest of Cambrai. In all, it was one of the most successful Allied battles of the war, which not only defeated the enemy but exhausted him and absorbed his reserves. Since 26 August the Canadian Corps had advanced 23 miles and broken through the redoubtable German defensive system. It was a costly victory, some 30 000 Canadian casualties, but the Germans, even though in defence, had lost many more. They had also given up 19 000 prisoners, 370 guns and 2000 machine guns.[28] Together with successes to the north by the British, to the south by the French and Americans, and across the Alps by the Italians, the Central Powers began suing for peace.

The Advance to Mons and the March to the Rhine

The 1st Division then went into rest and reserve until 12 October. When the Division again entered the fray it was slightly north of where it finished, positioning itself for an advance from Douai to Mons, the important Belgian coal and industrial town. In retreat the Germans laid waste to the Belgian countryside, stripping it of all farm animals and destroying all the bridges, canals, locks and by flooding the country. Even so their retreat was rapid, and it was difficult for the Canadians to keep in contact with them. Supply under such circumstances was the major problem. As Currie said of this:

> "Because the advances were so substantial, [the] enormous
> logistical demand was hard to anticipate, and supplies and
> replacements had to be moved further and faster to be at
> the right place at the right time."[29]

Division headquarters moved daily. Although this and the supply problems became routine it still involved Buster and his men in a lot of work which was carried out very efficiently. In fact, the war of movement was completely different and introduced many more variables to the problems of supply.[30] Nevertheless, the Q staff of the Canadian Corps and particularly the 1st Division, Buster and staff, coped so well with the problems they set an example of how this should be handled.[31]

The Corps had orders not to engage the enemy but to bypass him if he put up any serious resistance. Casualties were to be avoided, contrary to Sam Hughes' assertions. During this advance many of the senior staff had brief leaves including General Macdonell who returned on 23 October. The Prince of Wales lunched at Division HQ on 27 October after which Buster left on his leave returning a month later, well after Armistice was declared on 11 November. He had been with Clare in London for the enthusiastic celebration including attending plays such as Chu Chin Chow. The war was over and most thought the Allies troubles were about to end. Buster was amongst those who didn't think so, as his thoughts over the next few years reveal.

When he returned to the front Buster's chief challenge was arranging supplies for the rapidly advancing Division during its 'March to the Rhine'. The transport system had been significantly destroyed even in Germany. The columns' paths were through the Ardennes in France and the Eifel in Germany, both of which were dissected hilly terrain with a paucity of roads. Furthermore, these regions were already substantially short of food because of the naval blockade and the scorched earth policy of the enemy. At least ammunition was not much of a problem anymore and the weather was fine until the end of the month. The troops' spirits were high even though they were short of rations during their rapid rough march and frequently forced to sleep at night in wet bivouacs. Still, with victory at hand and the prospect of survival real, the first agitations to get home arose.

The 1st Division marched through Namur and Huy and crossed the border into Germany at Petit Thier, on 4 December, with Generals Currie and Macdonell mounted in the lead (Photo 6-8) followed by three lancers, then Buster and other staff in front of the smart and disciplined infantry marching with fixed bayonets (Photo 6-7). The only audience was a few Corps troops of the cavalry screen and a gaggle of German children whose parents were nowhere to be seen. The Generals and their staff, including Buster, probably dismounted just beyond the border to review and encourage the Division troops (Photo 6-9). The reception at the German frontier contrasts sharply from the rapturous one the Canadian Army had received everywhere in Belgium and eastern France. For example, in Denain on the route to Mons, the Prince of Wales with General Currie and Major General David Watson, GOC of the 4th Division, reviewed the troops with the ecstatic populace in the distance (Photo 6-7). The 1st Division reached the Rhine River at Cologne on 9 December at 09:30 hours after covering 250 miles in 21 days. On a rainy 13th December they crossed the river with fixed bayonets and bands playing before the GOC II Army, General Herbert Plumer, taking the salute. It was planned they were to be part of the Army of the Rhine.[32]

Photo 6 - 7. The Prince of Wales taking the salute with General Currie and Maj. Gen. David Watson, GOC 4th Division, at Denain, France on the Division's advance to Mons in the Hundred Days, 19 October 1918.

Soon after they arrived at Cologne, Buster received news he was to return to Ottawa immediately to become Director of Organization. There was much celebration on his behalf and on 18 December General Macdonell had a party for his farewell at which General Currie, the Brigadiers Farmar, Tuxford, Griesbach, Hayter, and Thacker as well as Buster's fellow Colonels, Parsons, MacPhail, Mathews, Palmer, Harris and Dunlop. Batty Mac, the GOC, said in his diary the party was a great success.[33] Buster left the next day, perhaps with a headache.

Buster had served in senior Q-staff positions under Alderson, Byng, Currie, Lippset and Macdonell. They all had recognized and praised his abilities, encouraged and befriended him. Alderson recommended him in late 1915 for the DSO, among the earliest in the war for Canadian officers. Given their differences in rank and origin, Alderson was very affable towards him even offering personal advice. Buster worked directly with Byng only a short time but he too befriended Buster and early in their association, in a show of appreciation, gave him a signed portrait. Their friendship continued through the post-war period while Buster was at the Imperial Defence College and later when Lord Byng was Governor General of Canada. Currie was a curious mixture of folksiness and austerity. Buster was not as close to him as he was to the others but he too gave Buster a signed portrait. They also had exchanges of friendly correspondence after the war largely concerning the unjustified slander to which Currie was subjected concerning his leadership (*see later*). Buster was closest of all to Archie Macdonell who recommended him for the CMG and promotion, was Godfather to James' and Clare's second son, and used Buster not only as his AAQMG but also in some respects like a GSO 1. This may have been one source of problems between Parsons and Buster (Photo 6-6) in the 1930s at the staff of Military District No. 11 at Work Point Barracks in Victoria (*see later*). Buster's close friendship with the General continued with frequent exchanges of letters until the latter died.

The war had crystallized many facets of Buster's personality. Attributes present earlier had grown and strengthened. His ability to work thoughtfully for long hours was evident to all. His sang-froid in the face of danger had been clearly demonstrated; his acuity had developed and his fund of relevant knowledge had expanded greatly. Buster's friendliness and openness with his colleagues was attested to by the way both his superiors and fellow officers treated and respected him. Also, he had a great ability to treat the troops with consideration, fairly and familiarly but maintaining decorum and discipline. Coincidentally, his ambition and jealousy of his status were sometimes revealed. However, it was Buster's organizational ability, always strong, which had increased

Photo 6 - 8. Gen. Currie and Gen. Macdonell crossing the German frontier at Petit Thier at the head of the 1st Division on the march to the Rhine, December 1919. Following the Generals are three lancers and then in the right hand column, Lt.Col. Sutherland Brown. NAC, PA-00.

Photo 6 - 9. General Currie taking the salute with Maj.Gen. Macdonell and staff of the First Division near the German border, Col. James Sutherland Brown on left with the chin strap of his cap in use after just dismounting, December 1918. IWM. CO 3723

markedly so as to become the characteristic his superiors and colleagues most associated with him. At the end of the war he was still one of the few Canadians who occupied senior Q-staff positions in the Corps. That this ability was exceptional is confirmed in a letter from Brigadier General G. Jasper Farmar dated 26 April, 1919, while he was a lecturer at the Staff College at Camberley. In a long, newsy and friendly letter he acknowledges that his own lecture on preparations for an offensive is based substantially on Buster's report to Macdonell on organization of the 1st Division for the 'Hundred Days'.[34] Surely then, the Canadian Corps victorious advance, and particularly the First Division's part in it, depended to a considerable degree for its striking success on Buster Sutherland Brown's meticulous staff work. This was recognized in a memo by E.C. Ashton on his file dated 1919-09-23 which stated, " This letter [referred to above] shows General Farmar's lecture... was based to a great extent on the way Colonel Brown solved ... the problems of ... the battles of the Hundred Days [which] were to a great extent administrative battles, that is, they depended almost entirely on the supply of ammunition, of trench munitions, the rapid movement of supplies, and the movement and quartering of troops and traffic control, all of which are dealt with by the A&Q Branch [Buster].[35]

Subsequently, Currie and his other superiors recognized that here was a man to merit a prominent role in organizing the postwar Canadian Army, and somewhat belatedly, promoted him to full Colonel. Buster was a good example of Bond's observation that, "Routine good work [by staff officers] passes unrecorded while errors and costly omissions receive the glare of publicity."[36]

Buster's good routine work, in fact, had been noted because he had been awarded the DSO on 14 January, 1916, and the CMG on 6 March, 1918. He also had been Mentioned in Dispatches five times: 1 January, 1916; 28 May 1917; 18 May 1918; 31 December 1918 and 11 July 1919. Still, many of his colleagues, such as Jaspar Farmar, thought he had not had his due. In his letter previously quoted he says, "I only hope they played the game with you and made you a full Colonel." Well, they did and they didn't, as he was promoted to Brevet Lieutenant Colonel and Acting Colonel.

7   Capital Ideas

Buster returned to Wimbledon before Christmas and throughout January concerned himself with winding up affairs in Britain, including purchasing household goods for a new life in Ottawa, arranging travel plans for his pregnant wife, infant son, Malcolm, and Miss C.A. Blackwell, nurse and general servant (Photo 7-1), who stayed with the family until 1936. He had been appointed Director of Organization of the new army, about which some thinking had been done but about which there was great divergence of views. First though, the CEF had to be demobilized and this occupied all his attention. When, after a false start, the Command's preferred policy on demobilization was agreed to by the government it went ahead swiftly and efficiently under Buster and the Adjutant General's office.[1] After demobilization the major problem centred upon the role and size of the army. The government was reluctant to decide on this so in effect National Defence Headquarters (NDHQ) made assumptions so that some action could be taken. These involved integration of the best parts of the returning Canadian Expeditionary Force to establish a new Militia and the Permanent Force.

The nine years from January 1919 to December 1927, while Buster was on the staff of NDHQ, was a challenging period in his life. Initially he was Director of Organization during demobilization and planning for the new army. Then, in late 1920, he was appointed to the senior post of Director of Military Operations and Intelligence, during which he produced Defence Scheme No. 1, designed to defend against an attack by the USA directed against Canada and the United Kingdom. He produced this secret plan under orders from the Chief of the General Staff but since the scheme was discovered in the 1960s, amongst the Sutherland Brown papers in the Queen's University Archives, it has been the subject of criticism and ridicule by some academic historians who regarded it as lunacy. However, the consensus of senior Canadian military staff who knew about it, and the situation for which it was designed, considered it the only feasible way to defend the nation. During this period Buster worked closely with the two Chiefs of the General Staff who rewarded him with their trust by appointing him to the Imperial Defence College in London, a precursor to most high ranking posts at NDHQ.

Photo 7 – 1. Baba Blackwell, the boy's nurse and cook on guard, Buster's idea of a joke.

Director of Organization

Buster, together with his RCR colleague and friend, Col. W.W.W. Gibsone, were directed on 7 January, 1919, by the Minister of Militia, Major General S.C. Mewburn, in a telegram to Sir Edward Kemp, the Overseas Minister at Argyle House in London, to be shown the files concerning their respective appointments before proceeding to Canada as rapidly as possible.[2] Buster and family embarked on the SS Olympic on 23 January bound for Halifax then on to Ottawa. On the same day his appointment was confirmed with the temporary rank of Colonel, but confusion ensued about whether the appointment was acting, whether the grade was Class 2 or 3, whether the rate of pay was $4,100 or $4,600 per annum, and also whether he was on the roster of the Militia or the CEF. With all this he was definitely caught up in the military bureaucracy of Ottawa in a period of extreme confusion. The immediate post-war period would have been confusing even if the military and political authorities with their best wills tried to solve their problems regarding the military. These included: organizing demobilization, planning the size and nature of the future army, determining the relationship between the Militia, CEF and the Permanent Force, deciding what battalions and regiments should be retained with what names, staffing headquarters and the commands as well as arranging accommodation and training facilities. The Cabinet, concerned with the country's economic and political problems, took scant interest in these questions and the Prime Minister's attention was riveted on the Peace Conference in Paris and creation of the League of Nations.

Before General Currie left Europe he had been feted in Belgium, France and Britain as a hero and a successful commander. Nevertheless, he returned home to receptions in Halifax and Ottawa that were almost hostile, an indication that politicians and the military were not going to work well together on these problems. The calumnies against Currie emanating from General Hughes and his clique of sycophants both within and outside the government poisoned the atmosphere. Eventually Currie received part of what was due him when the Minister of Defence, Major General Mewburn, who knew without doubt what Currie had accomplished, congratulated him warmly on behalf of the government at a reception in Ottawa and asked him to become Inspector General of the Militia Forces in Canada. The government probably expected him to treat this appointment as a sinecure to reward him for his service but this was not Currie's style. Nevertheless, it was the Canadian government's way - to give no rewards even remotely comparable to that which the UK had presented to Haig and other British commanders. The post and the atmosphere of the appointment frustrated him, consequently Currie left within a year to accept the position of Principal of McGill University.

One of Buster's major accomplishments following the war was his efficient organization of demobilization. Wartime deterioration of the Canadian railways and the paucity of ice-free ports in winter made this difficult. However, Buster was as much a master of railway demobilization as the Germans were of railway mobilization and movement. Although some planning for demobilization had taken place in Canada since 1915 on the peripheral problems of pensions and re-employment, when the exigency occurred it was one of the government's biggest post-war problems.[3] Demobilization difficulties were compounded by the earlier laying off of munition workers and the rampant flu epidemic.

While Currie was still in Europe he and his senior officers including Buster wanted the CEF brought back to Britain in their units and then quickly returned to Canada to be dispatched to their points of origin and disbanded. This, they believed, would avoid having them sit in camps with nothing to do, which would lead to boredom, trouble and riot. Ottawa wanted the troops returned individually on a basis of points dependent on time overseas and not as units nor related to experience at the front. The government was seemingly unconcerned with expediency as

Photo 7 - 2. Buster in Toronto for the return of the Third (Toronto) and Fourth (Central Ontario) Battalions on 23 April 1919. The two battalions arrived on four trains and were marched away for demobilization within an hour. Officers from left to right; Brig. Gen. J.A. Gunn, DSO; Lt. Col. G Gibson; Buster, Director of Organization; Lt. Col. J.D. Sharples; Trustee C.A.B. Brown; and, Brig. Gen. Sir Henry Pellatt. Toronto Daily Star, 24 April 1919.

their scheme would require more time to organize. Hence the result was as predicted by the Corps command and disturbances and riots irrupted.[4] These events did trigger an acceleration of repatriation and demobilization so that the CEF was all returned to Canada by July, 1919. Nevertheless, the politicians seemed little interested in the future of the army even though the CEF was recognized by the Allies and the former enemy as one of the most effective fighting forces on the Western Front, and they were for a short time the toast of Canada.

Buster arranged that the troops entrain as units at the ports, travel directly to their points of origin, detrain and march away to be dismissed immediately. The following day they were demobilized, possible because the delays in England had enabled their documentation to be completed already. Photo 7-2 shows Buster and colleagues waiting on 24 April, 1919, for the arrival of the four trains containing both the Third (Toronto Regiment) and Fourth (Central Ontario) Battalions of his beloved First Division at the North Toronto Station (Toronto Daily Star).

The government soon had other troubles in a turbulent post-war period with labour unrest caused by growing unemployment, resulting from shutting down munitions factories and the demobilization of returned soldiers. The legitimate labour concerns amongst the workers and unemployed was exacerbated by the declared intention in January, 1919, by the Bolshevik authorities in Russia to establish the Communist International (Comintern), an organization dedicated to the spread of revolutionary doctrines and practice throughout the world. In the minds of the government and the army command this assumed significance disproportionate to political and social realities. The birth of the One Big Union (OBU) at the Western Labour conference in Calgary in March, 1919, with its references to the Russian revolution, alarmed the government which called for the army to aid the Mounted Police in maintaining civil powers after troubles erupted in Winnipeg on 15 March, 1919. Labour there called a general strike that lasted until 26 June and resulted in serious confrontations, arrests and casualties.[5] Among the fallout from the perceived riots the Permanent Force was authorized to grow to a maximum strength of 10 000 men, although it never exceeded 6000.

A committee was formed under retired Major General Otter to examine the desired strength and organization of the Militia.[6] Previously, other officers including the former CGS, General Gwatkin and the immediate post-war CGS, Major General MacBrien, had studied the desired form and size of the permanent Force and the Militia; Gwatkin in anticipation of need in 1917 and MacBrien in 1919. They both proposed large standing armies (20 000 to 30 000 men) supported by conscription of able bodied men for a short training period followed by two to three years service in the militia. The justification for these plans was to cause the US government to pause before embarking on any adventuresome action regarding Canada's sovereignty as well as to be ready to contribute rapidly to Imperial defence with an expeditionary force.[7] The Canadian army was proposed to consist of 15 Divisions of which seven were expected to be ready for rapid deployment overseas. The government was not kept well informed of the thinking of either of the Chiefs of the General Staff on these matters. However, Sir Edward Kemp, the Overseas Minister, was given MacBrien's plan and later cautioned him about its advocacy. Nevertheless, MacBrien, the Canadian delegate to the Post-Bellum Conference on Imperial Defence held at the War Office in 1919, used these figures which thereafter were taken as the Canadian position.

After occupying an office in the Department of National Defence HQ in the Woods Building, one of the first jobs Buster tackled was an appraisal of existing training facilities, armouries and barracks for the Permanent Force and Militia. He examined facilities within MD No. 2 in Toronto, including the Old St. Andrews College, Long Branch Range, Stanley Barracks, Brant House Burlington, East Hamilton, Hamilton Armoury and recommended how they should be used or expanded. He followed the same procedure for MD No. 1, London, No. 3, Kingston, and No. 4, Montreal, and on through the list to MD No. 13, in Calgary. Initiated as part of the Otter Committee deliberations and coincident with them, the review was completed by the end of the summer of 1919.[8]

Buster, Clare and Malcolm, with nurse Blackwell, moved into a rental house on 61 Robert Street near the Driveway for several years during which a second son, Ian Macdonell, was born on 16 August, 1919; clearly a celebration of Peace. In April, 1922, they moved to 396 Daly Avenue in the Sandy Hill neighbourhood, just a short walk across the Rideau Canal to National Defence Headquarters. Although Buster worked long hours, there was a social life in the evenings and canoeing and hiking on weekends. One early disaster occurred when Buster, eager to try out a newly purchased canoe, launched it with Clare, Blackwell and Malcolm to find that, although it looked fine, it was completely dried out and leaked copiously along every join. Beaching quickly followed launching with concatenate soaked skirts and possibly a bawling Malcolm. When the latter was old enough to listen to nursery rhymes he confused 'black sheep' in the rhyme with Blackwell so that her family nickname became Baba. Clare was a bridge enthusiast and frequently played with Mabel McNaughton, wife to Brigadier Andrew McNaughton. Mabel and Clare became acquainted in England while both their husbands were serving with the CEF in France and they renewed their friendship in Ottawa after the War. Although the husbands, Andy and Buster, were in social contact their interests and personalities differed considerably and they did not pursue mutual friendship (Photo 7-3).

During the War Buster and Andy were both in the First Contingent and First Division. Later they were almost continuously in contact when McNaughton was made Counter-Battery Staff Officer of the Canadian Corps in January, 1917, and Buster was at Corps HQ in March and April, 1917, planning for the attack of Vimy Ridge. It was at this battle that McNaughton's skill as a scientific gunner really came to Currie's attention. Later when Buster was AA&QMG of the First Division, and he was responsible for all supply including artillery shells, they would have had to constantly confer. Andy McNaughton was made a Brigadier in charge of Heavy Artillery at Corps HQ in 1918, under Currie who called him, 'without a doubt the greatest gunner in the world.'[9] Currie also recommended to MacBrien in December, 1919, that Andy should be appointed the Director of Military Training and Staff Duties (DMT&SD) but MacBrien answered this with the following:

> "I cabled you regarding the [DMT&SD]. I know McNaughton is a clever officer, but his experience has been entirely with the artillery, and I therefore considered, with his expert knowledge of that branch, much better suited to be Director of Artillery than Director of Training of all Branches of the Service and the organization of General Staff Duties. Buster Brown is an officer with a particularly good general knowledge of military organization in all its branches. He was unfortunate in the War not having General Staff experience, but always devoted a great deal of attention to training and operations. I feel that he would be of more assistance to me owing to his broader knowledge than McNaughton, and therefore recommended accordingly. In case Brown cannot be spared from the Adjutant General's Branch, I would be agreeable of course to McNaughton's appointment, as I know that he is a student and would gain the necessary general knowledge."[10]

Although this letter almost certainly was not read by either Buster or Andy it reflects the start of their rivalry which, in spite of this seeming early set back, Andy won hands down. McNaughton became the DMT&ST in January 1920 on Currie's recommendation despite MacBrien's misgivings. Later, on 4 December 1920, Buster was made Director of Military Operations and Intelligence [DMO&I], an appointment that ranked just below McNaughton's which, in turn, ranked just below the Chief of the General Staff.[11] When General McNaughton was belatedly appointed to the Staff College, Camberley, in 1921 Buster was appointed to act in his absence as DMT&SD.[12]

Currie believed the Otter Committee's mandate was set too narrowly to address the fundamental issues of the necessary levels of war and peace establishments for Canada.[13] The committee seemed more concerned with integrating what was left of the CEF with the Militia, integrating Overseas battalions with previously established and named regiments. It was proceeding with this and conferring battle honours from the Great War to these entities. As most of the CEF Regiments had a home

Photo 7 - 3. Buster and Andy McNaughton in breeches with the Station Commander of Camp Borden, probably Major J.A. Glenn in the CAF's dark blue uniform. With them are some substantial businessmen who were supporters of the re-birth of the Canadian Air Force, 6 April 1922.

base this was not too difficult. However, the result was just another fall-out of the misguided mobilization policy initiated by the Minister, General Hughes. As part of the Otter Committee's main work a subcommittee was struck to assign honours to the appropriate and deserving regiments from the Second Battle of Ypres to the Pursuit to Mons. The committee originally was chaired by Col. W.W.W. Gibsone and later by Buster. It included Col. A.F. Duguid, later official historian of CEF, and Lt. Col. H.J. Coghill. They considered all the designated regiments and other applicable units, but like Duguid's history, it dragged on.

The Canadian Expeditionary Force had been completely repatriated by mid summer, 1919, and its units were immediately disbanded as they returned. Sam Hughes' mobilization scheme of 1914, resulted in the general abandonment of traditional regimental names and the creation of sequentially numbered battalions and brigades. This was all very logical and orderly. Only a few PF units avoided this fate: the RCR, Princess Patricia's Canadian Light Infantry (PPCLI), Strathcona's Horse for example. Hughes would have also liked to get rid of these in his desire to humiliate the permanent force. After the war his mobilization scheme led to the problem of how to award battle honours. The disappearance of the numbered battalions would have left much of the gallant Canadian army without significant recognition. Hence units raised, for example in Montreal, would be identified with the most appropriate pre-war militia unit, perhaps even one that was converted to a numbered battalion or which provided most of its troops. This process naturally went in parallel with reorganizing the post-war militia, therefore Buster as Director of Organization was basically in charge of it. The old regiments, the Seaforths (Vancouver), Black Watch (Montreal), Queen's Own Rifles of Canada (Toronto) *etc.*, when reconstituted were awarded the appropriate honours. Buster and others believed the old identities were important for *esprit de corps*. They considered that pride in a regiment and cohesion among the troops of similar origin and kinship induced high morale. Buster was an opponent of the concept of an Infantry Corps, which led to the filling of the ranks with the most readily available troops regardless of origin or allegiance. Happily, most of Buster's superiors agreed with him as he developed the plan to reconstruct the Permanent Force.

The Otter Committee's recommendations on strength and organization were very similar to those of General MacBrien's earlier study, and were also what General Currie desired before he resigned as Inspector General in August, 1920. Probably MacBrien had a strong influence on the committee. The report recommended to the government that the post-war active reserve consist of 300 000 troops, whose strength would be maintained by conscription. The army would be organized into 15 divisions, very much larger than its pre-war strength.[14] Although the Borden government received the report it did not seem to consider it very seriously and neither acted on it nor actively rejected it except for the idea of conscription. Nevertheless, the concepts remained as the ideal at NDHQ for years, and were the basis for planning. In June, 1920, the Minister increased the establishment of the PF because of alarm about the possibility of Communist stimulated riots or disturbances. However, neither the PF nor Militia came close to approaching in size the recommendations of the Otter Report for the defence of Canada, to maintain civil powers or to provide for an expeditionary force available for Empire defence.

While writing the Report, General Otter was asked to serve on a selection board initiated by General Currie to review applications for permanent commissions. It was the method by which Currie and MacBrien were determined to get rid of the deadwood in the army, officers who had served without distinction in Canada and Britain, and who were never active in the CEF. This attempt became part of the dispute between General Hughes, or more particularly, his old Militia cronies with headquarters. The Hughes faction still had much political clout, so the review was scarcely acted upon. Another frustration for Currie and MacBrien was that the government, far from equipping the proposed 15 divisions, only grudgingly accepted the offer of the British War Office to return equipment for four divisions minus their mechanical transport. Although the government was overwhelmed by its financial problems this was a curious approach to take to a gift. As Director of Organization Buster was an advocate of the army point of view in all these activities in 1919 and 1920.

Military aviation in Canada had a fitful start. The earliest flying in Canada before the war, the Aerial Experimental Association of Alexander Graham Bell, Glen Curtiss, J.A.D. McCurdy and F.W. Baldwin, was watched but not strongly supported by the military or the government.[15] The organizational confusion and lack of Canadian government commitment continued during and after the war in spite of Canada's major role in providing aircrew to the Royal Flying Corps (RFC), Royal Naval Air Service (RNAS) and then the combined Royal Air Force (RAF).[16] The birth of a real Canadian Air Force (CAF) with two, potentially operational squadrons was stillborn because of this lack of commitment in spite of the support of the Overseas Minister, Kemp, and GOC Canadian Forces in England, General Turner.

Buster as Director of Organization naturally, was also involved in the post-war history of the CAF. On 26 May 1919 he wrote to the Adjutant

General:

> "It is understood that a Bill is now prepared to amend the Militia Act, to increase the strength of the Permanent Force from 5000 to 10 000. The [CGS] considers that the constitution of the Air Force should be commenced at once, and that nothing be said at present as to whether the establishments will be included in the strength of the Permanent Force, or be included in the present strength... . In any case the question of officers makes no difference. The men would be included in the present establishment by making deductions from the present authorized units, in case the above amendments to the Militia Act are not approved.
>
> The [CGS] considers that the less said at the present time about the composition and the duties of its officers the better. I have just put down the numbers of officers and men required. The establishments, distribution, *etc.* could be drawn up in a future Order in Council, for publication in a General Order.
>
> It is recommended that an officer with sufficient technical knowledge [Col. Reginald H. Mullock, DSO was the candidate in mind] be recalled from overseas to help with organization."[17]

The proposed Order in Council to the Governor General of the same date states:

> WHEREAS no provision has been made for the constitution of an Air Service in Canada; and
>
> WHEREAS a large percentage of officers of the [RAF] were Canadians, and many of these officers desire permanent employment; and
>
> WHEREAS two squadrons and technical sections of the [CAF] are maintained in Great Britain, with a view to their being absorbed in a permanent establishment in Canada; and
>
> WHEREAS an Air Force is a necessary part of the Forces of every Country which maintains Military and Naval establishments; and

WHEREAS no pioneer organization has been established in Canada to give stimulus and encouragement to commercial, naval or military flying:

The under signed has the honour to recommend:-

(1) That the Canadian Air Force be constituted as a Corps of the Permanent Force of Canada;

(2) That the strength of the said Force be 72 officers and 440 men;

(3) That the composition, the establishment, the distribution, organization and pay and allowances of the said Force be left to the discretion of the Minister of Militia in Council;

(4) That the application be made to His Majesty's Government for permission to use the word "Royal" in connection with the Air Force in Canada.

Respectfully submitted,
Minister of Militia

The letter and the drafted Order in Council confirm that Buster and the CGS were supporters of an Air Force as part of the PF, that they appreciated its importance in the future of both military and civil aviation, that they understood the vital role of Canadian aviators in WWI and that they believed these elements meant the service should be entitled "Royal". It also shows something of the lack of frankness between government and the army and the reverse. The letter also included Buster's rough draft of an Organization for the CAF that included at least one more squadron.

Regardless of the favourable opinions of General Currie, the CGS, the Overseas Minister and General Turner, the CAF was not shipped back to Canada but was disbanded and demobilized on the date of the proposed Order in Council, 26 May, 1919. For some reason the Canadian Air Force found no favour with the Minister of Militia, Major General Mewburn, possibly because of the realization of the high continuing costs involved. Nevertheless, an Air Board was created and later the CAF was recreated in small incremental stages starting on 23 April, 1920.[18] Photo 7-3 shows Buster and Andy McNaughton in civies at Camp Borden on 6 April, 1922, with a senior CAF officer dressed in that Force's dark blue uniform. This may be Major J.A. Glenn who was the Station CO at the time. With them are some important supporters of the renewal of the air force.

During the summer of 1920, Buster's wartime malady, rheumatic fever and tonsillitis, returned seriously. Without wonder drugs the only cure was rest. Buster was invalided for the three months, from 7 June to early September. He then returned to work as Director of Organization until his appointment as Director of Military Operations and Intelligence on 3 December, 1920. During the last months in Organization he had two minor irritations: constant problems regarding pay and another regarding a compass he was accused of not returning to stores when he left the Staff College in August, 1914. Buster denied this completely in a hot letter, suggested they were in confusion at the outbreak of war and were now trying to account for old discrepancies. The correspondence went on for quite a time. In retrospect, it might have been easier to pay for it but his acute sense of justice did not permit him to do so.

Director of Military Operations and Intelligence

Buster was the CGS's choice for this second most important position in NDHQ. Earlier he had been MacBrien's choice for the most senior post but the CGS yielded to General Currie's opinion and McNaughton was appointed instead. MacBrien had known Buster for ten years, had attended Staff College with him and had worked closely with him at NDHQ for the last two. It is inconceivable that MacBrien did not know Buster's deficiencies as well as his capabilities. For such a position Buster must also have been acceptable to the Minister, although he might not have known precisely what was expected of Sutherland Brown. Buster's first project, plans for the defence of Canada, was accorded the highest priority of the CGS, Currie and possibly the Minister.[19]

Since Colonial days the defence of Canada from its powerful and sometimes aggressive neighbour to the south had been a natural concern. The War of 1812, the Fenian Raids and the growth in the USA of the tenet of Manifest Destiny following the annexation of Texas from Mexico in 1845, all generated feelings in Canada of apprehension concerning the Republic's intentions. These were heightened after Canadian Confederation by the continuing presence to the south of a large unemployed Union army; by a number of boundary disputes between the two countries and by the Venezuelan Incident of 1898. In all of these it was obvious that Canada could be invaded as a proxy for Britain. In the Venezuela Incident the US Government felt it should enforce the Monroe Doctrine in the dis-

Photo 7 - 4. Canadian 'spies' in 1923 on the road between Keene and upper Jay in New York State; from left to right they are Lt.Col. F.O. Hodgins, DSO; Lt.Col. E. Forde, DSO; Lt.Col. J.M. Prower, DSO. Photographer was probably Col. James Sutherland Brown, CMG, DSO.

pute over boundaries between the colony of British Guiana and Venezuela.

Those who worried most about Canada's defence were the British military establishment in Canada; the GOC, his compatriot staff officers and the garrison commanders of Halifax and Quebec.[20] At times some Canadian politicians such as Sir John A. MacDonald were also greatly concerned. Nevertheless, planning for the defence of Canada was only carried out fitfully in spite of some distinct possibilities of aggression. In London, opinions of War Office staff oscillated between thinking it was impossible to defend Canada in the event of hostility with the USA, trying to produce a plan and the wherewithal to defend the country or, alternatively, only produce a plan for the RN to attack the east coast of the USA.

A sketchy plan for the defence of Canada was produced in 1889 by Capt. Arthur Lee, Royal Artillery, which principally concerned the mobilization of the Militia. It included plans to despatch them to block access to Eastern Canada to delay American advance until help could arrive from the UK. It was a precursor to Defence Scheme No. 1 and also resembled the latter in that it was not fully disclosed to the Government.

In the next decade or so, most British and Canadian military staffs in Canada and the War Office regarding Canada were concerned with policy, protocol and the interaction between separate interests of Canada and Great Britain, or they were concerned with the Boer War. Defence planning was minimal until a Commission was set up under Maj. Gen. E.P. Leach of the Royal Engineers' Halifax garrison to examine it. This inquiry was negative about the possibility of a successful defence, as well as about the Canadian Militia with its excessive political control and patronage. However, the inquiry was not very thorough for it did not consider the Prairies or the West Coast.

The next significant examination was by Col. Willoughby Gwatkin in 1911, which was principally concerned with planning mobilization of a Division possibly to serve overseas. He agreed that war with the USA was remote but planning should be made for the contingency. Being Allies during the Great War made hostilities with the USA even more remote but the NDHQ still regarded it as a possibility for which they should prepare. It became Buster's responsibility.

Three general plans were conceived by NDHQ for the Director to work on:

- Defence Scheme No. 1, (DS No. 1), defence against a possible attack from the USA, judged the most important.
- DS No. 2, defence against possible attack by Japan.
- DS No. 3, organization and despatch of an Expeditionary Force to help the Empire in case of an attack by any combination of European powers or during a minor crisis.

NDHQ did not want Canada to be as unprepared as it was in 1914.[21]

When Defence Scheme No. 1 became known in the 1960s, through the Sutherland Brown papers deposited in Queen's University Archives, it was treated with ridicule by a number of academic historians. James Eayrs, for example, appears to have regarded the scheme as Buster's personal choice; a fantasy of an anti-American, United Empire Loyalist mind.[22] Eayrs clearly had little knowledge of my father's family background (see Chapter 1). The scheme was mocked as completely unrealistic without any consideration that it was drafted for a Canadian army of 15 Divisions as proposed by the Otter Committee and which Currie and MacBrien advocated and thought likely to be approved. Outside of academic circles the plan evoked some ridicule or whimsy.[23] Nevertheless, other historians such as Stephen J. Harris, on the basis of more complete research and better awareness of the contemporary situation in 1921, or Richard A. Preston by the realization that the US forces at the same time had plans to attack Canada, have treated the scheme with greater understanding.[24]

Eayrs makes the point that Buster was working alone and in secret. While both are true in certain respects they need qualification. Buster was not without help. The size of the DMO&I staff under McNaughton is not known. Soon after he was appointed to the post, McNaughton was sent to Camberley for a year to 'broaden his outlook'.[25] When Buster left the post of DMO&I in 1927 he had a staff of nine NCOs who signed a gracious letter congratulating him on being sent to the Imperial Defence College but regretting his departure.[26] This staff, amongst other things, reviewed an extensive literature and prepared it for Buster's retrieval and use. Furthermore, Lt. Col. H.H. Matthews was appointed as his assistant in 1926. Also there were Intelligence Officers (IOs) in the Military Districts. In 1929, the IO in MD No. 11 was a Major Rycroft who worked alone in a small office remote from the main administrative building. As a child I once glimpsed inside his office and was impressed by the walls covered with maps and the shelves filled with books. Secrecy of course is a necessity in intelligence work but what Eayrs inferred was that the Canadian government didn't know what Buster was doing and likely would not have approved if it had. Nevertheless, the government had laid down no policy regarding defence and little about the defence establishment but it must have expected the professional military to devise plans for the defence of Canada, no matter how unlikely such attacks were.[27] Most of Buster's critics also talked about Canada making war against the USA and appeared not to recognize that the plan was designed as a defence against an attack or declaration of war by that country against Great Britain with Canada as the initial target. The critics also ignored the main strategy that it was a plan to gain depth and time until aid came from Britain and the Commonwealth.

In 1913 Buster had been assigned a project while competing for entry into the Staff College, Camberley, that prepared him for DS No. 1. In this problem he was asked how he would defend central Canada (Red Force) against an attack from the USA (Blue Force). In his paper he stated that Canada's ability to mobilize quickly was an advantage which, coupled with the projection of the Erie Peninsula into the northern States, could enable the Dominion to seize the initiative and control of the Great Lakes. By deploying mobile columns ('flying columns' to him - rapid deployment force today?) into Blue territory to provide the depth for defence until expected help would arrive from Britain, at first through the Royal Navy.[28] This scheme was used in 1913 as the basis for the summer military exercises in MD No. 2 in which Buster acted as staff officer to the Red commander, Lt. Col. W.W. Burleigh. The exercise had extensive press coverage. Defence Scheme No. 1 was essentially an elaboration of the strategy of this exercise, the main problem being to develop a plan to cover all of Canada.

Harris states in his book;

> "Brown did not take the problem of defending Canada
> lightly. The long border with the United States could not
> be manned everywhere, while the vulnerability of the
> Dominion's population centres and transportation
> corridors was obvious. It was clear that British help was
> essential to offset the huge manpower advantage enjoyed
> by the Americans. The strategic problem, therefore, was
> how to gain time to allow the British to react before it was
> too late. ... Persuaded that a purely defensive strategy was
> doomed to failure, he preferred to throw the enemy off
> balance using surprise and shock action. 'Flying columns'
> of Militia battalions would be thrown across the border in
> a controlled penetration to a depth of a few hundred miles
> so that if all went well, and the US army was caught
> unprepared, the Canadian force would have a chance to
> prepare ground of its own choosing for a fighting

withdrawal. By the time it got pushed back to the border British operations should be underway... [and eventually] a reasonable peace settlement was likely to follow."[29]

The documents relating to DS No. 1 are found in Buster's papers in the Queen's University Archives.[30]

Included are background notes on Canadian Armed Forces history, the defence of Canada and its problems. Chapter 1 is an introduction with security rating and distribution; plans of mobilization, training and operations of war; problems such as the vulnerability of the prairies and Winnipeg; importance of central Canada, *etc*. Chapter 2 is an outline of the organization and proposed distribution of the army (12 divisions) as well as the organization of the 'flying columns'. Chapter 3 elaborates on Chapter 2 by identifying units to be involved, up to Brigades and Divisions, and their commanders and staffs; lays out plans for recruiting and training as well as their composition and organization; details the uses and the special training of the flying columns; describes channels of communication for mobilization, railways, remounts, *etc*; suggests creating a signals communication board; insists on registration of vehicles and horses; outlines the importance of mobile machine gun units and mechanized infantry. Chapters 4 and 5 are missing, but they dealt with American Army strength and distribution; with the objectives for the flying columns (Spokane, Seattle, Portland, Great Falls, and Butte in the West; Minneapolis and St. Paul in the Midwest; Albany and Maine in the East), method of advance *etc*. Chapter 6 concerns strategy, for example the importance of Edmonton, Quebec and Halifax as fall-back centres. If the initial actions of the Canadian army were unsuccessful, the forces should retire to those three strategic centres. It also appraises the probable strength of the opposing forces, estimates of the length of time to mobilize the National Guard (up to 2 months) and the time for the regular army to reach the target areas or the border.

Defence Scheme No. 1 was able to be written quickly, between December 1920 and April 1921, because of the preceding preparatory work. Following completion of the document, Buster and his colleagues conducted several reconnaissances of the northern States in civilian clothes; characterized as 'spies' by Eayrs and Taylor. The first reconnaissance included Buster, the Director of Signals and the three GSO 1s of MDs No. 3, 4 and 5 (Photo 7-4). Taylor suggested they did not look much like tourists in their suits and ties as they conducted their appraisals. He also gives some details of their trips.[31] During 1922-23 the scheme was refined as a result of information on US installations, US military budgets and geographic reconnaissance. Critics mocked their use of gas station road maps but the lack of topographic maps of the USA was a topic familiar to

Buster and one at which he scoffed. Consequently, he also recommended reconnaissance by senior staff in the various Military Districts and this became so popular that it soon had to be forbidden by the CGS because of budget constraint.[32] The plan was secret with copies given only to the DOCs and complete access was only shared with GSO 1s, others were to know only what they needed. This would have made preparing local plans difficult.

The scheme was never updated although Buster pleaded to do so to take cognisance of the changed conditions, including the much reduced strength of the Canadian army. Although this was not done, the scheme remained the army's plan for the defence of the nation from a potential attack by the USA until after Buster's resignation in 1933.

During this period factors, which influenced thinking about DS No. 1 in the military and possibly government minds, included a visit and report of Admiral Lord Jellicoe, contrary opinion of the CIGS, Sir Henry Wilson, and the opinions of the Canadian Deputy Chief of Staff and the DOCs. Jellicoe thought that war between the USA and the Commonwealth was very unlikely and that in any case Canada could not count on the RN for support. His opinion reflected wartime cooperation between the two country's navies. On the contrary, the CIGS reaffirmed the British army's support in case of invasion and opined that it might be needed.[33] As late as 1923, McNaughton, as Deputy CGS, was supportive of the scheme because he was apprehensive of American imperialistic policy. Later, in 1928, he appeared to have forgotten this and called the scheme lunacy.[34] In between, his protege, Lt. Col. H.D.G. Crerar, on exchange at the War Office in 1925 said that "war with the USA would place Canada in a more than desperate situation but it would not be altogether hopeless."[35] The DOCs initially approved the thrust of the document and its daring proposals.[36] Some were apprehensive of what was required of them and naturally this increased as the prospect of a 15 Division army faded and, late in the decade, the Great Depression further collapsed the military budgets.

The defence of Canada against an attack by the USA would have been a formidable undertaking. Buster's approach held considerable risk of failure but as he said, a purely defensive approach was certainly doomed to failure. Buster's knowledgeable colleagues agreed. For example, Major General George Pearkes , VC, in 1929 Buster's GSO 1, and later Minister of Defence in the Diefenbaker government, is quoted by Taylor as saying, "It was a fantastic, desperate plan but it might just have worked. The Americans had very few troops close to the Border. We might have been able to divert their forces to the flanks, and to hold them out of central Canada until Britain intervened, or second thoughts prevailed in Washington."[37]

It appears there were no alternative proposals to Buster or the senior staff of NDHQ to change the plan. The scheme, under the conditions proposed, was probably as good as could have been developed. Failure of the CGS or the former Inspector General to inform the Minister, the PM and Cabinet, and get them on side in regard to the need of a strong militia, bore seriously upon the possibility of a successful defence. The question of the possible intentions of the USA in the early and mid 1920s caused alarm in the senior staff of NDHQ even if it didn't with the government's advisors on foreign affairs such as Loring, Christie and O.D. Skelton.[38] Perhaps if these advisors knew what modern day historians know about American offensive planning they too might have been alarmed.[39] At the same time as DS No. 1 was drafted, the US War Plans Division drew up a series of offensive plans with one directed against Britain (Red) and Canada (Crimson). Richard Preston of Duke University has stated, "Colonel Sutherland Brown's Defence Scheme Number One does not appear quite so ludicrous against this background [of American plans]."... "In the 1920s, when memories of the First World War were bitter and when Canada's economy was sliding into the Great Depression, Brown's [DS No. 1] may have kept the Militia alive."[40]

Was Buster Anti-American? This question could as well be asked of Currie and MacBrien who directed Buster to plan for the defence of Canada against attack from the USA. However, in many respects Buster could be considered Anti-American, but this was a learned attitude not a family inculcated one as most of his critics avowed. He grew up in a community composed of many UE Loyalists and his family indeed had moved to Canada from Massachusetts but they kept strong family and business ties to the USA. They were also keenly Whig and Presbyterian, and not Tory and Anglican, members of which were at that time considered more likely to be Anti-American. Buster's apprehension about the intentions of the USA stemmed from attitudes probably acquired while in the Militia and PF, reinforced by his experiences with the RCR in Sydney when dealing with the strike induced by the United Mine Workers of America. The leaders of this American union provoked mayhem and murder in Nova Scotia. Buster also thought many Americans in high places still believed in 'Manifest Destiny', and he was alarmed at the large budgets for the American armed forces with no enemy in sight except Canada as a proxy for Great Britain. Buster was not paranoid, as could be inferred in Eayrs' work, although he was very suspicious of American intent in regard to both territory and resources.[41] He was fiercely Canadian and a believing Imperialist but then so was Stephen Leacock who was never considered paranoid. Leacock said, "I ...am an Imperialist because I will not be a Colonial." As Taylor says, "In short, Canadian Imperialism was a genuine form of Canadian Patriotism."[42]

Defence Scheme No. 1 appears to have a life of its own. Although it appeared to 'die' in 1933, it was discovered alive by James Eayrs in the early 1960s, about ten years after Buster had indeed died. Since then it keeps on being rediscovered by journalists who then write editorial page articles couched in mocking terms: for example, Richard Starnes in the *Toronto Globe* (*ca.* 1985), Nick Auf der Maur in the *Montreal Gazette* in November, 1987, and Michael Kaufman the *New York Times* in April, 1995. Usually these are just restatements of the overall plan displaying incredulity and commonly including errors such as, for example, that Buster worked on the project on his own initiative or that he had only one clerk. They are mostly traceable to quick reads of Eayrs' or Taylor's books. In September, 1989, *Pacific Northwest* magazine published a better researched article by Michael Murphey with some different perspectives. Later, in April, 1991, the *London Daily Telegraph* printed an article by Fred Lanagan about the USA plan Red and Crimson, invasion of Canada in a war between Britain and the USA, which is probably traceable to the discovery of Richard Preston's article. In addition to following Preston, it cites Keegan that every nation creates these plans as exercises. However, Preston seems to have thought the US schemes were the visible halo of more serious secret plans. The *Telegraph's* article generated three letters to the editor, two of which were serious and one drew attention to DS No. 1. The article suggested the USA's dependence on Canadian resources would be the cause of American adventures. Also, Eayrs wrote an article printed in the *Kingston Whig-Standard* July, 1974, which justified his own work in the light of James Preston's. He mockingly suggests, "Why not celebrate Buster Brown Day" on the Fourth of July.

Another facet of the Scheme's life is an hour long CBC radio docudrama on Buster and the DS No. 1 created in the early 1980s.[43] The play entitled, *The Attack of the Killer Mouse*, was part of a series on Canadian Cranks. This was written by John Douglas, produced by Stephen Katz with Gordon Pinsent playing Buster and David Calderusi as McNaughton, Don Herron as MacKenzie King, Elva May Hoover as Clare with an original score by Lucio Agostini. It is centred around DS No. 1 and inferred duplicity and opportunism by McNaughton, wiliness by MacKenzie King, and sincere but naive efforts by Buster to prepare a defence of Canada. The author seems to have done more research than just reading Taylor and Eayrs but some of his timing is wrong and he used considerable artistic licence in some imaged scenes. Douglas clearly had no personal knowledge of the Sutherland Brown family because he has Clare swearing like a barracking wife, something she was not. The play near the end incorporates a dream sequence with Buster staring into the dying fire from burning copies of the scheme but fancying that the attack had occurred, the enemy had been repelled and Buster honoured. It ends at General Thacker's death bed after the documents had been destroyed asking the old General if he, Buster, had misguidedly wasted his time and was assured he had not. If Douglas had more insight into military lives he would have had Archie Macdonell as the old General because he was like an uncle or older brother to Buster. True, General Thacker was Buster's superior as CGS but only in the late twenties. He was not that much older than Buster (Photo 6-6) and lived three years after Buster. An epilogue to the play states that, at the time the scheme was written and with its limited objectives, most military experts thought it might have been successful. Incidentally, the CBC Archive no longer has a script or recording of the play, so:

> ... "These our actors,
>   as I foretold you, were all spirits, and
>   Are melted into air, into thin air:"

A different view of Defence Scheme No. 1 was aired on CBC radio on 29 March, 1983, on their series Ideas. This was a quite separate docudrama and commentary and the relationship, if any, between the two is unknown. The Ideas program was called *The Great Unfinished Task of Colonel J. Sutherland Brown*. The impression given by it is confusing. It started with military fife and drum music, followed by a fairly long and reasonable commentary by Bill Ruckett. It then swung into the play, which in every sense was a gross lampoon of the idea of the scheme, and, furthermore, it was badly done with unbelievably pompous voices, exaggerated accents, unreal characterization and ridiculous scenarios.

A quite separate manifestation of the continuing life of DS No. 1 was a protest movement against US influence in the 1970s using James' nick name as a banner. Farley Mowat and his colleagues formed what they called the Colonel J. Sutherland Brown Volunteer Brigade which tended to raise Buster to the status of a folk hero of anti-Americanism. Their intent was to object, amongst other things, to low level flights by US B52 and B58 bombers over Saskatchewan.[44] Their ideology was far from Buster's. I am not sure whether he would have been angry before he lapsed into amusement.

Although Buster was something of a workaholic he and Clare had a pleasant life during the 1920s that revolved principally around social gatherings with army friends. Because of Buster's former association with Viscount Byng of Vimy, who became Canada's Governor General in

Photo 7 - 5. Buster with his family camping at Petawawa in 1926; Ian with Buster, Atholl on Clare's lap and Malcolm at right.

1921, they received frequent invitations to Rideau Hall, which pleased Clare and may have trained Buster for his period as Senior Aide at Government House in Victoria. His association with Byng was close enough so that he was asked to lunch with Lord Byng at his club while the latter was commissioner of the London Metropolitan Police in 1928. For recreation Buster and Clare regularly played badminton, although probably not the vigorous game played today, and they also frequently enjoyed Scottish country dancing which was as vigorous. During this period Clare and Buster had their third and last son, Atholl, born 20 June 1923. They had almost no resources beyond Buster's salary, one reason he frequently disputed his pay or allowances. Because of their lack of private income and capital they did not compete with the likes of the McNaughtons or the Ashtons (E.C. Ashton, Adjutant General and later CGS, a qualified Physician and one of Atholl's godfathers, Photo 11-3). Buster and Clare spent their money on items they regarded as important. Their house was not prepossessing but their furniture was excellent, much still in use today, and they had solid silver flat wear and candelabra on the table. They had the services of Baba Blackwell as a nurse, cook and maid of all sorts, who was kitted out in a mauve uniform during the day and a black dress and white apron at night (Photo 7-1). Buster and Clare both dressed well. He had every uniform to be had (full dress, blues, frock coat) as well as bespoke civies ordered from Hawkes Bros. in Saville Row. To a degree, he was a dandy with a silk handkerchief tucked into his sleeve which had buttons on the cuffs, which really did up. In due time, they also spent money on their sons' education. However, Buster was careful with his money when it came to items such as automobiles, summer cottages or vacations (leave), even though they had to endure the hot and humid Ottawa summers. Often, the only holidays were at the invitation of friends such as the Ashtons or alternatively setting up an elaborate camp on army grounds, such as Petawawa (Photo 7-5). In the 1920s alcohol in Hull was more available, of better variety and cheaper than in Ottawa, which for a period was dry, so Buster, owning no vehicle, would combine a walk with a lark, by wheeling Ian across the bridge to Hull in a large English pram and return with an overload - child plus booze.

After the completion of Defence Scheme No. 1, the other schemes were not worked upon immediately. A first test of Canada's willingness and preparedness to carry out its commitments with the Commonwealth occurred in 1922 upon the irruption of the Chanak (Canakkale) affair. In this incident Britain, without prior consultation, called for Dominions to supply detachments in support when a small British garrison was pinned down on the Dardanelles in Turkey, which was still under Allied occupation. The affair passed quickly but the new Canadian Prime Minister, Mackenzie King, declined to respond in one of the first demonstrations of

Canadian independence from Whitehall in foreign affairs. Furthermore, the military were as unprepared as the government was unwilling to live up to their commitments. Buster wrote to the CGS to say the Army had Sam Hughes to blame for the mess of the mobilization in 1914 but they would now have no one to blame except themselves in this case or any other serious event.[45]

Later, in 1925, Buster with a committee, prepared a mobilization plan for the PF and Militia and still later in 1926 he was directed to work on DS No. 3, which called for the despatch of a full Expeditionary Force to help in the event of a European or Empire crisis. This scheme was not completed until 1933 by Buster's successor and former assistant, Col. H.H. Matthews (also a godfather to Atholl). DS No. 2, defence against an invasion by Japan, was thought not to be germane after the Washington Treaty appeased Japan. In the next few years Buster had many duties besides his principle one of keeping abreast of intelligence and political information. He advocated a number of essential but diverse projects, such as expediting Canadian topographic surveys, producing a National map index system or strengthening the harbour defences in Halifax and Esquimalt. He wrote studies on subjects as varied as the Baghdad Railway and the causes of the NW Rebellion. He was on many committees such as the Defence, the Mobilization, the Tri Services and the on-going Battle Honours Committee. Buster was chairman or secretary of a number of these, as for example, the Mobilization Committee which consisted of the CGS; Commodore Hose, the Chief of Navel Staff (CNS); Maj. Gen. Ashton, the Quartermaster General; the Adjutant General, and the Director of the Canadian Air Force, and himself as secretary. Also in the absence of the CGS, Buster acted for him.

Buster wrote a good number of appreciations and briefing notes for the CGS, for the various committees or articles for military journals. In the Proceedings of the Defence Committee on 29 December, 1923, Buster wrote that, "It is the primary duty of every country to provide for its own defence, and secondly, to provide for any commitments by way of alliances or international agreements.... . The [UK] and the Dominions ... have a secondary duty of [coming] to each others aid... ." He then outlined the serious deficiencies in armament, munitions and equipment for the existing, let alone the potential Canadian forces, but which considering the financial state of the country, could not be rectified all at once. His point was that stores were needed for the rapid expansion of the army were it to be mobilized and that the stores had to be properly housed in secure, dry and fireproof accommodation. He followed this with criticism of the Deputy Chief of Staff's memo of 21 October, 1923, that advocated among other things that the Militia in effect consist of a single Division and its stores. This criticism would not make him loved by McNaughton who now held the post. A main point of Buster's comments was that NDHQ shouldn't request less than was realistically required but should present the facts to the government, and let it decide and take responsibility for any negative political fallout. Finally, he reviewed foreign relations with the USA, emphasizing fishing disputes, boundary disputes, the St. Lawrence Seaway and its financing, railway problems in the Maritimes, and most significantly, the US Army's great size and abundant financing.[46] In 1923, Buster wrote an article for the Canadian Defence Quarterly on Military Policy of Canada, 1905-1924. In it he states:

> "The Union Government went out of power in December, 1921, before it completed a military policy and the present [Liberal] Government has been so involved with intricate and disturbing questions and faced the necessity for economy that it has not found the moment opportune to consider the question of Military Policy... .The Department of National Defence has made some progress in consolidation. The Canadian Air Force has been put on a permanent and military basis. The Naval Service, however, still needs either a bit of wooing or caveman pressure to bring it into line."[47]

Buster continued with a survey of current needs, reiterating:

> "The government of every other civilized country... has taken its military problem in hand and put its military house in order. Canada has not yet done so. [He followed this with a section on present needs which he summarized as follows]:

1. A complete consolidation and unification of the Department of National Defence.
2. A policy to form a well balanced [and organized] force with its proper proportion of all arms of the service for the defence of the frontiers of Canada, or for the despatch of an expeditionary force, should an emergency arise.
3. In order to properly organize, administer, command, train, mobilize and use such a force for home defence, the military organization of Canadian territory to meet geographical and strategic requirements needs immediate attention.
4. Schemes for the organization of the Reserve Militia should be considered and the most effective, economical and efficient one adopted.
5. A definite policy is needed concerning the Permanent Force with respect to -
   (a) Stabilization, so that officers and other ranks may have some

idea of the future.

(b) A decision as to its duties and then furnish it with sufficient personnel to carry out these duties efficiently.

(c) A definite decision as to its distribution to prevent the present pernicious dispersal and at the same time provide arrangements for the proper barrack accommodation of the force.

6. A definite policy as to fortified naval stations and the garrisons required for each.

7. A definite policy for armament, munitions, number and location of arsenals and magazines.

8. A policy for co-operation of the different Departments of the Government and the Provincial Governments in case of war and the preparation [to control public works, transportation and communication facilities].

9. A proper scheme for registration of horses and vehicles [so they could be available] in case of general mobilization.

> Headquarters staff can do, and have done, a lot of spade work along these lines, but little can be put into force until it is has approval of the Cabinet."

Other facets of his army life, at this time, included such things as a request by the DOC of MD No.1 to attend and speak to the RCR on an important anniversary for them, Paardeberg Day, celebrating the regiment's successful battle in South Africa. Also, he accompanied the CGS, General MacBrien, on a month long western tour in 1924, particularly to inspect Military District No. 11, BC and Yukon. Buster also received several extensions of his appointment as DMO&I until he was sent to the Imperial Defence College at the end of 1927. His appointment to the IDC came as suddenly as his appointment to the Staff College in 1914. In all probability it partly resulted from General MacBrien turning down an offer from his Minister to attend the college as a way to keep him in the Service.[48]

Buster's sense of the need for justice was strong as some of his correspondence shows. For years General Currie was subjected to considerable abuse by Sir Sam Hughes and his henchmen, which led the General eventually to bring a slander suit against the owner of a small newspaper, the *Port Hope Guide*, and W.T.R. Preston, the author of an article in the paper in June, 1927. The critique accused the General of, 'deliberate and useless waste of life', particularly in the capture of Mons on 11 November, 1918.[49] Buster wrote Currie several letters about the case and received thoughtful replies, the last on 28 November, 1927, just before Buster left for England. After the case was settled in the General's favour Buster wrote again from England congratulating Currie and saying, "Your case was ours as you were fighting the battle of all respectable personnel of the Old Corps. ... It is a pleasure [to us that you have] turned down a rascal like Preston, whom I have known since childhood."[50]

Buster also wrote a letter on 18 March, 1927, to Malcolm's principal at the Model School, W.J. Neale, because the children had been asked to contribute funds to the striking steel plant workers in Cape Breton. Buster said he was in touch with the situation in Sydney from his own experience. He went on to write:

> "I stand fore-square for the British Empire. I don't believe in Bolshevism, Labourism, Socialism, or any other sort of "isms" that stand for the disruption of society or pulling down our present institutions. At the same time, I have no brief for the British Empire Steel Company which is dominated by a Montreal Jew by the name of Wolfin. They undoubtedly have not dealt with their labour in proper ways, but, nevertheless, most of the trouble in Cape Breton has been caused by one McLaughlin and others of his ilk, who have never done an honest day's work in their lives and sucked their substance from people who were foolish enough to listen to them or cowed into a state of non-resistance." [51]

Taylor quotes the above and goes on to say:

> "Here it all is - the love of Britain and British ways, the deep suspicion of American interference, a suggestion of anti-Semitism and a firm adherence to conservative politics, including a belief in the virtues of honest toil and a defence of the working class in the face of liberal-capitalist greed. In one great surge of feeling directed at the hapless headmaster, Sutherland Brown had nailed his colours to the mast." [52]

Buster's opinions were not much more politically correct then than they would be now but they were honest statements of how he felt. Buster also said that relief should be in the hands of the municipalities, the Provincial and Federal governments, not the school children of Ottawa. Curiously, Neale answered Buster's rant by saying he only intended the collection as an outlet for the children's 'charitable instincts'. Later, when Malcolm left the school to travel to England, he wrote a pleasant letter of praise to Buster about his son.

The Canadian Army had hedged its bets regarding the rank and pay of its officers for decades. An officer might only have the gazetted rank of Captain but be a brevet and temporary Colonel, as was the case of one of Buster's brother officers in the RCR, R.O. Alexander, DSO. Buster, ever mindful of his status and pay, wrote a memo to the new CGS, appointed in 1927, Major General H.C. Thacker, ". ... It apparently has been in the interest of the service to have kept me seconded [from the RCR] from September, 1914, drawing rates of pay higher than regimental rates. I have been a Director in the department for nine years since January, 1919, commencing at a rate of $4,600 a year and rising by annual increases to a maximum of $5,500 which I reached in April 1924. ... I have held the rank of Temporary and Brevet Colonel since January, 1919. I have been a substantive Lt. Colonel in my regiment since 15 October, 1924. Having been seconded so long there is no place for me on the regimental establishment, it would be unfair to me to return to regimental rates, particularly when my expenses are going to be higher. Brig. General McNaughton while attending the [IDC] has been allowed to draw the pay of a Colonel on the Staff [equivalent to Brigadier] and it would be fair to allow me to enjoy the same rate of pay. ... In attending the [IDC] and performing duties of Liaison Officer at the Office of the Canadian High Commissioner my duties will not be less."[53] Thacker and the Adjutant General, Maj. Gen. H.A. Panet, agreed.

Buster had established himself with his peers as a hard working, well read, thoughtful man; something of a genius at strategy and organization but also a bold risk-taker. He did not tolerate incompetence or laziness. Some thought as a leader he would demand too much of them or wondered if they could perform what he might require of them. His trait of frankness and lack of guile was admired by most, not least by the two Chiefs of the General Staff for whom he worked. They trusted him but they too must have wondered what might come from Buster's lack of diplomacy, or was it a lack of guile? Nevertheless, they saw him as a potential leader of the Canadian militia or neither would have recommended him for the Imperial Defence College. It is difficult on surveying all his activities at NDHQ, his membership or position as secretary of so many important committees, and as a trusted advisor to two CGSs, to agree with Eayrs or Gimblett when they say Buster worked alone on the outside and scarcely in contact with the main circle of NDHQ.[54] Nevertheless, Buster's frankness had already moved his immediate chief, and potential rival, from friend to a latent enemy.

Buster at work had once again established his ability to create great enthusiasm and respect of soldiers who reported to him. When Buster left the Directorate his staff of nine wrote and signed the following letter, probably composed by Quarter Master Sergeant Thomas Bee;

"On behalf of the sub-staff of the Directorate and the staff of the Departmental library I have been asked to present this gift, as a token of our esteem for you.

We are all very sorry to see you leave the department and probably I feel just a little more deeply than the others at your departure. However, we must not grieve over your going because it is to your advantage in a professional way and loving you as we do we are glad to see you climb the ladder of military achievement. From Company Commander to a high post on the General Staff is the culmination of long and laborious study on your part, and it must indeed be a happy future that awaits you.

I have watched for a number of years and know the difficulties and perplexities that have confronted you in your official duties and I have seen a great many of those same difficulties and perplexities surmounted by your never waning courage, when you felt that the cause for which you were striving was fair and just.

We will welcome then your departure, may God speed you and yours on the way, bless an preserve you all whilst in England, and when you return to Canada in 1929 may it be with greater enthusiasm than ever to resume your work here, fortified with still higher and broader knowledge derived from associations at the Imperial Defence College. I vouch for all when I say - how happy our lot will be if, in the future, we are again associated with you.

We wish also to take this opportunity to welcome our future Director of Military Operations and Intelligence - Lt. Colonel H.H. Matthews, CMG, DSO, wishing him every success in his appointment, and promising him also the same unswerving loyalty and devotion to duty as we have tried to render to you in the past."[55]

8 Imperial Defence

Buster and Clare entered one of the happiest and most fulfilling periods of their lives, in 1928, when his appointment to the Imperial Defence College (IDC) took them to London, England for a year. Left behind were the niggling military bureaucracy, the restrictive budgets, the back-biting competition of HQ, and the weight of trivial routine duties. To a considerable degree he was liberated. He and Clare were living in the heart of an engaging and exciting metropolitan capital. They had a new stimulating social life in the city that they knew quite well but which was now renewed, bustling and prosperous. The work at the College was very demanding in time and energy with intensive reading, writing, listening to and preparing lectures. However, there was still time for a pleasant social life which they enjoyed to the full. There was also a good break between terms for travel. They had superior accommodation off Kensington Gardens in central London, just a long walk through the Parks to the IDC at 9 Buckingham Gate. Consequently, no time was wasted commuting. Clare's relatives were not far away in Southampton and the Channel Islands. The two older boys attended a good Public School in Bromley, Kent and the youngest was carefully looked after by Baba Blackwell. Buster's colleagues were a compatible group, amongst whom were a number of friends from Camberley days. Also, competition was more muted compared with the Staff College, and everyone was self-driven. As Jack Dill (then a Major General and an instructor at the college) said in a letter to Buster on 9 January, 1928, "it will be like old times only pleasanter". They were all imbued with feelings of having achieved a personal level of success together with a feeling of satisfaction from working towards the security of the Commonwealth. Buster's duties also included acting as a liaison officer to the Canadian High Commissioner, which lent interest and variety to his work.

The family, with Miss Blackwell and a cousin of Clare's, left St. John, New Brunswick, on 6 December, 1927, aboard the S.S. Montclare for Liverpool. Buster had made all the arrangements in advance and they turned out to be excellent. Their life in London is best mirrored in a letter he wrote in response to a request about living arrangements from Lt. Col. W.G. 'Rab' Beeman, DSO, who was to attend the college two years after Buster. No one was sent in 1929.

Photo 8 - 1. Imperial Defence College, class of 1928 at 9 Buckingham Gate. Commandant, Admiral Sir Herbert Richmond, RN, seated centre, to his left, Maj. Gen. Jack C. Dill then Brigadier James Sutherland Brown; to his right two over A/C Joubert de la Ferte; first row behind, second from the right W/C A.W. Tedder.

"Victoria, B.C., 9 December 1929.

My dear "Rab"

I have your letter of 2 December this morning and make haste to reply. We stayed in England at a pension at 62 Queensborough Terrace, Bayswater, London, W2. This was within a hundred yards of Kensington Gardens which is a delightful place for the children to play and get a breather. It is within five minutes walk to either the 'underground' or the district railway and you can catch a bus on Bayswater Road, which is about fifty yards away, so in all ways it was a most convenient place to live. It was run by a certain Madame Lapotres, who was very congenial and a very nice Frenchwoman. She has since sold out to another proprietress who ran another pension across the road and who I believe was capable and respectable. In any case Madam Lapotres has written to my wife telling her she has sold out and saying that she has no hesitation in recommending that 62 Queensborough Terrace would still be a delightful place for her old Canadian patrons to go.

We had three rooms, quite a nice double room for ourselves, another good room in which the nurse and Atholl, our youngest who was just about five, used and we had another room in which the other two boys used when they were home from school. It cost me about 18 gns. a week when they were all home and about 12 or 14 gns. when the boys were away at school. There was a large drawing-room on the [second] floor which was well furnished and it was scarcely used as most people preferred to use the bigger room on the first floor. We found it a very congenial place all told, of course, it did not have all the conveniences that one would like but the servants were very good ones. We can look back and say that we thoroughly enjoyed ourselves at 62 Queensborough Terrace.

It would take you about 35 minutes to walk through the parks to 9 Buckingham Gate, the Imperial Defence College. I often walked but more often took the bus part way... They asked me to do liaison work. This I undertook in as far as it did not interfere with the work at IDC and I should be sure to make that proviso.

125

I found there was very little money for enjoyment. Of course I had three husky boys and when we went around it took a considerable amount for bus fares and as I took them around quite a lot to see the sights of London we rather spent our money in that way rather than going to the theatres which are very expensive. The cost of everything, except men's and women's clothes which are cheaper, was very much as you would find in Eastern Canada. It cost me well over a thousand dollars for the boys schooling. I had saved up a little money before I went over, possibly about $1000 in cash and my wife had about $1000. Most of this money we spent on things to bring home and cannot legitimately be charged to our expenses in England. We just managed to struggle through. You will find your pay and allowances will just about make things meet. Don't forget they give you an extra $2.00 a day when living in London. You will have nothing left to spread yourself unless it comes from private funds. With reference to clubs, they will probably put you up at the 'Rag'. This I found the nicest of clubs, the most congenial, the best food at very reasonable prices and they have a nice ladies part where you can entertain your friends to luncheon or dinner at costs very much below the West End hotels and restaurants. You get transportation when you travel around and your allowances go up to the higher rate (you draw travelling allowances which of course reduce after 15 days in one place so if you go away from London they go up to the higher rate for days away).

You will thoroughly enjoy your work at the [IDC]. It is unnecessary for me to say to be moderate in your views. Stick up for Canada, squelch any uninformed criticism and I think they will appreciate you all the more if you do that. ..."[1]

The family arrived, on 15 December, to learn General Edwin Alderson had just died. Brigadier McNaughton had not yet left for Canada so he and Buster attended the laying to rest of the General. Subsequently, Lady Alderson wrote to the Canadian High Commissioner to say how deeply touched she was by their attendance. She also asked for their addresses. Buster then wrote her a personal letter stating his admiration of the General, his leadership, acuity and kindness, as well expressing sympathy for her loss. She answered this immediately with a note saying she would like to see him and give him a memento of the General's.[2]

126

Just as Buster left for England he received a long friendly letter from Archie Macdonell saying, "You are the man for that job [attendance at the second course of the IDC] and I am glad and proud you have been selected." He continued writing about the war and how he would like to be in London with its theatres and also to visit the Canadian cemeteries in France. He then writes he felt he let Alderson down, [that] fine English gentleman and that he was betrayed by Foxy Gran'pa [Hughes?]. He finishes by saying, "that he can't speak too highly of my own staff who made a success of the Old Red Patch in spite of their GOC. I love you. God bless you Buster."[3]

The studies at the IDC took precedence in Buster's year in the UK. The curriculum included a heavy reading schedule with, for example, 20 books to review during the four week mid-summer break. The members were all senior officers (Photo 8-1) and were expected to lecture on their specialities. For example, two of Buster's lectures were on the constitutional development of Canada and on Canadian military affairs. They also had a heavy load of secret intelligence reports to digest. Opportunities were available to visit UK units and facilities and one of Buster's choices was to observe experimental Armoured Corps manoeuvres on Salisbury Plain; another was to the Gloucestershire Regiment, which was aligned with the RCR. The latter invitation was made especially appealing because it coincided with a race meet. Admiral Sir Herbert Richmond was the Commandant and the staff included Major General Jack Dill, Captain Gerald Dickens, RN, and Air Cmdre Joubert de la Ferte. A lot was expected to be accomplished by seminar discussion. The class of 26 included among others, Wing Commander A.W. Tedder. Whether Buster got indications of his progress from the College, he got some by way of a letter from his colleague Harry Coghill, in Ottawa, in May:

> "From your letter I take it you are very busy, and working long hours. Of course, that would never hurt you because you live to work and the knowledge that you gather up over there will be a great help to us all on your return. ... A chit did arrive from the High Commissioner's Office, with regard to you, and it was one of the best and was seen by the Minister and the Prime Minister, General Thacker and the Adjutant-General. They all spoke very highly of your activities."[4]

Although Buster did not rate his liaison work at the Canadian High Commission highly, compared with study at the College, there is no doubt that some of it was very important and much of it stimulating and interesting. He was directed by the Deputy Minister of National Defence on 5 January, to attend the Overseas Defence Committee with General

Photo 8 - 2. Clare in Court dress before presentation to Their Majesties, June, 1928.

McNaughton and to take over when the latter left.[5] A letter from General Milne to CGS and copied to Buster said:

"I was glad to meet Col. Sutherland Brown here the other day and I hope he will get full value from his time at the IDC. It is a great advantage from my point of view that the successor to General McNaughton is another officer of recent experience at NDHQ - who will know the views and be able to represent Canadian interests at meetings of the Overseas Defence Committee and similar bodies. ..."[6]

Buster also became an informant to the distinguished military historian, Liddell Hart, initially in regard to articles he was writing for the Encyclopaedia Britannica. Buster and Liddell Hart became firm friends and they lunched together a numerous of times at the "Rag".

Another assignment from the CGS, through the High Commission, was to give technical support to the sculptor of the National Commemorative Canadian War Memorial, Mr. Vernon March.[7] Buster answered the CGS with a long letter saying he had met with March and reviewed the work in progress. His letter is full of suggestions for the sculptor and request to the CGS for material to increase the accuracy of some aspects. He also praised the work. Not all Buster's recommendation were followed but a number were and are evident in the finished work.[8] March wrote to Buster on 28 November, 1928, saying, "I am ever so grateful to you for the masterly way in which you have solved for me numerous problems in regard to the historical data for the Canadian National Memorial."

He also asked Buster to lunch to inspect the memorial again but Buster declined as he had little time before he had to return to Canada.

Buster also maintained a vigorous correspondence with army colleagues in Canada. This ranged from matters such as the continuing saga of Battle Honours, an organization chart for the Air Service and a name for a Canadian Guards unit [Buster's suggestion - the Governor General's Body Guard]. It included quasi-business dealings with such organizations as the Red Chevron Association (original members of the 1st Canadian Division), or the Canadian Cavalry Association, and letters to the CO of the RCR about his being dropped from the regimental role (see earlier), or to the CO of the Norfolk Regiment about new badges now that the unit was no longer a rifle regiment. Otherwise, most of Buster's correspondence received consisted of gossip about appointments and vacancies for DOCs and Directors. Buster's outgoing letters included congratulations to General Currie on winning his slander suit or sociable letters to General Macdonell.

For the most part Buster and Clare's social life during their stay in London was largely restricted to weekends and divided into contacts with Clare's family or Buster's colleagues. It included small dinner parties for Clare and club lunches for Buster. A memorable highlight for Clare was her presentation at June Court to Their Majesties, at Buckingham Palace (Photo 8-2). Family outings included educational excursions to St. Paul's Cathedral, the Knightsbridge Museums or the Houses of Parliament. Family entertainment included military tattoos, horse shows or picnics in outer London parks such as Croydon, Box Hill or at Kew Gardens. In the mid-summer break, the family had a seashore holiday on the Isle of Wight, a cut above camping at Petawawa. Buster and Clare had a week to themselves while the older boys stayed with their Aunt Kate Hoskyn and I went with Baba Blackwell to her home village, Shipston-on-Stour. From here he was taken for visits to Banbury Cross, of nursery rhyme note, and Stratford-upon-Avon in his first introduction to the Bard. Residence at the pension was memorable even to a child because of the French cuisine. Although Atholl seldom dined with his parents, Sunday lunch was a family event at which roast pheasant was commonly featured followed by a splendid dessert.

As the course approached its end, Buster was left wondering what his next appointment would be. Letters from colleagues assured him he would be appointed DOC of MD No. 11 but official word did not come. On 18 October, the CGS, Maj. Gen. H.C. Thacker, sent the Adjutant-General, Maj. Gen. Panet, a memo that Sutherland Brown should be informed of his posting after the course. On the 21 November, Panet sent messages to McNaughton in Victoria and the High Commissioner in London that Sutherland Brown would replace McNaughton as DOC of MD No. 11.[9] Buster was not informed until 28 November and it was gazetted and announced in the Globe on 1 December that the appointment would be effective as of 1 January, 1929. Buster received many robust congratulatory telegrams and letters, however, his joy was tempered because Thacker retired as of that date and McNaughton became CGS and his boss.

The second term ended with Buster making his mark, achieving a fine report from the Commandant, Admiral Sir Herbert Richmond. At the final dinner for the course members at the Cavalry Club on Piccadilly, Buster was designated to propose the toast to the Commandant and to give what could be called a valedictory address, a thing he would relish. Soon after, on 4 January 1929, he and his family left from Liverpool for Victoria, British Columbia. On arrival in that temperate city they were greeted by six inches of snow.

9   Work Point

Buster arrived in Victoria with his family on 23 January, 1929, to take up his duties as District Officer Commanding (DOC) of Military District Number 11 (MD No.11) which consisted of BC and Yukon. He was now commanding troops again, something his early history showed he did well but which had been denied him for more than a decade whilst a staff officer. The problems of command and control of a small force in the vast western terrain was a task he relished and he applied himself to it with diligence and vigour.

The family was surprised to see snow on the ground when they arrived and Clare was disappointed that some staff member had booked them into the 3rd class Glenshield Hotel. She said it would have been her only chance to stay at the Empress. The officer's quarters at the barracks were a row of adjoined, white clapboard houses stretching eastward along the small peninsula of Work Point (Photo 9-1). The quarters housed five families in addition to a centrally located Mess for single officers. This contained a large dining room for entertaining as well as a library, lounge and billiard room. When the family furniture arrived and was installed in the DOC's quarters, it became a pleasant home. Being at the south eastern end of the row it was light because it had windows on three sides. One had fine views of the harbour and the snow capped Olympic Mountains, in Washington, across the Strait Juan de Fuca. All the family quickly became enthusiastic about the town and their new home at Work Point.

The Barracks were originally built for the British Garrison late in the 19th Century. It was still relatively small in the 1930s before McCauley Point Golf Course and adjacent lands were incorporated at the start of WWII. On entering, one passed a manned guardhouse at the end of Lampson Street to a large square incorporating a grass playing field at the west, a parade ground in the centre and a grass tennis court at the east. Next to the court was a low crenulated wooden Administration building, and beyond this the Officers' quarters. Men's brick barrack blocks, NCOs' married quarters and a hospital surrounded the open space. The whole was quite pleasing in appearance.

Photo 9 - 1. Buster on his way back from his office encounters Mrs Colquhoun's children's party in the officers quarters, Work Point Barracks, 1932. Ian, Atholl and Malcolm in the centre. The DOC's quarters beyond the fence.

Buster and Clare enjoyed the service of several military servants, as well as the redoubtable Baba. The driver of the Dodge staff car assigned to them was Cpl. Nicholas who was like an ancient family retainer to us boys. We encouraged him to drive as fast as possible but it was hard to get him to exceed the speed limit. The furnace man who stoked the coal boiler that heated the officer's residential block was Mr. Flanagan, who was a CEF veteran and full of mechanical information for us. My father's batman was Pte. Badger, whose job seemed to be to remove any trace of silver on the family plate. The ancient gardener for the officer's quarters was always just called 'Gardener'. He may not have had another name but he loved his job and a fine garden resulted. Photo 9-1 shows the officer's quarters, gardens and some of what Americans call Army brats at a party given for them by Mrs Colquhoun, wife of a company commander of the PPCLI. Buster encountered the children as he walked back from his office late on a summer afternoon.

Buster when he reached this lotus land, so different from conditions at NDHQ, did not fall into a slumbering dream. He knew his responsibilities in this new position were broad but he quickly determined the need to obtain the Non-Permanent Active Militia's (NPAM or Militia) support as the most important element required to create a skeleton but viable defence force. His ideas on this were similar to Currie's, which is quoted by Hyatt as thinking, "In order to have a useful militia force it was necessary... to have an efficient staff organization and a small but well organized PF."[1] The latter at Work Point was limited to a Battalion of the Princess Patricia's Canadian Light Infantry (PPCLI) (Photo 9-2) with detachments of Coast Artillery, Engineers, Signals and supporting headquarters units such as a military hospital, ordinance and Army Service Corps. These PF units were well trained, well commanded and efficient, even if they were deficient in motor transport and had no fighting vehicles. Buster considered himself fortunate to inherit an experienced staff headed by Lt. Col. George Pearkes, VC, as GSO 1. The Militia, however, was undermanned, had relatively few enthusiastic young officers, was starved for funds even before the onset of the Depression, and was without adequate training sites, armouries or field camps. They were demoralized by the public's antipathy towards them. The philosophy of disarmament that emerged at the end of the Great War meant that even defensive activity was scorned. However, there were numerous established regiments such as the two battalions of 16th Canadian Scottish (Photo 9-3) on Vancouver Island, the Seaforths, Westminster Regiment, the BC Dragoons and others on the lower mainland, some cavalry in the southern Interior as well as a few batteries of coast and field artillery. Buster's solution to these problems was to work hard to provide adequate facilities during a period of decreasing budgets, to spend much time recruiting prospective officers, and to search for rich men with the

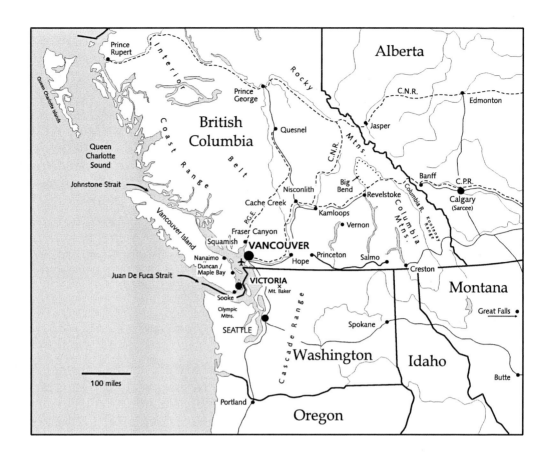

Map 2. The West Coast Region during the 1930s.

credentials to become Honorary Colonels who were then expected to pick up some of the Militia's costs. He was remarkably successful in all these endeavours.

Buster believed a most important aspect of his job was to anticipate potential emergencies and provide protection for western Canada. He saw major strategic problems in being able to do this. Harbour defence for the RCN base of Naden, at Esquimalt, was in a relatively poor state and this, coupled with the inadequacy of means to deter entry through the Strait of Juan de Fuca to Vancouver, could be a major problem. The Navy was not strong enough and the coastal artillery batteries were equipped with ancient 7.5 inch disappearing guns that could not reach the opposite coast. Curiously, Roy in his biography of Pearkes says, "[He, Pearkes,] got the strong impression that [Buster] would have wished their range could have reached the American coast," as an illustration of Buster's anti-Americanism and not as strategic perception. Buster also decried the total absence of any defence against entry toward Vancouver through Queen Charlotte Sound and Johnstone Strait at the northwest

Photo 9 - 2. PPCLI troops at rest during manoeuvres, 1930.

end of Vancouver Island, which was not corrected until WWII. He also worried about the extreme vulnerability of the highway and the two national railways in the Fraser Canyon to landslides or enemy action and the lack of connection to the Pacific Great Eastern railroad (PGE).[2] In his appraisal, he also advocated setting up an efficient and secure system of communication between the elements of his command, the acquisition of some modern anti-aircraft guns and the establishment of an RCAF base closer to Victoria.[3] Buster, throughout his tenure, emphasized the tactical importance of combined operations training for three reasons: British Columbia's extensive, indented and sparsely populated coast; the possibility, however remote, of a Japanese invasion; and finally, the need to be prepared for the possibility of having to create an Expeditionary Force capable of landing on a hostile shore, should the Commonwealth become embroiled in another conflict. Consequently, every year of his command he applied most of his small training budget to joint exercises of the Militia and PF in co-operation with the RCN and RN, and the pitifully small RCAF (Photo 9-5). To further tri-service cooperation, Buster worked hard at establishing good relations with the RCN, the RN and RCAF.

Since the command bordered the Pacific, it received many important military and political visitors from the Far East, the Commonwealth, foreign countries as well as Canada. Just as BC's Government House acted as a western proxy for Rideau Hall to such visitors, so too did the DOC and his wife act as hosts to the many important personages who arrived at this outpost of Empire. Amongst the significant visitors were reigning monarchs, Vice-Regal couples, Canadian Ministers and their Deputies, as well as many high ranking Commonwealth and foreign officers. In addition to these VIPs, Buster and Clare saw their social duties as extending to community leaders in Victoria and Vancouver so that the military would be welcomed and supported by them. Some of their social functions were also planned to engender comradeship between the Militia and the PF officers. Buster and Clare were good at entertaining and took this responsibility so seriously that they drew upon their own meagre resources because the army's allowances were non-existent. Buster worked diligently at his job and enjoyed it so much that in the five years as DOC he only took three weeks leave; this in spite of the fact that he was good at delegating. He also thought why go on a holiday while you're living in Paradise. Family life was centred around his work but his boys' education and social activity were also important. Buster and Clare were happy in Victoria which was then a small provincial capital with passable cultural activities and a benign climate. The possibility of his eclipse was scarcely perceived and, at first, his relationship with the CGS seemed normal. Ottawa was a continent away and the Great Depression scarcely a cloud on the horizon.

'Calling' was still an important aspect of social activity in the inter-war years and Buster began by visiting the Provincial politicians, city and municipal mayors, church and business leaders. He made hundreds of calls in Victoria and Vancouver in his first few months and, in a letter to the Adjutant General (AG), Buster wrote that he and Clare had received over 400 calls at Work Point.

Apart from meeting the local establishment and, in turn getting himself known, it was also an exercise in which he could appraise possible recruits for Militia officers or wealthy men suitable to become Honorary Colonels. Such activities involved intelligence, insight and diplomacy. In due course he persuaded the Premier, Simon Fraser Tolmie, and the Leader of the Opposition and next Premier, Thomas D. Patullo, to both become honorary members of the Garrison Mess. Within a year or so he had recruited a considerable number of officers for the Militia, many of whom had CEF experience. They, along with others, became the core of militia personnel in WWII. These included Mickey Maguire for the Rocky Mountain Rangers, J.M. Green of the BC Police for the BC Dragoons, Russell Ker for the field Artillery, Fred Cabeldu and Reg Kingham for the Canadian Scottish. Buster also managed to obtain the ex-Lt. Governor, Randolph Bruce, Richard Malkin, Austin Taylor, W.C. Woodward as well as others to become Honorary Colonels of Militia units with the understanding of what was implied.[4] Buster also encouraged the senior Militia officers in Vancouver, Col. W.W. Foster, DSO and Lt. Col. Harry Letson to take active roles in the District. Pearkes in a letter to Buster on 1 February, 1930, said, "the news about the other units [of the NPAM] sounds excellent and, if I may say so, any progress is due to your personality. The BC people [Militia] will play up for anyone they like."[5] Charles Taylor interviewed Pearkes in 1976 and quoted him as saying, "He worked the Militia hard, but unlike some commanding officers, he also really cared for them. They all loved him, and their morale was never higher."[6]

As soon as Buster arrived he began informal visits to the military units followed immediately by formal inspections. He quickly formed opinions of his subordinates, the status of the western Militia and the general military environment. His review showed how badly off the NPAM was for armouries and field camps, as well its broad dispersal and lack of critical training. On the other hand, the PF were moderately well housed and well trained. Buster felt fortunate that his senior officers and staff were almost all experienced and efficient. Most of the unit OCs were decorated CEF veterans, only ten years older than they were at the Armistice, and therefore still in their prime. The GSO 1 when Buster arrived was Col. G.R. Pearkes, VC, DSO, MC who was followed by Col. J.L.R.

Parsons, CMG, DSO. The CO of the PPCLI Battalion at first was Lt. Col. Hugh Niven, DSO, MC followed, when he retired, by Lt. Col. W.G. Colquhoun, MC. Senior artillery officers included Majors H.M. Reynolds, W.C. Thackery, CBE and Victor Tremaine. His chief of staff was Lt. Col. Horace Greer, a Cavalry man. Major Drum served as the Senior Medical Officer until he retired and was replaced by Major Hunter. Major, and later Lt. Col., Pat Hennessy, DSO, MC was OC of the Army Service Corps. Major E.C.G. Chambers, MC, was District Engineering Officer. Other staff included Lt. Col. Turner and Major Rycroft, Intelligence Officer. Major Ken Stuart, later CGS, was GSO 2 for the first year and a half before being posted to RMC. The Garrison in Victoria may have been small but was of superior quality and well led. Buster's opinion of the Canadian army is advanced in the conclusion of an article that was published in the Journal of the Royal United Services Institution, in 1929.

> "1929 finds the Canadian Militia generally efficient, well organized and well officered, strongly Canadian in its make-up but deeply Imperialist in its outlook, hoping for continual peace, for the development of Canada and the Empire but ever ready to respond to a call if a great emergency should overtake us again."[7]

This sounded rather grand and possibly ostentatious at the time, so much so that the CGS authorized a disclaimer that these were the writer's personal views, but they were proven remarkably true in 1939. Then, although the Militia was small and pitifully armed, its mobilization was well organized and during WWII it produced many skilled leaders. Also the army was truly Canadian, discrete from the British or Americans.

Relations between the CGS, General A.G.L. McNaughton and the DOC of MD No. 11 were not cordial before they took up their respective posts, in 1929, but at least they both disguised any antipathy. It did not take long before this started to change. Soon after Buster was in place he found his GSO 1, George Pearkes, whom he liked and trusted, was to be removed from that position to become GSO 1 at RMC. That was an unpleasant surprise made worse by the fact Buster read about it in the newspapers before he was notified officially. Consequently, Buster wrote a confidential letter to Andy McNaughton on 2 April, 1929, which said in part:

> "The newspapers of March 29th announced the move of Pearkes to Kingston and Parsons here. The AG's letter dated 26th arrived here yesterday. That is the whole of Canada knew the move of my General Staff Officer before I received official notice (or private notice either) of it.

There was a time also when Defence Headquarters notified DOCs of the intention of sending a staff officer to them and asked for objections. In this case I have serious objections to Parsons. He has never been loyal to anybody and he certainly will not be loyal to me. I could give many more objections but I shall abide by your decision."

Buster then goes on to make some other suggestions for changes including that Ken Stuart, already in Victoria, could be made GSO 1. Buster then reports on his activities saying he has completed all the inspections including recently the COTC [at UBC] which he praised. He then describes his calling program saying:

"I called on the Lt. Governor, the Premier, some Ministers particularly the Minister of Lands, the Chief Justice and the Bishops. We are having the Governor General to dinner in the Mess on Friday the 12th and Clare and I are going to Government House on Friday night to [one] for the Willingtons."

Buster concluded with some news about the weather, the gardens surrounding the officers quarters and wished kindest regards to Mabel.[8]

The CGS replied on 9 April addressing him as 'My Dear Buster' and says:

"I have your letter of April 2nd, this morning, and I note what you say in respect to the AG's letter notifying these moves not arriving before the information was made public. This is unfortunate but there were special [unspecified] reasons not under my control.

With respect to prior consultation with the DOC when moves are in contemplation: this, of course, I will not do as it is contrary to the principles by which Staff duties should be regulated, and it is highly desirable that the responsibility in these matters should be centralized to the end that no outside pressure can be brought to bear on the General Staff in this important military matter."

McNaughton also replies to Buster's remarks about Parsons and says, confidentially, he has other plans for Stuart within a year. He comments on Buster's remarks about the OTC and goes on to conclude with:

Photo 9 - 3. Memorial Church Parade of the Second Battalion, 16th Canadian Scottish Regiment and veterans at the Duncan Cenotaph with Buster, left, leading the salute, 1930.

"With kindest regards to you all, in which Mabel joins me."

Signed A. McNaughton[9]

Both officers maintained decorum but the letters resonate with potential conflict. It is implicit that Buster believed Parsons was expected to be a mole for the CGS. Buster's opposition to Parsons was not a casual thing for they knew each other very well, both having been on Gen. Macdonell's First Division staff at the same time during the war (Photo 6-6). It is also likely that Parsons was upset at being Buster's GSO 1, especially after holding the same appointment under Macdonell, while Buster was AA&QMG.

The next indication of serious problems for Buster was in his confidential report for 1929. In this Buster was judged to be 'satisfactory'. He received much higher appraisals from Andy's two predecessors, MacBrien and Thacker. In a following item in his appraisal, (4) 'Is he fully qualified for (a) Both Major General's Command and Appointment', Buster is judged not to be except in due course subject to selection and that he was best suited for a Command of a District. Buster was unused to such marginal approval. In a letter to NDHQ he stated:

> "Major General Thacker, who had good opportunity of judging me, recommended me for both a Major General's Command and Appointment. As I am better qualified now ... wherein have I failed?"

There is no record of an answer but about the same date he received separate evaluation by General E.C. Ashton, QMG, who stated:

> "This officer is energetic and painstaking [with] good powers of command and his administration of his District appears to be satisfactory.
>
> He is well trained in staff duties and his knowledge of military matters is above average. The "Q" services in his District were found in satisfactory condition.
>
> The discipline of the PF troops inspected appeared excellent."

Signed E.C. Ashton,
20/1/1930[10]

Photo 9 - 4. Buster at cavalry camp at Vernon in 1931.

Buster's Annual Confidential Report, for 1931, is similar to his first one by McNaughton but it states:

"(7). The work of this officer has exhibited a definite improvement since the report of last year.

He is now commanding his district satisfactorily and is recommended to continue in the appointment of District Officer Commanding.

(8). 'For what particular employment either in his present or in higher rank or grade do you recommend him?' Employment as a District Officer Commanding in his present rank."

Signed A. McNaughton[11]

Another revelation of attitudes at NDHQ was a letter dated 6 May, 1929, from the AG, Col. Clyde Caldwell, discussing whether Buster should have a staff car for his use. Buster answered immediately in a full letter:

"My dear Clyde:

I always held while at [NDHQ] that a motor was one of the perquisites of a DOC. If not his pay and allowances should be materially increased. ...

General McNaughton told me when I came through Ottawa [on the way here] that we had to have a car and he would defend its use by the DOC. I am doing just what he did and his predecessors and what is being done by all other DOCs."

Buster then goes into details on how the staff car is used, how difficult it would be isolated at Work Point without a vehicle, how it would be a wasteful duplication to have a separate private car, how he could not afford it, and how a driver is necessary at many functions. He then enumerates all the visitors he has had on NDHQ's behalf in the five months he had been in place. He finishes with thanks for sending Chimey Chambers, the new District Engineering Officer. Buster does not say that neither he nor Clare had learnt to drive. His arguments were accepted.

During Buster's tenure as DOC he tried with some success to improve the military facilities in his District. Work Point Barracks was a fairly good base but he got the NCOs' Mess improved, a recreation hall for the troops and a squash court for the officers. More importantly, he got the oil tank farm on the adjacent McLoughlin Point to surround their facility with a concrete retaining wall to protect the base and harbour from a seaborne fire in case of accident or attack. In addition, he was very successful in creating new facilities in the lower mainland. Buster's advocacy resulted in three fine new armouries built for the Seaforths, the Westminster Regiment and the BC Dragoons. During this period Buster also engaged in a long fight to create a new cavalry and infantry camp at Vernon (Photo 9-4), in spite of much politicking from other interior towns and their MPs, as well as the opposition of the CGS who wanted a new camp that included an artillery range in the Nisconlith Forest Reserve northwest of Kamloops.[12] In Buster's opinion the Nisconlith site was not suitable for a range because of fire hazard created by exploding shells in that Interior Dry Belt area of the Province. Also, Vernon was considerably more accessible by road and rail than the undeveloped Nisconlith area. Furthermore, MD No. 11 artillery camps could continue to be held at Sarcee, near Calgary (MD No.13), without further expenditure. Finally, much of the land for the Vernon camp would be donated by the city.

Photo 9 - 5. HMS Dauntless discovered and attacked in Satellite Channel on the approaches to Maple Bay, Vancouver Island during Combined Operations training, 1930.

Buster prevailed in this disagreement with the CGS but it undoubtedly did not improve their relationship. What was achieved, however, was that the state of preparedness and early response of the Militia in BC on the outbreak of WWII owed much to his foresight, his capability to argue succinctly, and his diligence in getting modern facilities in place in addition to his recruiting troops and officers for the Militia.

As a convinced Imperialist, Buster believed that the navy was the first line of defence for the Commonwealth, including Canada and when he was complimented for supporting the RCN Volunteer Reserve by Brig. A.H. Bell, CMG, DSO, the current AG, he replied, "the more we can do for them the better."[13] Buster, when asked to store 70 naval guns for possible use for armed merchantmen in time of war, regretted he had no suitable space and outlined to NDHQ what would be needed for such a depot, of which they seemed unaware. His personal relationship with the CO of Naden, Commander Len Murray (Photo 9-7), was excellent although not so with his successor.[14] Buster got strong cooperation from the RCN, which wholeheartedly supported the attempts at Combined Operations training for the Militia, although, as he said, there was little in it for the Navy. The RN also joined in the operations at the DOC's behest because most summers they had a cruiser from the Caribbean station in BC waters (Photo 9-5) and Buster knew how to turn on the Imperial tap. Most of the RN Captains became his firm friends. In addition, Buster strongly backed the RCAF. In a speech to the United Service Institute in Vancouver on 7 May, 1933, he decried the reduced establishment for the air force. Not only did he see them as an essential armed force but he was also a strong believer in their aerial photography and mapping program. At the same time, he compared the lack of topographic mapping in the USA with Canada's better efforts. Buster's attitude to the Navy and Air Force had a completely different emphasis to that of the CGS's who wanted them to be subservient to his command; in fact, he wished to be Chief of a Combined Staff.[15] Also to help maintain the army funding he recommended to the government there should be severe cuts to navy and air force budgets.[16]

Combined Operations were the main focus of field training for the Militia from 1929 until Buster left in 1933. The initial idea may well have been Pearkes', as Roy states, but it was embraced by Buster and he carried it forward with variations every year.[17] In the light of WWII operations these exercises were pathetically small and simple but they had elements of realism for the forces available. All the infantry and auxiliary units of the Island and lower Mainland were represented with the navy transporting up to a thousand men from the Mainland. A crucial element in the exercises in 1929 and 1930 was to practice a quick and skillful landing

Photo 9 - 6. Six wheel Leyland lorry tried out during field maneuvers at Maple Bay with scarcely any chance of buying them.

against limited resistance at Maple Bay, near Duncan 30 miles north of Victoria. Like Gallipoli, the sea borne force only had the ship's boats to carry the troops ashore. The RCN destroyer HMCS Vancouver and mine-sweepers, together with the visiting RN cruisers HMS Dragon in 1929 and Dauntless in 1930, all took part. Some RCAF Vickers Vedettes (Photo 9-5) carried out reconnaissance and simulated bombing.[18] In 1931, the exercise was to seize Esquimalt and its forts by night landings at Cordova Bay north of Victoria and Parry Bay near William Head to the south (see Map 3). The RCAF simulated a coordinated bombing of the forts. Col. W.W. Foster was in command of the Mainland forces and Lt. Col. Martyn the Island ones. HMS Dragon was again involved. The exercises got considerable press coverage and were judged to be both fairly realistic and useful. The Mainland forces were judged to have captured the forts. The budget was limited to $1,500 and the Militia forsook their pay to enable the exercise to go ahead.[19] Next year budgets for the RN forbade their Pacific cruise, consequently the exercises were changed again to landings near Nanaimo in mid-Island. For realism, they were conducted during the rainy autumn days in November. The lack of any contemporary all-terrain troop transports or fighting vehicles at the island manoeuvres or the cavalry camp at Vernon, was coped with in various ways. At Maple Bay the army 'tried out' six wheel Leyland transports (Photo 9-6), with little hope of purchasing them if they proved to be suitable. At Vernon the BC Dragoons in their enthusiasm made some trucks resemble armoured cars. Buster got as little credit as he got money from NDHQ for these innovative and forward looking programs.

A constant succession of very important visitors to Victoria and Work Point required acute diplomatic attention or considerable entertaining. The most important visitors were the King and Queen of Siam who, with an extensive retinue, arrived in April 1931. They were the first reigning monarchs to visit Canada. The King was suffering from malaria when he came so that the Queen and her parents, HRH Prince and Princess Svasti, were waited upon (Photo 9-7). Three Vice Regal couples also came to BC: the Willingtons, the Byngs, and the Bessboroughs. Buster had a convivial meeting with 'Bungo' Byng while the others occasions proceeded according to strict protocol. In addition, there were visits from two different Ministers of National Defence, Col. J.L. Ralston and Lt. Col. D.M. Sutherland, both of whom Buster knew well, and the Deputy Minister G.J. Desbarats. Besides these official visitors there were a host of military and diplomatic persons travelling back to the UK from Far East postings or tours. Amongst these were some personal friends like Maj. Gen. Jack Dill, a future CIGS, then on the staff at Camberley. As Buster had gone to Staff College and the IDC with Dill he devoted a lot of attention to him, arranging visits to all the Military Districts and writing the DOCs to look after him as he too was under severe travel cost restrictions. Buster had a long letter from him when he left Canada thanking him and describing his impressions and his fine welcome everywhere.

Buster was asked also to give many addresses to Militia units, military organizations, veterans groups and service clubs. He never refused, must have enjoyed it, and saw it as part of his support of the Militia and the PF. He was inclined to be a rather fulsome speaker but, since he kept being asked, people must have appreciated his talks.

While Buster was at Work Point he kept up a vigorous correspondence with a wide array of people: colleagues, veterans, petitioners, international visitors and old friends. His important confidential letters he wrote and also copied longhand. At the start of his tenure he received and acknowledged dozens of letters of congratulation for his appointment as DOC, including ones from Maj. Gen. James MacBrien, CB, CMG, DSO and Lt. Col. G.P. Vanier, DSO, MC, later Governor General, and from Maj. Generals Dill and Lavarack in the UK. Buster also was appealed to repeatedly to support requests for rank or pension adjustments. Usually he considered such appeals worthy, and did what he could to help, sometimes successfully. These actions provided another reason why he was well thought of by his officers and men. Starting in 1930, Buster started receiving confidential letters complaining about NDHQ in general and in particular the CGS 'as a one man show'.[20] Many went on to say they were hoping or expecting he would be the next CGS to clear up the mess. Such letters came from among others Rab Beeman and T.V. Anderson who later, when he was CGS, would have his own chance to clean up the mess. Some of the letters complained about the absence of infantry or cavalry officers in NDHQ. One from Geoffrey Morton after a conference of MD GSO 1s at Sarcee said, "There is a strong feeling amongst GSOs here, that you should go to Ottawa if there is a reshuffle. Such a move would have the backing of the PF and restore confidence in it. I find we are not the only ones who feel as we do about NDHQ."[21]

Most the officers knew that Buster agreed with them about the status and staffing of Headquarters but initially he did not lend much encouragement. Replying to a letter from Lt. Col. R.O. Alexander in September, 1929, he stated, "Your prognostications are not to be... I do not expect the other job [CGS but he did that of AG].... [and he agreed] the gunners do seem to be getting an extra dose of everything..."[22]

The whole controversy of skewed staffing and preference for those of high academic standing rather than experience and proven leadership in McNaughton's regime is covered thoroughly by Harris.[23]

"Some of the carping was undoubtedly directed at McNaughton himself. Considered by many to be a 'super-engineer and college professor', not a soldier, [and] despite his own limited command experience he had risen to the top ahead of more senior officers with good records as colonels and brigadiers in France, and this caused considerable resentment... . As Sutherland Brown observed, the coterie of officers the new CGS gathered around him had 'entirely too much of the university, gunner, and engineering complex,' with scarcely an infantryman or cavalryman to be found. Sutherland Brown was always worried that academic qualifications would be the criteria for selecting brigade and divisional commanders of the next Canadian expeditionary force [and this turned out to be the case]. ...In short, McNaughton argued against the existence of a unique profession of arms if that entailed full-time, life long and concentrated study on the part of its members to learn how to manage violence in war. ...[The group that emerged under McNaughton's criteria for WWII] had insufficient opportunity to learn their profession before they became senior commanders. Unfortunately, they failed because of this."

However, as time advanced Buster became less cautious in his criticism in talks and letters of the CGS and NDHQ. At least one of Buster's confidants gave one or more of these later critical letters to the CGS, which certainly increased their personal estrangement. Buster wrote such a letter to MacBrien, then Commissioner of the RCMP, on 29 August 1932, after his brief visit to Victoria. Following some pleasantries Buster said:

"I hope you will be able to give Donald Sutherland, [Minister DND] some good advice. I am afraid he will not get the best. McNaughton, Bell and Caldwell are not an imposing trio. McN has plenty of brains but lacks personality. He is uncouth and slovenly in his make up and is decidedly unpopular with the Militia and forgets he is dealing with men [not as smart] as him but with more balance and knowledge of [others] and more business acumen. He was a rotten battery commander...[as opposed to a scientific gunner]. Bell is a mere rubber stamp and Clyde is an out and out politician.

Photo 9 - 7. Buster with Commander Leonard W. Murray, Senior Naval Officer, Esquimalt, and the Honourable Mr. Lemaire, Secretary to the Privy Council, representing the Prime Minister attending HRH Prince Svasti, father of the Queen. in April 1931 during visit of the reigning the King and Queen of Siam to North America, Victoria Daily Colonist photo.

It was a bad day for our department when it lost men like you, Thacker, Ashton... and Panet." Buster then rails at the triumvirate's lack of regimental experience and goes on to say,

> "McNaughton never liked me personally but was never in a place to do me much harm until he was CGS. Now he has come out in his true colours as a vindictive and conceited man. He doesn't like advice and does not ask it and is much annoyed if anyone has different views to himself. I expect I [will get] no fair dealings with the present hierarchy. I won't end up as AG. I can do that job better than anyone I know [because of my legal training]... . I am afraid McNaughton

will not recommend me and the Minister will not know of my existence."

He then asks for MacBrien's help in drawing his qualifications to the attention of the Minister.[24]

It is sad that Buster felt backed into a corner and that he was constrained to make this appeal. His period as DOC had started with such optimism and vigour. He had achieved almost a rebirth of the Militia in the West, yet here he was seemingly defeated in his quest to improve the status of the army in the service of the nation, as well as achieving the apex of his career. The frustrating situation undoubtedly had arisen partly through flaws in his own character, blind trust and a certain naivety. However, it was chiefly the result of an unfortunate fate that he should find himself under such a triumvirate headed by a person who relished power, disliked him and who was so clearly vindictive.

McNaughton had achieved his high reputation based on his scientific excellence and superb gunnery rather than leadership or broad military knowledge and experience. His status was enhanced by the press and secured by his political skills which included an amount of duplicity. Even McNaughton's admiring biographer, Swettenham, described him as manipulative. Harris describes his political manoeuvring in detail, first with the Tories and Prime Minister Bennett and then with the Liberals and Mackenzie King.[25] But it is Shirley Render who unfrocks him. Only on reading her book, *The Inside Story of the Double Cross*, would you obtain a clear view of this other side of McNaughton's personality and behaviour. In describing McNaughton, as well as the course he took in aborting James Richardson's desire to create a national airline, she says of the former, "The puzzling part of all this is that McNaughton undoubtedly would have described himself as a man of integrity. Did his lack of the most elementary business sense... distort his thinking? ... Once McNaughton decided on a course of action nothing could stop him - after all he was doing it for the good of Canada. This unwavering belief in his own rightness so warped his judgement during World War II that he was relieved of his command and brought back to Canada."[26]

In the late spring of 1932, the Great Depression was obviously not retreating as Prime Minister Bennett and others thought or hoped, but actually was intensifying. Military budgets, although already greatly reduced were, as usual, targeted for further reduction. Buster received a letter from Harold Matthews, DMO&I and acting as McNaughton's secretary, asking the PF officers to volunteer to take a ten percent pay cut. Salaries for the military were already minimal and below equivalent ranks in the civil service or in civilian life. Yet, generosity to the Canadian armed forces was unheard of. Not only had Currie received no reward for his extraordinary service and successful generalship, but also his salary was so modest as Inspector General he readily accepted McGill's offer when it came to become the University Principal.[27] Furthermore, among the reason MacBrien resigned as CGS, the highest ranking officer in the army, was because of pay. As Commissioner of the RCMP, he would receive a much more adequate compensation.[28]

Buster's response to Matthews was immediate. He called a meeting of all the PF officers of the garrison to inform them of the CGS's suggestion and then wrote a five page letter in reply.[29]

"My Dear Harold,

I make haste to answer your letter of April 12 which arrived yesterday morning. ... If the government in its wisdom considers that a 10% cut is necessary in behalf of the present conditions I presume that it will be taken philosophically but at the same time will be most disappointing.

The officers here are absolutely unanimous against any volunteering towards reduction. Our attitude always has been that the P.F. has been underpaid, particularly the higher officers and some of the W.O.s and N.C.O.s. ... The officers are underpaid compared with the British Army and the United States [Army]. ...

I shall develop arguments later on in this letter but before doing so I shall refer to my own case which is... similar to all [DOCs]. We do not live an extravagant life. It has cost me $2000 more than my total pay and allowances during the last three years. ... Most of this [has had to be taken from our small capital]. ... In order to keep up with the situation we have had to forgo all sorts of pleasures. I have had exactly 17 days' leave since being in B.C. The main reason for that is I cannot afford to go any place and take my family. ... General McNaughton, I understand, realized this situation and some three years ago recommended that all D.O.C.s should have an increase of $1000 a year."

Buster goes on to take up Matthew's letter point by point, much of which makes comparisons between civil service pay, duties, degree of difficulty and hazard with that of the military equivalent positions. Among his arguments he states:

> "9. The pay of higher officers of the army was reduced right after the war. ...

> 11. In 1924 the pay of the private soldier was reduced from $1.70 to $1.20 per diem, about 30%."

Buster concludes:

> 21. I trust that the Minister will make a most determined effort to see that no calamity like this falls upon His Majesty's Service in the Dominion of Canada."

This letter is consistent with Buster's whole philosophy: willingness to endure sacrifice on behalf of the army and the nation but demanding that the proper political authority acknowledge responsibility. To place upon his men voluntary acceptance of an additional reduction in pay was to Buster unfair and manipulative. Buster must have wondered if McNaughton was recommending this volunteering to ingratiate himself with the Minister or the Prime Minister. Certainly, the General knew the whole Militia was underpaid. Buster believed superiors should be seen to be responsible for their acts.

Buster was about to encounter the most testing period of his life. This was not due to military affairs but rather that his relationship with the CGS deteriorated greatly as a result of severe differences about how to manage Unemployment Relief Camps that NDHQ created to help fight some of the effects of the Great Depression. Regardless of this coming confrontation, Buster's stewardship of MD No. 11 in the early thirties, despite the near crippling financial cut backs, made the District much better prepared for WWII than it had been. The Militia was as active and as well trained and staffed as budgets allowed. It had expanded and was now led by more enthusiastic officers. Against the fiscal trend and all odds Buster had secured new armouries and training grounds. He had helped generate co-operation between the services which became the normal way of operating on the West Coast. Buster had secured the infrastructure and the men to enable the District to go on a war-footing rapidly when, in six short years, the Second World War irrupted.

10 Hard Times

In 1933 Buster's world became unstitched. The collapse of the New York Stock exchange on Thursday, 24 October, 1929, did not immediately have full impact on Canada. The consequent Great Depression developed somewhat slower in this country, even if it was eventually deeper and more severe than in most western countries. Buster was not affected directly by the Crash because he had few investments. However, he soon felt the sharp edge of hard times himself. The effects that impinged on him were mostly beyond his control. The first was the progressively restricting budgets for the army under his command. This was soon followed by the ten percent salary cuts across the board for officers. Then, at the end of 1932, as a result of General McNaughton's influence on the Prime Minister, the Military Districts became responsible for setting up and administrating camps for unemployed single men. One third of these men were in British Columbia which already had a camp system. Although Buster was a great organizer he faced a real problem because the BC camps had generous provisions and required little work compared to the Spartan ideas that the NDHQ had in mind. McNaughton and Buster had completely different philosophies concerning the camps. Consequently, the existing rift between Andy and Buster quickly became wider and more serious, particularly for Buster.

The Great Depression

Canada's economy in the post-war period depended significantly on the sale of commodities: grains, fish, forest products and metals. In 1929 the economy was buoyant but in 1930 the strain began to show. As the Depression decline steepened, the markets for these commodities eroded rapidly, throwing Canada into a desperate situation.[1] Thirty three percent of the Gross National Income depended on these exports. Between 1929 and 1933 it is estimated that Canada's Gross National Expenditure was reduced by 42 per cent and its Gross National Product must have been similarly reduced.[2] In the 1930s there was no adequate social safety net in Canada. Public welfare scarcely existed and charitable organizations and individuals were thrown to extemporaneous attempts to alleviate the worst effects by establishing soup kitchens, breadlines and other relief organizations. These were completely inadequate to cope with the mounting crisis. In the Canadian way the Federal government declared that welfare was a Provincial responsibility and the Provinces responded that it was a national one. Most local governments, which were generally impoverished in any case, refused or were unable to help. Although the burden of the Depression was spread fairly broadly, one of its worst effects, unemployment, rested most heavily on young single men. Married ones were preferentially retained in commerce and government and if laid off could receive a dole, which in BC, would be between $12.50 and $30 a month depending on the number of children. The Depression was intensified by coincident drought and crop failure in the Prairies. Hence, its effects were not evenly distributed geographically because the Western Provinces were the principle producers of commodities and their economies depended almost entirely on their sale. This created a multi-faceted social and financial crisis most heavily felt in the west and not least in British Columbia.

In 1929 this westernmost Province was booming in a way it hadn't since the Gold Rush so comparisons based against performance that year look particularly bad. By January 1930 unemployment increased 300 percent. Disturbances started almost immediately. The Province was already $102 million in debt and would not act until after the next Federal election which brought the Conservatives and Prime Minister R.B. Bennett to power. By February 1931, BC had 67,128 people on relief. By the Spring of 1932 the Province was $143 million in debt and was spending $2.4 million a year on relief without effective programs to rectify the desperate situation. The attributes of mass unemployment were already widely evident: transient populations of single men, hobo jungles, soup kitchens, despair, general anxiety and disturbances. The West Coast, because of its milder climate, seemed like a better place to face the winter so there was an influx of laid off farm workers from the Prairies, loggers from the BC Coast and Interior and factory hands and miners from Ontario. The main problem with transient unemployed men was initially evident in Vancouver but it soon spread to most Interior towns. As a partial solution the Province started setting up camps for these men with some Federal money designated for relief.[3] However, the problem was exacerbated by the Dominion government terminating its emergency relief program in March 1931, followed by the Provinces doing the same. To reduce their responsibility the Municipalities insisted on six months residence before any relief was available. All this inter-governmental squabbling did little to relieve the distress of men, women and children caught in the crisis.

The Federal Cabinet was finally convinced by the Minister of Labour, Gideon Robertson, of the continuing nature of the crisis and so enacted a new *Unemployment Relief Act* in July 1931, but they still insisted the Provinces and Municipalities were responsible. Funds (proposed at $50 million of which only $28 million was paid) were given to the Provinces to manage relief because they were nearly bankrupt. They were required to set up commissions to direct relief and most Provinces did so. In British Columbia the Commission was chaired by Major J.G. Fordham whom Buster rated a first class fellow. The other members were Dr. W.A. Carruthers of UBC, whom he described as an impractical university professor and Socialist, and Col. D.W.B. Spry, whom he rated as effective.

As much as the Provincial Governments were alarmed about the state of their economies and the effects upon them of widespread unemployment, they were equally anxious that transients in the cities could lead to disturbances, riot and the growth of Communism. Consequently, the BC Government at the urging of the Fordham Commission, continued setting up unemployment relief camps in the hinterland to get the transients out of the cities. The men got $2 a day of which they paid 85 cents for board and accommodation. By September 1931 the Province had set up 237 camps with a potential capacity to house 18 340 men, about a third of all the single unemployed men cared for in Canada. The idea was that the unemployed would build roads and other public works. The program was not well managed for a number of reasons, including its stop and start operation resulting from Dominion Government policy as well as Municipal and Provincial nepotism and political-based favouritism. Most men did little or no work and complained of isolation and boredom. Here was fertile ground for social strife and the sprouting of Communism which the authorities feared.

An Imperial Economic Conference, a Federal - Provincial Conference, many less formal meetings, as well as abundant official and impromptu studies were conducted in 1931-32 without much resolution. Charlotte Whitton, acerbic social worker and later Mayor of Ottawa, in her report to the government uncharacteristically for her profession, advocated unemployment relief camps. In the early Fall of 1932, for different reasons, so did General McNaugton, now a confidential advisor to Prime Minister Bennett, and as such judged 'perhaps the most powerful public servant in the country'.[4] In the summer the General had, in the course of his Canada-wide travels, seen the distress caused by unemployment. He later said he was motivated to save the nation's young men as well as to remove a potential menace of riot and rebellion.[5] He proposed to the new Minister of Labour, W.A. Gordon, a scheme of Federally supported work camps administered by DND. These camps would accept able-bodied single homeless unemployed men at their own request. At the Opening of the House on 6 October, displaying his power,

Photo 10 - 1. General A.G.L. McNaughton, CGS 1929-36, portrait while GOC Canadian Army about 1943. NAC photo PA 132548.

McNaughton sat by Bennett. The PM leaned over and told the General that the Cabinet liked 'his' ideas and wished to apply them. Two days later they were implemented by order-in-council. Bennett wanted the scheme to be limited initially to 2000 men and the cost limited to $1.00 per man per day including food, shelter and clothing, with a 20 cents allowance. By 8 October 1932 Buster started receiving wires asking about the organization of UR camps in BC.[6] Buster replied in a full letter on 15 October with a detailed list of camp locations and construction status in which 3743 men were housed with a further 103 in hospitals. He also stated the total in camps the previous winter had been between 6000 and 7000.

DND Unemployment Relief Camps

Neither McNaughton nor the Government saw, or worried, about having two sets of unemployment relief camps in BC that had different aims, qualifications for entry and scale of welfare. This became a real problem and a source of discontent and discord that continued even after DND eventually took over the BC camps in June 1933. It bedevilled the administrators of both organizations and was a substantial element of the breech that developed between Buster and the CGS.

McNaughton's first projects were the restoration of the historic citadels of Quebec City and Halifax. His decision ignored the fact that the worst of the unemployment problem was in BC. When projects in that Province were started in the winter of 1932-33 the relative generosity of BC camps was in stark contrast with the stringency of the DND ones. The BC camps were supposedly directed to public works and the construction of new roads aimed at better communication within the Province; for example, the Big Bend 'highway' along the Columbia River to connect Revelstoke and the Interior with the Rocky Mountain Trench and the Hope-Princeton 'highway' to connect the Coast with the Interior and provide an alternative to the vulnerable Fraser Canyon route (see Map 2). McNaughton also favoured these projects as well as preparation of landing fields to support his other chosen objective, a national airline. After the initial thrust to re-build the citadels involved him in conflict with labour unions he turned to these other schemes which required axes, shovels and wheelbarrows, and not machinery or trade skills. The DND camp scheme, however, faced more subtle obstacles than labour union objections. The camps were characterized by their detractors, led by the Communist Party, that they were the thin edge of the wedge of militarism and would lead inevitably to conscription. Alternatively, they were described as slave labour camps. Both these charges were substantially untrue but they caused much ferment. Military officers and men connected with the camps consequently wore civilian clothes and avoided any hint of military discipline or recruiting. Unemployed men could join the camps or leave at will although a few trouble-makers were ejected permanently. The objection that 20 cents a day constituted slave labour was tested in the Federal courts where it was argued that the sum was an allowance and not a wage, and given for personal effects as part of relief. Nevertheless, those who decried the scheme mocked the camps and labelled them and their occupants as 'the Royal Twenty Centers', inferring both militarism and stinginess.

McNaughton convinced the cabinet that DND was the only government agency that had the overall capability to run the camps: *i.e.* engineering, accounting, procurement, management ability *etc.* McNaughton always took a rosy view of the camps and their accomplishments in work and in avoiding disturbances and public mischief. He argued strongly to the PM that without them the Militia and the government would have to face riot and possibly Communist insurgency. He also stated that military rations and accommodation were sufficient and could be provided at a dollar per man per day. In the Pacific Province the DND camps initially worked along side the BC-run camps, which were more generous in food, clothing, and allowances. It invariably followed that the men would make comparisons that led to complaints or worse. When DND took over all the BC Government run camps on 1 June, 1933, it evoked a strong protest from the unemployed men in them about their decreased welfare, poorer clothes and, to some, increased work load.

From January 1933 Buster and his senior staff, particularly Colonels Greer, Pope and Major Chambers, DEO, became heavily involved in the Unemployed Relief Camp direction and problems. Priority and orders for managing and controlling UR camps stemmed from NDHQ. Nevertheless, the regular work of the District had to continue including a good deal of attention to the NPAM. Buster saw the Militia as another way of helping the unemployed men. He succeeded in getting unemployed militiamen on direct relief so they could still report to their regiments. In MD No. 11 unemployment relief was particularly sensitive because of the relative generosity of the BC program and the slackness of its works program compared to DND camps. Disturbances irrupted almost immediately, particularly in the DND camp at Princeton where men stopped work on 4 January, 1933.

To deal with this matter Buster immediately dispatched Major Chambers and Colonel Greer to investigate and correct the situation. Princeton was then two days travel by ferry and rail from Victoria. After they reported to him he wrote a three page letter on 10 January to the Secretary, DND, in other words the CGS, which in part stated:

"... 4. Before dealing with the specific complaints I desire to point out that all complaints of the 'Militia Camps' conditions will be compared to what has been done by the Provincial Government. As far as I know [BC] is the only Province that has gone in for unemployed camps on a very large scale, and it has treated unemployed men on a more generous scale than that at present in vogue by [DND]. For instance, they get $7.50 per month instead of 20 cents per diem. They get an issue of tobacco, full medical attention, a very generous issue of boots and clothing. ... Their cooking utensils are more modern... and of the type used in lumber and mining camps... earthenware [in contrast to our much chipped enamel dishes]. ...

9. There will always be complaints about army ration, which is not on the scale issued by the Province... nor in accordance with the normal diet of those men in lumber and mining camps in this Province. It would be better if [Greer] were allowed a specific sum to buy rations rather than to adhere to the standard ration. Probably no more would be required than at present being expended.... It is important that bath towels be issued. ... [Some] leather boots should be issued as some men cannot wear rubber boots owing to the effect on their feet.

10. Greatcoats will now be issued [even it is not politic to turn men out in khaki. ...There is no way to have them dyed in Princeton].

There were a number of other reasonable requests such as the need for barbers tools and Coleman lamps rather than storm lanterns. ...

13. The situation appears to have been dealt with firmly and reasonably by Major Chambers and Mr. Lowe, the foreman. The men returned to work the following day. ... The men as a whole appear to be a reasonable body of young men, but many are of foreign extraction ... and misguided by agitators [of which] one or two may still be in the camp. ...the situation is being watched by the BC Police. Two men have already been expelled. ...

16. Everything that I have in my power to attend to locally will be done."[7]

Buster's request to the CGS to increase the scale and variety of food in the DND camps was turned down by him and the Minister of Labour.

Buster commented that McNaughton was annoyed with him for asking and for being persistent in giving him information, as he saw it, concerning the troubles and their causes. He reported on problems in the Sooke camp, and that half of the men in the DND camp at Hope had left.[8] Buster informally said to friends that McNaughton's vision of the Camps was that they should be similar to those for PoWs. In comparison, Buster's view was certainly more humane. Charles Taylor considered that:

> "As a conservative, Sutherland Brown believed that human society was an organic entity in which every member had responsibilities to his fellow citizens. So he held that the unemployed should be treated with dignity, compassion and as much generosity as circumstances would permit."[9]

To increase general security and his staff's ability to act swiftly in case of trouble, Buster, early in the year wrote to the BC Attorney General, R.H. Pooley, and Col. J.H. Mullins, Commissioner of BC Police, requesting that he, Greer and Chambers be made constables. Buster's experience with the fierce strikes in Cape Breton in 1909 confirmed how useful this could be. His request was granted, and Major Chambers was also appointed Justice of the Peace, enabling him to swear in Special Constables during an emergency.[10] Buster wished to counter any trouble before it spread and to avoid, if possible, calling out the troops as an aid to the civil powers.

General McNaughton wrote to Harold Matthews who was acting as Secretary to NDHQ on 8 February 1933:

> "Dear Harold:
>
> I have your letter of 4 February and I most sincerely appreciate your kind congratulations on the extension of my appointment [as CGS]. ...
>
> With regard to BC I am well aware of the situation in respect to the over elaborate arrangements the BC Government had made for the unemployed, and I was anxious to bring the matter to a show down. The best way to do this it was to approve projects for a reasonable number of men and then clearly demonstrate that they would not be forthcoming so long as BC provided camps with good meals and without work, so what we want to do is to make reasonable efforts to get men but not to over stress the matter....
>
> Very sincerely yours,"[11]

In contrast, Buster wrote on 9 February 1933 to the AG, Clyde Caldwell elaborating upon his assessment of the situation in BC:

> "Feeding is at the bottom of most of our troubles. The men in the two camp systems knew all about the comparisons. The men in the Provincial camps get twice as much sugar, much more milk and butter, spices and fruit. They have ham and eggs, sausages and kippers for breakfast. In other words they have a varied diet instead of the same thing day in and day out. ... [They have] no kick about quality of our rations, just its sameness."[12]

Although URC direction and concerns dominated his life during the early months of 1933 there was some relief. Buster was asked by Brig. D.M. Ormond to give the Vimy Dinner address in Calgary to the Military Institute on 9 April 1933. The invitation addressed to the Secretary of DND according to protocol went the rounds of the CGS, QMG, and Deputy Minister. Desbarets and Bell approved and Matthews, on behalf of the CGS, concurred as long as there was no expense to the Public and that no publicity be given to the address.[13] Another major concern of the DOC's was the formation of 11 Squadron Non-Permanent Active RCAF at Sea Island, Vancouver. Even though the unit would have no aircraft for some time, quarters and command had to be established. Buster also had a regular slate of inspections of Militia regiments including the Second Battalion of the 16th Canadian Scottish in Duncan of 30 May, the same day he received critical telegrams from the CGS.[14]

Many events were compressed between the beginning of May and the end of June 1933. Buster had little respite from the deluge of letters and telegrams from NDHQ requiring immediate action as well as requests for reports. In thirteen days to 12 June he received 42 telegrams of instruction and comment. Charles Taylor acknowledges the situation and notes Buster's reaction:

> "The main torrent of abuse and impractical orders were [chiefly levelled] at me. As I had the confidence of almost everyone in British Columbia I can only take it that the Chief of the General Staff was trying to drive me into a corner where I would resign"(see Appendix E).[15]

McNaughton by his constant directions from Ottawa inferred the camps in BC were not being well run. In contrast, the *Victoria Daily Colonist* on 3 June ran a full page account of the DND camps in BC in which they were judged to be successful and well run, confirming Buster's view rather than that of the CGS.

On 24 May Buster submitted to NDHQ a three page penetrating appraisal of the contemporary situation in BC of Unemployment Relief that covered:

1. Limits of responsibilities for UR;
2. Distribution of the homeless unemployed;
3. Political situation in BC;
4. Patronage;
5. Homeless unemployed in cities;
6. Situation in camps;
7. Rations;
8. Segregation of malcontents;
9. Administration of homeless men in urban centres;
10. Road construction and selection of engineers;
11. Present complex disposition of the administrative staff of the Province concerned with UR.

The full report which forms Appendix C of this volume was answered by a complex two page telegram referring to the numbered items with uninformative and cryptic comments such as '2. noted', or '4. covered by Policy and Instruction', or '8. regulations under consideration'.

On 30 May Buster got a telegram in caps from the CGS which, after a prelude states:

> McNaughton will take over four thousand men in his camps by twenty second June and will increase this number as rapidly as possible thereafter possibly at the rate of two thousand a month stop Commission is only asked to function as heretofore in respect to men now under its care until they can be absorbed in the National Defence camps stop Regarding increased rations this matter wholly under the jurisdiction of General McNaughton and present scale has my full approval and twenty cents cash gratuity to meet such extras as tobacco etc Stop Would suggest further that there is utmost need for the Commissions ration being brought in conformity with army ration obtaining in National Defence camps if any disparity between the two ends addressed commanding eleven repeated commanding thirteen Stop Acknowledge
>
> Chief General Staff

The growing conflict between the views and CGS and Buster is further illustrated by two telegrams the following day, 31 May 1933. The

Photo 10 - 2. DND Unemployment Relief Camp at Michel, BC, Project No. 61. Men lining up at stores for tobacco, February 1934. NAC photo PA 35996.

CGS to DOC MD No 11 said:

> "Telegram received by Government from Tolmie [the Premier, sic], Bruhn, [Chief Engineer BC Ministry of Public Works], and others indicate you have expressed views to Provincial Ministers that approved scale of Army rations is inadequate for relief camps. Have you made any statement to this effect? Reply by wire."

Buster replied the same day:

> "In conference with Provincial Authorities I have pointed out the undesirability of having two scales of rations issued at the same time in camps in close proximity. I have not stated that the Army scale is insufficient but have dwelt on the psychological effect of the change over.
>
> Telegram of Mr. Gordon [Federal Minister of Labour] to Mr. Bruhn seems not to have rectified this matter."[16]

The unfortunate clash of these two strong men was due to their very different personalities and abilities.

The one brilliant academically, technically and politically skilled, sure he is right but needing it played back by yes men. He was also manipulative, inconsiderate, vindictive and missing some qualities of leadership. The other: intelligent, pragmatic, broadly experienced, organizationally and socially skilled, consultative and a leader. However, he was also to a degree naive, vain and inflexible, was open to indiscretion, and impatient. They shared some characteristics such as a love of the army, being hard working, devoted and patriotic but these were not enough to bring them together. The last set was played over how to run the Relief Camps. McNaughton, the boss, had the serve and won the match.

During this period Buster learned he was going to be moved to Winnipeg. He wrote to General MacBrien on 1 May:

> "I got a rude shock a couple of days ago. Confidentially, I have been notified I am being transferred to command MD No.10 ... and Ashton is to coming here. ... Where Victor Anderson goes I don't know. ... McNaughton, of course, dislikes me personally and probably will not be sympathetic to the protest I am going to put forward. ... He gets $2,000 more a year [with his extension] ...while we get ten percent less."

He goes on to say the CGS deserves the money but the contrast is stark.[17]

Matthews who had moved from DMO &I and Secretary of NDHQ to DOC, MD No. 13, Calgary, was a further agent of the distressing news. He wrote 6 May 1933 that:

"I heard Ashton was slated for MD No. 11... although Mrs. A. said she was trying to get him to retire... [as he needed a rest]. I thought possibly you would change places with him at Toronto and Victor [Anderson] would go to AG. You certainly should be in line for NDHQ any time now and it will be bad luck for you and the service as a whole if personalities are to enter into the question and prevent it. ... [This not long after congratulating McNaughton on his extension as CGS]. I can understand what the move to Wp'g would make as regards the boys education compared to where you are now. Perhaps this big road project task will result in your staying in Victoria some time longer. With it in hand I can't see where Ashton will find MD No. 11 a place to rest in. ...

I've just got your wire outlining a proposal for our respective spheres on the unemployment road project. [This is referring to Buster's proposal to share work in East Kootenay with MD 13 as he was directed] ... I think you have been more than generous."[18]

It is not clear what the CGS's intention was in taking most of the Kootenays UR camps from MD No. 11 and giving them to No.13. In some ways access from Calgary was slightly easier than from Victoria but a vindictive diminishing of Buster's authority may well have been part of it.

On 8 May Buster wrote to the Secretary of DND, AG's Branch, asking that they reconsider his new appointment on compassionate grounds. Paraphrasing his letter he stated that if there was no further advance for him, that he be allowed to serve out his career in MD No. 11. Secondly, in regard to the education of his sons, he could not afford their travel and board at University School in Victoria if he was in Winnipeg. Thirdly, he knew thoroughly all the politicians, civil servants and the engineering projects in the area and that it would take a newcomer some time to achieve the same degree of knowledge. He stressed he was vigorous and in good health. Finally, that the district was in excellent shape and he had the full confidence of the Militia.[19]

On 6 May he got a reply from MacBrien with some good advice:

> "I think you should look on the transfer to Winnipeg in the light of a promotion. An old friend's advice would be not to protest against the move in fear of upsetting the Minister of Defence, who I know is well disposed towards yourself. Later, as you are still a young man...[you] will be given one of the promotions on the Defence Council."[20]

Unfortunately Buster, for whatever reason, was not disposed to wait and take his chances. He was being harassed by McNaughton and, strong as he was, it was affecting him. He used to return late from the office and recline on the divan in the library unlike his normal vigorous behaviour. Even as a child I recognized something was wrong. In retrospect, I realize he was suffering from emotional exhaustion and was trying to decide how he should respond to the various challenges. In spite of what MacBrien said, the transfer to Winnipeg was anything but a promotion, but if he had accepted it, he might well have outlasted his tormentor. He was certainly partly responsible for the breach with McNaughton because he had repeatedly expressed his confidential opinion of the CGS, and naively thought none of his friends would relay his comments to the General. In fact, Buster had been warned by Bell of his use of intemperate language about his seniors, including a letter on 20 May which stated that the information was sufficiently vague it required nothing but a warning. Buster's reply stated he had never criticized his superiors publicly. He also said loyalty was one of his best qualities.[21]

Late in June Buster must have been thinking of resigning. No documentation has been found in his papers at the Queen's University Archives nor amongst the papers acquired from DND by Access to Information. The only source about such a letter was told to me by my brother Malcolm who said that our father late in the month wrote to the CGS with a list of recommendations for the management of the UR camps together with the statement, "Accept my recommendations or accept my resignation." According to Malcolm the General accepted both. No documentation is known for this either. Charles Taylor writes that Buster's rheumatic fever had returned and that he was wracked by over work and worry. He decided after a long talk with Clare to resign on his birthday, 28 June, at the age of fifty-two (*see* Appendix D).[22] For a career soldier who believed he still had something to contribute, it must have been the most wrenching decision of his life.

Soon after Buster resigned Matthews came to Victoria to temporarily take over MD No. 11 and to report to the CGS on the status of the District and the UR camps in BC. He addressed his letter to the Secretary of DND and reported:

> "I have the honour to report that in accordance with the in-
> structions conveyed to me personally by yourself, over long dis-
> tance phone...on 4 June... [I proceeded on 6 July to Victoria to
> take command].

> On arrival on 8 July I found the situation at District Headquar-
> ters somewhat disturbed due to the unusual circumstances
> which led up to the recent resignation of Brigadier J. Sutherland
> Brown.

> Thanks to the hearty support of all ranks of the District Staff,
> and to the friendly cooperation accorded me from Ottawa in
> disposing of some outstanding controversial points, an improve-
> ment in the general attitude and morale of all concerned soon
> became noticeable."

Matthews stayed in Victoria because he said he knew the condition of
the camps and thought it would be advantageous for the staff to circulate
about the camps. His letter continued:

> "I found the general organization of the Relief work in the Dis-
> trict to have been planned on sound lines, for which Major
> E.C.G. Chambers, MC, the DEO, deserves great credit. ... I
> found the organization of Relief Work duties at Work Point Bar-
> racks somewhat different to that at MD No. 13. What
> amounted to a separate organization from the normal Military
> Staff had been set up in a building apart from the [HQ] offices
> with the GSO 3 in charge... ."

Matthews covers a number of other points including the cooperation
he received from the Provincial Government and its civil service. As well,
he commented on Col. Spry's helpfulness, the only remaining member of
the Fordham Commission. He also states Spry was subject to almost daily
abuse from radical organizations. He ends by commenting on Brig.
Beeman's arrival to take over from him.[23]

In his report Matthews failed to draw attention to the fact that MD
No. 11 was dealing with one third of all the unemployed single men in
Canada. In these circumstances the special headquarters Buster had set
up without being able to employ additional manpower was a wise
course. It is difficult to avoid the view that Matthews report appears to be
designed to please the CGS. If the staff's morale was bad it was largely be-

cause they had just lost a Commanding Officer whom they admired and even loved (*see* Appendix D). They understood something of his travail. Buster was upset that during Matthews' stay in Victoria he had almost no contact with him and did not visit him socially even though Buster had been his mentor as DMO&I. Buster was deeply hurt by what he interpreted as his cowed, delinquent and discourteous behaviour.[24] He damned Buster with faint praise if not actually stabbing him in the back. Buster could not understand how one so brave in war could be such a coward in peace.

Troubles with the unemployed did not decrease after Buster resigned, rather the reverse. The DND Unemployment Relief program continued until it was terminated by the government on 1 July 1936. Arguably the worst incidents occurred during the 'On-to-Ottawa Trek' that followed a strike in BC camps in April 1935. The most disaffected and militant unemployed travelled by box car and other means eastward until the Bennett government, on the advice of the CGS and against that of the Commissioner of the RCMP, MacBrien, tried to stop them forcibly in Regina. During the subsequent riot and police action two RCMP were seriously injured and a city policeman was beaten to death.[25] Another serious incident followed closure of most of the camps in 1937 when over 600 rioters occupied both the Vancouver Post Office and the Art Gallery. The general conclusion seems to have been that the camp program, and particularly the NDHQ camps, were not as successful as the Civilian Conservation Corps (CCC) camps in the USA. These were supposed to be modelled after the Canadian ones but were far more costly. This incremental money came from President Roosevelt's Pump Priming Program.[26] Perhaps a bit more generosity in Canada would have had a better effect rather than McNaughton's austere program.

Charles Taylor called McNaughton, 'a brilliant and outspoken officer who was to prove Sutherland Brown's sternest adversary in later years, and the agent of his downfall'.[27] Shirley Render has been quoted previously about McNaughton's single mindedness and propensity to break his word if he thought it was for some greater good. Probably the most telling indictment of him is in J.L. Granatstein's book, *The Generals*, where he discusses McNaughton's role in WWII under the heading '*The God that Failed*'. He quotes Field Marshal Sir Alan Brooke, who knew McNaughton well during and following WWI, as saying,

> "A man of exceptional abilities where scientific matters were concerned, but lacking the required qualities of command."

Granatstein also quotes Defence Minister Colonel J.L. Ralston as saying,

> "Has chosen several very capable men but on the whole has surrounded himself with men of average ability. Does not brook opposition easily, resulting in 'yes men' having more influence than they should."[28]

General Crerar, McNaughton's protege and successor as CGS and then as GOC of the Canadian Army overseas in 1941, is reported to have said to Col. Ralston; "[that it was impossible for McNaughton] to effectively do so many jobs - command, research and development, ...political functions, and ... Senior Canadian Officer."[29] All these comments were, after all, the conclusions reached and charges made and reported to have been made by Buster in the 1920s and early 1930s.

11 Old Sweats and Aide-de-Camp, 1933 -1951

Buster's resignation on 28 June must have been a surprise to the bulk of the Militia in the District as he had been carrying out his military duties with them up to that date and the knowledgeable few at Work Point did not broadcast the problems he was having with the CGS. After the resignation the news soon spread rapidly to be followed by a movement among the Militia officers in Vancouver and Victoria to resign their commissions in protest. Buster's reaction was immediate and positive - this was wrong and not helpful to him, the Army or the nation. The movement was stopped before it gathered any momentum (*see* Appendix D).[1] Quite a contrast from the delusions of Sam Hughes in 1916 or McNaughton in 1943 who told their respective Prime Ministers that the army would rise up in revolt if they were removed.

The Militia and the PF were thus limited to showering Buster and Clare with gifts to show how they felt; for example, Clare was given a large silver plated tray from the Garrison Sergeant's Mess, while the Vancouver Militia wished to give them an automobile, a gesture which Buster discouraged. Instead they accepted a pair of very large handsome Queen Anne candelabra. They scarcely needed them but they could not turn down everything when the intentions of the donors to express sincere regret for Buster's fate were so manifestly evident.

In June, the destiny of the family was in balance; were we to go to Winnipeg, possibly to Toronto or retire in Victoria? Each option required moving so packing began before the destination was decided. Late in the month the decision was made in consultation to resign and stay in Victoria. They had flirted with the idea of moving to Toronto and enquired about Buster's entitlements but they loved Victoria so they opted to remain. The state of the economy and the depressed housing market in the city made it easy to find a suitable house. Paying for it was a different matter. They had enough for the down payment but Buster had to take on a mortgage at 52 years of age with no income except his pension from which deductions were still being made. In spite of the bad blood between himself and the triumvirate he still expected to be raised to a Major General on retirement as his colleagues had. This would have made a great difference. Instead, they had to live in a very reduced state; my brothers left University School and provision for Malcolm to go to RMC in Kingston the following year was in doubt.

When he wasn't promoted Buster appealed to Matthews, Acting DOC, and asked him to forward his request to the AG which Mathews did. The AG then wrote a letter to Matthews as follows:

> 1. "Having reference to your letter dated 14th July instant, forwarding an application from Brigadier J. Sutherland Brown, CMG, DSO, for promotion to the rank of Major General with effect of 1st January, 1933, I am to inform you that such is not approved.

> 2. It is pointed out for the information of Brigadier J.S. Brown that he held the appointment of [DOC] for approximately 4 years and 6 months only, consequently it is the intention to grant him the honorary rank of Brigadier on retirement."

This letter was sent to the CGS for approval. On it McNaughton signed a note in his own hand to the AG:

> "I concur with para 1 but think para 2 should be left out as it is unwise to start an argument."

The letter without paragraph 2 was sent.[2] Even the revised letter makes it abundantly clear Buster was *persona non grata* with McNaughton and his supporters at NDHQ. It also infers Buster had a case which was being rejected by the CGS.

Buster and Clare had better luck with their home. It was the second oldest house in what later became Oak Bay Municipality, three miles east of downtown Victoria or Fort Victoria as it was when the house was started. The oldest part of the house was built before 1870 by John S. Bowker. He and his family came across Haro Strait by Indian dugout canoe to Willows Beach in Oak Bay from the San Juan Islands where he had been raising stock. His wife was the daughter of John Tod, HBC factor, owner of the oldest house in Oak Bay.[3] The history of the house, Bowker Place, appealed to Buster. It had been restored and added to in 1912 by the distinguished West Coast architect, Samuel Maclure and was upgraded again in 1932. However, in many ways even more attractive to them than the charming white clapboard semi-bungalow was its view. This looked eastward across fields, shore and the Strait to the low forested islands, Discovery and Chatham, named after Captain Vancouver's

RN ships. Beyond the islands soaring above the Cascade Range was the young snow-capped strato-volcano, Mount Baker. The house accorded with Buster's personality:

> "I will hold my house in the high wood
> Within a walk of the sea,
> And the men that were boys when I was a boy
> Shall sit and drink with me."

Hilaire Belloc

Before Buster had much time to think he was asked by Premier S.F. Tolmie and Attorney General Pooley to stand as a candidate in Victoria, a four seat constituency, for the Unionist Party (Conservative) in the up coming Provincial General Election. Both men knew Buster well and appreciated what he had done with the unemployment program and thought he would be a strong candidate. However, Buster had little time or money to prepare for such a contest as the Provincial election was scheduled for November 1933. In the unaccustomed milieu of politics Buster was not at ease. His talks were too long and too full of data. Also, all Canadian governments that held power during the Great Depression were defeated when they stood for re-election, the Unionist Party included. This party had the additional disadvantage that it was rent in two during the run up to the election. Even the Premier lost his seat as the Unionists were soundly defeated. An additional disadvantage for Buster was that the Victoria vote was delayed three weeks so the results from the rest of the Province had already determined the outcome. Buster was defeated, coming in the middle of the pack of 23 candidates for the four seats. However, his strong beliefs led him to continue political activities after the election as an executive member for the Conservative Party in Victoria from 1934 to 1938.

Later Buster was asked by the Conservatives to be their candidate in Victoria in the Federal election of 1940 in which Prime Minister Mackenzie King and the Liberal Party were returned to power with a landslide victory. In this election Buster's chief adversary was Robert Mayhew, a wealthy and pleasant entrepreneur who was later Minister of Fisheries, then Canadian Ambassador to Japan. It was a difficult task for Buster because, once again, he had little money for advertising whilst his opponent ran regular ads in the Conservative paper, the Daily Colonist. Buster did relatively well in this his last political venture. He received 8423 votes to 13 170 for Mayhew and 3258 for the CCF candidate, Ken McAlister before the Service vote was countered. He shared with Andy McNaughton a lack of success in getting elected.

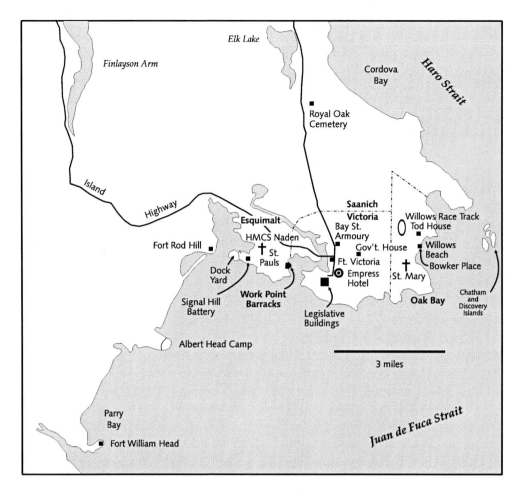

Map 3. Victoria in the 1930s.

During the first Summer and Fall of retirement Buster was unsuccessful in another venture. He was asked by his old friend, General Victor Odlum, to become a stock broker in his firm. Buster had no particular training for this but did have good business sense learned from his father. He put up a small amount of capital for the post but, as the only activity on the market was in gold mining which, in his opinion, included a deal of fraudulence, he soon resigned and abandoned his investment.

Buster's life then adapted to a trifold focus of gardening, aid to and association with veterans and acting as Senior Aide-de-Camp to the Lieutenant Governor. He was involved with these disparate avocations for the rest of his life; each in its own way offering vigorous activity and satisfaction. Lesser aspects of his life of retirement were the social round of the city, of which his activity at Government House formed a part. He continued to be a prodigious reader. He scoffed at golf as a game that ruined a good walk but continued playing badminton and highland dancing with the Can Scots (16th Canadian Scottish Regimental Mess) at the Bay Street Armoury.

Buster and Clare's property at 1931 Bowker Place was over an acre and divided by a road, the old carriage driveway to the house. On the seaside small fields were left relatively wild with towering elms at the foot. About the house were lawns, holly trees and a monkey puzzle but at the rear Buster developed an orchard and a great vegetable garden. He, with induced help of his sons, dug the garden two feet deep into which was forked chopped kelp from the sea and recycled compost from the garden. The resulting vegetables were the largest and healthiest imaginable. Buster had, in fact, become a farmer if not for profit because much of the produce was given to friends and neighbours. As the youngest son I had the longest term of indenture but benefitted at the table and in other small ways. Buster's rural roots, to his satisfaction, penetrated deeply into his garden soil. In Spring, Summer and Fall he could be found there, his bald head, back and legs deeply tanned, clad only in stout boots and khaki shorts held up by an old regimental tie. Clare's interest in the garden extended only to the flowers and produce she might pick. Their semi-rustic life extended to regular tea in the garden and for her, in warm weather, a short swim in the chilling sea off their small beach. This same shore line provided the kelp after winter storms and abundant drift wood which I was responsible for turning into logs for the library fireplace with a ten foot crosscut saw.

Buster's life of service to and friendship with the 'old sweats' was another facet of his regular life. Here he showed his common touch and sympathy for the men who had served in the CEF and who had formed the Permanent Force at Work Point and the Militia. Relatively few officers took the vigorous interest in veteran's affairs that Buster did. Even before he was freed of his commitments in politics and his brief foray into the stock market Buster was active in raising money to build a new clubhouse for the Army and Navy and (later Air Force) Veterans Association of Canada. He had friends in the brewing business (the Molsons and the Sicks) whom he challenged. He was also a member of two Royal Canadian Legion Branches in the city but his heart was in the AN&AF Vets. For it he applied himself vigorously to help build a new building on Wharf Street overlooking Victoria's inner harbour. Buster's old friend General Griesbach laid the cornerstone in 1934 and the three story ferro-concrete building was completed within a year, at a time when few new buildings were being constructed in the depression wracked city. In the 20s and 30s, as a remnant of the late war temperance movement, Victoria was dry except for clubs downtown and pubs in the suburb of Esquimalt dour enough to make a Scot cry. How different from the town's rowdy pioneering days. As a result of the near prohibition the AN&AFVA Branch, though built in part by gifts and great expectations, floated on a sea of beer. Buster was one of the best customers.

Buster also represented many veterans in disputes with the Federal government and took part in their festivities (Photo 11-1). He also took up roles in administration advancing in Branch activities to President, then to that of the Region. Towards the end of his life he was made a 'life' member. To receive the award he, in effect, rose from his potential death-bed in September 1950 to go to the national convention in Winnipeg to accept this honour. The minutes of that meeting record the presentation.[4]

> "Chairman: Before carrying on with our regular business I have a pleasant duty to perform. Will someone please ask Brig. Sutherland Brown to come to the front?
>
> Comrade Brig. Sutherland Brown: What is the charge — refusing to fight? (said jocularly.)
>
> Chairman: Comrades, this is a pleasant function that I have to perform, unfortunately we are not able just at the present time to present the honour that we were about to confer, and the reason that we are not in this position is because we have become so accustomed to seeing this youthful person during the past years, that we have overlooked the fact we are all getting older.
>
> Over a period of many years he has been a stalwart gentleman in all affairs of the veterans, and particularly in the affairs of our Association, that your Board of Directors have thought it proper, and I am sure that nobody here will question this... On this occasion when the Brigadier has climbed out of a hospital bed, and boarded a plane to be with us today.
>
> We appreciate the years of faithful service and the effort he has made to be here by conferring on you the Honorary Life Membership of our Association which will carry with it in due course, our gold medal, our life membership card and certificate.
>
> Comrade Sutherland Brown: This is a great honour.
>
> Chairman: It is a great honour for me today to confer this honour. I am sure you will add to the select group of our honorary members the same amount of dignity that you have brought to the Association as a whole. Now, may I

Photo 11 - 1. Comrade General Buster Brown at the Army, Navy and Air Force Vets presenting a prize to Comrade Cpl. Cuthbert, ca. 1945.

congratulate you, sir.

(Loud applause by the Membership followed by the singing of "For He's a Jolly Good Fellow" and three cheers... unanimous request for a speech.)

Comrade Brig. Sutherland Brown: Comrades, ladies and gentlemen: I don't know what I am under arrest for. (Laughter) I was with some dubious characters for awhile last night it is true. One of your esteemed citizens in the capital city of Manitoba who belongs to a certain political group in power was present — but he happened to be in command in London during all the war — so he must be a good man.

This little disability that I have is not very serious. About three months ago, I realized for the first time that I am

Photo 11 - 2. *Christmas Ball at Government House, Victoria, 1939. His Honour Eric Hamber, Lieutenant Governor of BC with his wife on his right and Clare on his left. Buster, as senior Aide, is behind and to Clare's left. BC Archives photo.*

getting to be an old man. I had rheumatic fever which this time got me around the ticker, and the doctor put me in hospital; however I got out.

It is a wonderful thing to be with you fellows again. A number of you I have known in the Army and Navy for a good many years, and the more I see of our organization, the more I like it. I know what we have done, and what we are trying to do; and as far as I am concerned I am with you to the very last tick I have in me... Thank you very much."

Soon after the Honourable Eric W. Hamber was appointed Lieutenant Governor of BC in May 1936 he asked Buster to serve as Senior Aide at Government House, a post that contrasted strongly with his other avocations but one for which he was well suited. He served so efficiently and graciously that Hamber's two successors, Lt. Col. William C. Woodward and Col. Charles Banks, asked him to continue. Buster was socially aware, knew the vice-regal protocol, and also a great many of notable business, professional and social personages of Victoria and Vancouver. He also knew a surprising number of the visitors from afar. Undoubtedly it pleased him to wear his uniforms again, and Clare and he enjoyed the work as much as the entertainment. They were good friends of all the Lt. Governors and their Chatelaines before they were appointed and had an easy but correct relationship with them all. Indeed, Buster had recruited them years before to be Honorary Colonels in the NPAM. They relied on Buster's advice as well as his service role as Aide. Buster or Clare frequently acted for them when they were unavailable. For instance, I have a photo of him on a blustery snowy day at the Cenotaph in top hat and mourning coat standing in for the Lieutenant Governor. Clare could as well represent one of the Chatelaines opening a charity bazaar without tremendous disappointment to the convenors. Having no car and little money for taxis they frequently travelled to Government House by bus or streetcar dressed in their finery. After alighting, they would then have to walk the half mile from Fort Street to the great house on Rockland Avenue. Photo 11-2 shows them in the Ballroom of Government House during a Christmas party at the beginning of the war with Clare on his Honour, Eric Hamber's, left with Buster standing behind.

After his eclipse from the PF, Buster did not frequent military establishments, especially Work Point, unless specially asked to attend functions. However, when General Erne Ashton took over as DOC in 1934 their old friendship resumed. Moreover, Ashton made a point of asking Buster to summer camps and manoeuvres for he, unlike his two predecessors was not afraid of what McNaughton would think or do.

*Photo 11 - 3. General **Ashton** with Buster (retired), Col. Martyn and Lt. Col. Brooke Stevens of the 16th Scottish at Militia summer camp at Maple Bay, BC in 1934.*

Photo 11-3 shows Buster in civies in 1934 with Ashton and the 16th Canadian Scottish Colonel D.B. Martyn and Lt. Col. Brooke Stevenson. The Navy also frequently asked Buster onboard their ships or to HMCS Naden, their base in Esquimalt and always treated him royally. When Craig Campbell, a family friend, was a lowly Midshipman aboard the destroyer HMCS Fraser in 1937 he was instructed by the First Lieutenant, Harold Groos, to see that at a noon reception on board, the General's glass was never empty of his chosen spirit, brandy and soda. Campbell relates:

> "[Buster] stood in the middle of the Wardroom with his right arm straight up grasping a steam pipe, and in his left [hand, his brandy. As the reception progressed] the ships officers were drifting away without lunch, as the table was never set, leaving the officer of the watch and myself to continue to entertain the great man. We both assumed it would be disastrous when he lost his grip on the pipe.

> About 14:00 he looked at the Wardroom clock, and made his way to the ladder leading to the upper deck, followed by both of us. The CPO piped him over the side. He saluted the Quarter Deck smartly.

> We were both aghast but elated by his steadiness and aplomb."[5]

They might not have known that Buster then had to walk to the Dockyard Gates and catch a streetcar home.

Buster did not reveal his basic beliefs often. He came from a strict Presbyterian family but he easily converted to the Anglican faith of which Clare was a staunch member. He believed in the Church as essentially a power for good and builder of morale for the troops. He also believed strongly in Christian ethics. At Work Point he regularly took part in the monthly Church Parade to St. Paul's Naval and Garrison Church. In retirement he less frequently accompanied Clare and their brood to Church. In particular, I remember him coming into the dining room one Sunday morning at breakfast dressed in his gardening clothes. Clare gently reminded him she was expecting him to accompany us to Matins at St. Mary's, Oak Bay. He equally gently said without prelude,

> "Here with a Loaf of Bread beneath the Bough,
> A Flask of Wine, a Book of Verse - and Thou [Clare]
> Beside me singing in the Wilderness -
> And Wilderness is Paradise enow."

> Fitzgerald / Khayyam

Naturally Buster followed Canadian politics and international affairs closely during the lead up to the start of WWII. He wasn't surprised at the success of the blitzkrieg on the Polish front although he thought 'General Mud' might have been more of a factor. He believed that the lightening quick Polish campaign was just the start of a long war. He also was convinced that he again would be needed, and that pleased him even if the events didn't. Perhaps because of anticipation that he could be useful again he was in good spirits in late September 1939. He even asked me if I would like to accompany him to the horse races at the Willows Fall Fair, which I did. We walked the mile to the race track, he dressed in white flannels and a striped RCR blazer. At the track he was greeted by many old sweats and others, especially Militia, and recently retired officers, all similarly clothed. They were also in similar spirits. Buster indulged himself with a two dollar bet on the nose of some nag in every race even though he knew a horse's capability, of which he was a judge, had nothing to do with winning on this track. I can't remember the results but I can recall the mettle of these old warhorses.

The regard for Buster was not everywhere as obvious or favourable as those reflected by his colleagues at the track. As Fall progressed Buster underwent another period of anguish and frustration. He truly believed he would be called upon quickly for some role, as perhaps an Inspector General or a DOC. He had few illusions he would be given a more active role. After a month or more when the call never came he took to inquiring discreetly through friends without results or word from Ottawa. Eventually he took direct action with an official letter to the DOC of MD. No. 11, Brigadier C.V. Stockwell offering his services. Stockwell responded by letter to NDHQ as follows:

"The Secretary, [NDHQ]

Hon. Brig. J. Sutherland Brown, CMG DSO

1. The marginally-named officer retired to pension from the Permanent Force of Canada in 1933. He is now a resident of Victoria, Vancouver Island.

2. This officer is 59 years of age, and physically fit. He had a distinguished career in the last war, is P.S.C. [sic] and I.D.C. [graduate of the Imperial Defence College], and held numerous appointments on the staff in peacetime.

3. I am aware of the circumstances which caused his retirement, but consider that in this state of national crisis his undoubted talents might be profitably employed.

[signed C. V. Stockwell
Brigadier, DOC MD No. 11]"

The Secretary in a note to the CGS on the bottom of the letter stated:

"Have you any comments in connection with the above?"

to which the CGS wrote:

"I don't agree with the views expressed in para 3." initialled H.D.G.C., CGS, Major-General Crerar.[6]

Thus Buster's hopes to play an active part in WWII were crushed and he was reduced to a role of a spectator of the profession for which he trained all his life and which, in many officers' opinion, he was better equipped than many of those in command. Although his disappointment was intense he kept it mostly to himself. He never displayed public bitterness or anger with McNaughton or his clique. In his own house it was different. As most senior officers paid him a visit when they came to Victoria there were sometimes rousing discussions. I can remember being permitted to be present at one such time when Generals Griesbach, Hertzberg and Schmidlin visited together. Buster regaled them with an anecdote about the PM that now, after the release of the Mackenzie King diary edited by J.W. Pickersgill and D.F. Foster, would no longer shock. However, when one of them said, "Buster you can't say that." Buster replied, "Even if it is true?"

Obviously Buster was not forgotten by many of the military brass; and nor was he overlooked by the local forces. Early in the war the Army developed a number of small bases along the Inside Passage to Alaska as he had long before recommended. To serve these they converted a seiner to become a tender and supply boat which was commissioned the Brigadier Sutherland Brown (Photo 11-4).

Buster's frustration at his rejection did not affect his health or his basically optimistic view of life. His immediate neighbour used to come over daily during the first three years of the war with a long face repeating tales of woe. Buster nicknamed him 'Old Calamity'. However without official sources, he was reduced to following the war as closely as he could by radio and newspaper. Also Clare and he got some solace from their sons' performances. Malcolm the eldest, an RMC graduate served with the RCE and went to the UK with the 1st Division. He was with the small group of Canadians dispatched to France in 1940 as an advance guard for the proposed deployment of the Division but which was quickly withdrawn when France collapsed. During the four years of training and waiting in the UK Malcolm advanced rapidly to the rank of Lt. Col. Soon after D Day in Normandy he was awarded the DSO for getting the first bridge across the Orne River while his field company was

Photo 11 - 4. The Brig. Sutherland Brown, an Army supply tender, on the inside passage, BC. Buster was not forgotten by the local command during the war. BC Archives photo.

under fire thus allowing the 3rd Division to advance. After fighting through Normandy and the polders of Holland he ended the war as CRE for the 5th Division. Their second son, Ian, was at RMC when war broke out. His class graduated prematurely at the end of 1939 and he entered flying training with the RCAF. On the award of his pilot's brevet, like most early graduates, he was posted as a flying instructor in the Commonwealth Air Training Scheme at No. 3 Service Flying Training School (SFTS) in Calgary. He was killed in a flying accident in the Rocky Mountains in July 1941. I was still at home and remember the ring of the doorbell and my father signing for the telegram which stated Ian was missing and believed killed. He went quietly into their sunny bedroom to tell the awful news to Clare. I remember her shriek. There is no way to soften such a message, nor any way to console a mother for such a loss. Tragically it was made worse by later news that aerial reconnaissance showed someone was alive at the crash site. It proved not to be Ian. Soon after I was eighteen and I too joined the RCAF as a pilot. My operational career took me to Burma flying Beaufighters in the 3rd Tactical Air Force where I was awarded the Distinguished Flying Cross in February 1945.[7] My parent's pride on my return in August 1945 is reflected on Photo 11-5 .

When back in Victoria I soon got into a heated argument with my father when I told him Churchill was going to be defeated in the coming election in Britain. He would not believe it. When the election news confirmed my prediction he apologized straightforwardly for his stubbornness and forever after treated me as an adult.

Life proceeded much the same during Buster's remaining years. After the war, with McNaughton gone, he was treated generously by NDHQ. They awarded him a liberal medical pension because of his chronic problem with rheumatic fever that he contracted at the front during WWI. Attacks of this disease became more frequent as he aged but otherwise with the additional income, his and Clare's lives were made much easier and pleasanter.

After his award in Winnipeg of the gold medal and life membership by the AN&AF Veterans Association Buster and Clare journeyed to Ottawa, and together with my brother and his wife, Peggy, visited my wife, Barbara, and I in Princeton in October 1950. This was the first time Buster had been in the USA for twenty years. Whatever he still thought about the States he certainly enjoyed Princeton because of the attractive University and the charming town. Buster was clearly tired after his travels so that on the second evening he did not join us attending an excellent public lecture by Professor Huxley at which many academic luminaries including Einstein were present. We left him sitting in front of the fire at our

Photo 11 - 5. Buster and Clare welcome their youngest son home from the air wars in Burma at the CPR docks in Victoria, summer 1945. Victoria Daily Colonist photo.

cottage where he seemed content and even cheery. They returned to Ottawa the next day. That was the last time I saw my father.

In the good times and hard, Buster was fortunate to receive immense support from Clare. Their happy marriage would shame most others. I never heard harsh words between them. Clare was a strong, capable and loving woman and Buster all his life thought he was exceptionally lucky to have won her. Undoubtedly she was part of the reason for his resilience in the later part of his life.

Buster's health deteriorated and in the Spring of 1951 he was admitted to the Veteran's Hospital in Victoria and shortly afterwards on 14 April died quietly in his seventieth year. The armed forces gave him a full military funeral officiated by Bishop H.E. Sexton with the assistance of Archdeacon A.E. de L. Nunns of St. Mary's Church, Oak Bay. The senior army officers in Victoria, all good friends and former subordinates, were his honorary pall bearers were Major General H.F.H. Hertzberg, CB, CMG, DSO, MC; Brig. C.V. Stockwell, DSO; Brig. W.G. Colquhoun, CBE,

MC; Brig. J.F. Preston, MC; Brig. W.C. Thackery, CBE; Brig. G.A. McCarter, CBE, CD; Col. R.B. Ker, OBE, ED; and Col. M.H. Turner, OBE, CD. The RCN band played the slow march as the gun carriage carrying his flag-draped coffin left St. Mary's for burial at Royal Oak Cemetery. Buster was laid to rest following a feu de joie, a piper playing Lament and Coronach and a bugler sounding *The Last Post*. A reception that followed at Bowker Place was as convivial as are some Celtic wakes. Both Victoria newspapers covered the story fully including photographs. The Times mentioned there were 400 mourners present while The Daily Colonist carried the motto at its masthead "Victoria is the poorer by the passing of Brigadier James Sutherland Brown."[8] Clearly Buster was popular in the city as well as with his old sweats.

Clare was prepared for Buster's death and coped well afterwards, out living him by twenty-two years, all but the last three in good health. She sold Bowker Place and then lived alone in an elegant apartment in the converted former Hobart Molson home on Rockland Avenue. She travelled frequently to see her friends and family in Ontario, occasionally to England and once to Israel to visit Malcolm who at that time was Canadian Military Attache in the Embassy at Tel Aviv. When she returned she frequently regaled her friends with stories of the Holy Lands which few of them had visited in those days. On constantly hearing these tales eventually I said,

> "Mom, wasn't there something that disappointed you in the Holy Lands."

She thought for a moment and then said,

> "Well the Jordan wasn't much."

In her life in Victoria she was very fond of my late wife, Doogie and loved our young son, Brian. She had a pleasant social life which included much bridge until she had a series of strokes that led to her death in September, 1973.

Epilogue

The Introduction of this biography asked whether James Sutherland Brown was a hero as Charles Taylor inferred in his recollection of my father and which I slowly came to believe. Will others agree? His life confirmed bravery and skill in his chosen role that advanced him near to the peak of his profession without his showing much hubris. From there he certainly suffered reversals of fortune by which heroes are tested, and he emerged from them without becoming bitter, morose or vindictive. He was an approachable beer-drinking hero to the old sweats and his colleagues admired his skills, bravery and directness in peace as much as war. His flaws were there for all to see as he made no attempt to hide them.

To military historians Buster's life is of interest in a number of ways. Many of them have placed much emphasis in their writings that the CEF in WWI and the Canadian Army in WWII were amateur armies, an inflated Militia, and that the PF played a minor and not very distinguished role. For the first comment it could scarcely have been otherwise considering the numbers and the expansion of the army in both conflicts. Nevertheless, many followed Sam Hughes in depreciating the permanent force, but with little justification. There were hardly better regiments on either side of the Western Front than the 'shino boys' of the RCR or the PPCLI. Also the PF produced a proportionate number of senior leaders such as Generals MacBrien, Macdonell and Morrison. Unquestionably too, most of the senior Militia officers owed their capability to training and preparation by the PF. Buster more than most represented both sides. He had a long history in the Militia and believed throughout his life that Canada needed a substantial active reserve rather than being burdened with a mid-sized standing army. He did all he could to support and encourage the Militia as well as the Navy and Air Force, especially when he was a DOC. At the same time he thought the nation needed a well-trained professional army as a core from which growth and leadership should spring during an emergency. He was exceptionally proud of the RCR believing it was all a good infantry regiment should be. Other regiments such as the PPCLI, Lord Strathcona's Horse and the Canadian Dragoons were in his estimation, only slightly less good.

The history of CEF has received and is still receiving much attention. Most of the research however, has been focused on the battles, the casualties and appalling service conditions, as well as individual units and their COs, the general war effort and most particularly on the commanders; Currie, Byng and Alderson. The Division Commanders have received only cursory treatment,[1] and the senior staff, upon whom their successes so heavily depended, have received almost none. This is particularly true of the Q Staff in which there were so few Canadians. Because of this and his efficiency Buster spent the whole war as one of these few which to some degree proved detrimental for his professional future.

Buster has been characterized as a colonel blimp by some academic historians as well as by newspaper columnists who reflected and exaggerated their views. Both groups revel in portraying army commanders and strategists as dwelling in the past by preparing for yesterday's battles or misidentifying the potential enemy.[2] It is doubtful that such charges are true of Buster for through reading, correspondence with General Fuller and attendance at Tank Corps exercises in England, he showed greater interest than most of his Canadian contemporaries in armoured forces. He also encouraged cavalry regiments to have trucks mocked up as armoured cars in his field exercises. Furthermore, while he was DOC he constantly stressed combined operations training and conducted what some of his colleagues called innovative field exercises. He advocated improving the defence of Vancouver by forts in Johnstone Strait and acquiring artillery for the Victoria coastal defence that had the range to cover the Strait of Juan de Fuca. He certainly was more concerned than most of his colleagues about the fragility of the lines of communication in the Fraser Canyon. In addition, Buster was a strong and consistent supporter of an adequate and independent Air Force. If Buster did dwell in the past it was because he was a consummate reader of military history. He may not have been an admirer of the USA but he was an expert on their Civil War.

Most successful generals such as Wellington and the Israeli generals in the Yom Kippur war have been very knowledgeable of past campaigns and their strategies, and have drawn upon many sources to forge new or appropriate approaches from this knowledge. Buster had limited chances to apply his skills in campaigns except in organization and supply, where he excelled. His Defence Scheme No. 1, which was so strongly scoffed at by academicians, was regarded by experts as an exceedingly risky response but possibly the only way to counter any potential aggressive action by the USA. Such an event was mocked or the possibility denied by many and yet we now know that such an eventuality was contemplated and prepared for by United States military planners. Buster deserves to be seen as the man he actually was; organized, skilled at his profession, brave and compassionate, one of Canada's most accomplished soldiers.

Reference Notes

Introduction (pp. 1 – 4)

1   George Lomis 1998.
2   Charles Taylor, 1977, p. I - iv.
3   Hattersly.
4   The family coat of arms my father instituted incorporated the Gaelic word in its banner *'Tireachadh"* which embraces both the idea of patriot and colonizer (*see later*).

1: Out of Scotland (pp. 5 – 11)

1   *Simcoe Reformer*, 1888-03-15.
2   Swettenham, 1968, p. 24.
3   *Simcoe Reformer*, 1900-05-31.
4   *idem*, 1889-04-04.
5   *idem*, 1889-04-04.
6   *idem*, 1890-09-09.
7   *idem*, 1886-11-04.
8   *idem*, 1891-02-26.
9   *idem*, 1901-04-18.
10 *idem*, 1900-12-27.
11 *idem*, 1889-04-04
12 *idem*, 1889-10-31.
13 *idem*, 1901-04-11.

2: Hatched (pp. 13 – 24)

1   Charles Taylor, p. 8.
2   *idem*, p. 11.
3   National Archives of Canada, random papers from J. Sutherland Brown's files by Access to Information from the Department of National Defence Central Registry HQ File 675-1, Vol. 1 and 2. The individual papers received are hand numbered in course pencil. These papers will be referred to as NDHQ 675-1, Vol. 1 or 2, page X etc. This reference, NDHQ 675-1, V1, p. 8.
4   *Simcoe Reformer*, 1916-01-06
5   *idem*, 1902-12-15.

6   *idem*, 1906-01-26.
7   NDHQ 675-1, V1, p.22.
8   *Simcoe Reformer*, 1903-11-27 and following.
9   *idem*, 1904-06-03.
10 *idem*, 1904-06-24.
11 *idem*, 1904-19-21.
12 NDHQ 675-1, Vol. 1, p. 11.
13 *Simcoe Reformer*, 1905-04-21.
14 *idem*, 1906-01-26.
15 NDHQ 675-1, Vol. 1, p. 6.
16 Queen's University Archives, James Sutherland Brown Papers. Reference will be in the style, QUA/JSB, Series (S), Box (B), Folder (F). This reference, QUA/JSB SI B1 F2.
17 QUA/JSB SI B3 F3.
18 Mackenzie, 1993, p. 44.

3: Regimental Officer (pp. 25 – 37)

1   Fraser, 1985, p. 26.
2   QUA/JSB SIV B8 F192; a reply dated 1932-11-09 by JSB to Col. A. F. Duguid, DSO.
3   *idem*, SI B3b F47.
4   *idem*, SIV B8 F192.
5   Featherstonehaugh, 1936, p. 180-81.
6   *idem*, p.182.
7   *Sydney Record*, between July 1909 through April 1910.
8   *idem*, 1909-07-10.
9   *Sydney Record*, 1909-07-07.
10 *idem*, 1910-02-22.
11 Featherstonehaugh, p.182.
12 *idem*, 182.
13 *Sydney Record*, 1910-04-04.
14 NDHQ 675-1, Vol. 1, p. 35-38, 1910-02-24.

15 NDHQ 675-1, Vol. 1, p. 38-43, Mar 1910.

16 QUA/JSB, SI B3 F45.

17 Featherstonehaugh, p. 189.

18 NDHQ 675-1, Vol. 1, p. 59-68.

19 *idem* p. 75-76.

20 *idem*, 72-73.

21 QUA/JSB, SI B3 F41.

4: Camberley *(pp. 39 – 43)*

1 Bond, p.280.

2 *idem*, p. 276.

3 *idem*, p. 288.

4 QUA/JSB, SII B3 F56.

5 Bond, p. 285.

6 *idem*, p. 294-95.

5: In the Great War, Canada's Apprenticeship 1914-1916
(pp. 45 – 68)

1 Keegan, 1998, Chapters 1, A European Tragedy, and 3, the Crisis of 1914.

2 Swettenham, 1965, p. 27-28.

3 *idem*, p.26.

4 Corns, Cathyrn and John Hughes-Wilson, p. 32-33.

5 *idem*, p.30-32, and NAC RG24, vol. 1754, Sutherland Brown to CGS, 1921-01-10.

6 Nicholson, p.36.

7 Pulsifer, p. 45- 57.

8 Swettenham, 1965, p. 36.

9 NDHQ 675-1, dated 1919-09-27, not numbered.

10 Appointments, rank, locations and presence during battles of the war years have been taken chiefly from J. Sutherland Brown's statement of war service (Form 2624) signed by himself, countersigned by Major General A.C. Macdonell and certified by Lt. Col. F.B. Ware, DA&QMG, 1st Canadian Division, 1919-09-26.

11 QUA/JSB SI B1 F5.

12 Fraser, p. 23.

13 Personal letter from Desmond Morton, 2003-03-31. He commented additionally that it was an awkward lump ...no one who ever dug dirt could have used it.

14 *idem*. p.25-26.

15 *idem*. p. 26.

16 QUA/JSB SI B1 F2, as labelled but probably really F1.

17 QUA/JSB SI B1 F2

18 Nicholson, p.34.

19 *idem*, p. 51-53.

20 Swettenham, 1965, p.79-81.

21 *idem*, p.84.

22 NAC RG24, vol. 1755, file DHS 10-10 pt. 2.

23 QUA/JSB, SI B1 F4.

24 Ashworth, 1980.

25 Morton and Granatstein, p.115.

26 *idem*, p.116.

27 Swettenham, 1975, p. 124-144.

28 NDHQ 675-1, Vol. 1, p. 113-14, 1917-08-04.

29 Swettenham, 1965, p. 141, and Robert Laird Borden: His Memoirs, I, p.463.

30 Eyre, p. 116 &121.

31 Bond, p. 305.

32 *idem*, p. 281.

33 Ashworth, 1980, Chap 9.

6: In the Great War, Canada's Triumph, 1917 - 1918 *(pp. 69 – 91)*

1 Nicholson, p. 249.

2 *idem*, p. 247-252.

3 Kegan, p. 326.

4 QUA/JSB SIII B6 F101.

5 QUA/JSB SIII B6 F103.

6 NDHQ 675-1, Vol. 1, p.113 & 117, 1917-06-05.

7 QUA/JSB SIII B6 F106.

8 Currie Diaries, NAC, RG150 & QUA/JSB SIII B6 F101.

9 Winter, p. 270-71.

10 McCulloch, CMH, 1998, Vol. 7, No. 4, p.11-28.

11 Swettenham,1965, p. 171-72.

12 QUA/JSB SIII B6 F105.

13 *idem*, SIII B6 F107.

14 Morton and Granatstein, p. 169-170 & Keegan p. 368.

15 Swettenham, 1965, p. 189.

16 QUA/JSB SIII B6 F109.

17 O'Connor, p.81.

18 *idem*, SIII B6 F135.

19 QUA/JSB SIII B6 F136.

20 *idem*, SIII B6 F137.

21 *idem*, SIII B6 F137.

22 *idem*, SIII B6 F140-41,

23 Swettenham, 1965, p. 205.

24 Wise, p. 522-23.

25 QUA/ JSB SIII B6 F142-43.
    Swettenham, 1965, p. 211.

26 Nicholson, p. 419.

27 QUA/JSB SIII B6 F143.

28 Swettenham, 1965, p. 226.

29 Hyatt, p. 119.

30 Eyre, p. 137.

31 NAC, MG30 - E133, Series II, 304
    Vol. 2.

32 QUA/JSB SIII B6 F145-46 and
    Nicholson, p. 524-27.

33 A.C. Macdonell diary, NAC MG30
    E20.

34 NDHQ 175-1, Vol. 1, not numbered,
    1919-04-26.

35 *idem*, not numbered dated
    1919-09-23.

36 Bond, p. 305.

7: Capital Ideas *(pp. 93 – 122)*

1 QUA/JSB SI B3 F47.

2 NDHQ 175-1 Vol. 1, p. 122.

3 Morton, 1992, p. 165-167,
   Morton and Granatstein,
   p. 150-156.

4 Swettenham, 1965, p. 237.

5 Masters, 1950,
   Rodney, 1968.

6 Morton, p. 165-68.

7 Harris, p. 141-46.

8 QUA/JSB SIII B7a F148.

9 Swettenham, 1968, p. 190.

10 NAC, MacBrien Papers,
    MG 30, E 63, Vol. 1, 1919-20.

11 Gimblett, p. 8.

12 NDHQ 175-1 Vol. 1, p. 38,
    1920-12-22.

13 Harris, p. 146-47.

14 *idem*, p. 147.

15 Wise, Chap 1-4.

16 Ralph, Chap 12,
    Wise, Chap 1-4

17 QUA/JSB, SIV B8 F159.

18 Eayrs, p. 199.

19 Harris, p. 170.

20 Harris, Chaps 3, 4 &5.
    Morton, 1992, p. 93-122.
    Morton, personal letter, March
    2003.
    Preston., p. 29-37.

21 QUA/JSB, SVI B9 F214.

22 Eayrs, p. 75-81.

23 CBC Radio, 1985, *The Attack of the
    Killer Mouse.*
    Watt, p. 95-96.

24 Gimblett, p. 22-36,
    Preston, p.29-37,
    Harris, Chapter 8.

25 NAC, Minutes of Military Council,
    1920 Vol. III, RG9.

26 QUA/JSB, SI B1 F2.

27 Eayrs, p. 75,
    QUA/JSB SIV B8 F176.

28 QUA/JSB SII B3 F56.

29 Harris, p. 170.

30 QUA/JSB SVI B9 F209-218. Copy
    14 of DS No.1 in the Archives was
    missing Chap 5 when I examined it.
    This report was among Buster's pri-
    vate papers when he died and was
    later deposited with his other mate-
    rial in the Archives. Buster clearly
    kept a copy of his own work when
    he resigned in June 1933 just before
    McNaughton ordered all the DOC's
    to destroy their reports in October
    of that year. After Buster's resigna-
    tion there was a period of confusion
    at MD No. 11 with three DOCs in
    quick succession so the order was
    not only not carried out but there
    appears to have been no follow up.
    Eayrs reproduces parts of the report
    in an appendix, Document 1.

31 Charles Taylor, p. 3-6.

32 Gimblett, p. 24.

33 Harris, p. 169-70.

34 *idem*, p. 171-72.

35 *idem*, p. 171.

36 Gimblett, p. 24.

37 Charles Taylor, p. 19.

38 Harris, p. 160-62.

39 Preston, 1974.

40 *idem*, p. 36.

41 *idem*, p.29.

42 Charles Taylor, p. 15-16.

43 CBC radio play, 1985.

44 James King, p. 258-59.

45 Harris, p. 171-73.

46 QUA/JSB SIV B8 F163,
    Harris, p. 172-174.

47 QUA/JSB SIV B8 F 176.

48 Hillmer and McAndrew, 1979.

49 Swettenham, 1965, p. 1-20.

50 QUA/JSB SI B1 F4.

51 QUA/JSB SI B1 F2.

52 Charles Taylor, p. 14-15.

53 NDHQ 175-1 Vol.1, p. 113-114.

54 Eayrs, p. 70-71,
    Gimblett, p. 23.

55 QUA/JSB SI B1 F2.

8: Imperial Defence (pp. 123 – 130)

1 QUA/JSB SI B1 F7.

2 QUA/JSB SI B1 F3.

3 QUA/JSB SI B1 F2.

4 QUA/JSB SI B1 F3.

5 NDHQ 675-1, p. 132.

6 QUA/JSB SI B1 F3.

7 QUA/JSB SI B3 F38.

8 Gardam, John and Geisler, Patricia,
   cf letter and photographs.

9 NDHQ/JSB 675-1, p.136-140.

9: Work Point (pp. 131 – 153)

1 Hyatt, p. 133.

2 QUA/JSB SIV B8 F168.

3 QUA/JSB SX B11 F246.

4 QUA/JSB SI B3 F52.

5 QUA/JSB SI B1 F9.

6 Charles Taylor, p. 26.

7 NDHQ 675-1, p. 165-180.

8 QUA/JSB SI B1 F6.

9 *idem*.

10 QUA/JSB SIV B8 F180.

11 *idem*.

12 QUA/JSB SI B3 F40, 50 &51.

13 QUA/JSB SI B1 F9.

14 QUA/JSB SI B3 F39.

15 Harris covers this and the next item
    thoroughly, p. 156-7.

16 *idem*.

17 Roy, p. 101.

18 QUA/JSB SIV B8 F172.

19 QUA/JSB SIV B8 F160.

20 QUA/JSB SI B1 F6-13.

21 QUA/JSB SI B3 F53.

22 QUA/JSB SI B1 F6.

23 Harris, p.206 -07.

24 QUA/JSB SI B2 F31.

25 Harris, p. 158.

26 Render, p. 185-86.

27 Hyatt, p. 134.

28 MacBrien Papers, NAC MG30 E63
    Vol. 1, File 1.

29 QUA/JSB SI B3 F42.

10: Hard Times (pp. 155 – 171)

1 Four secondary sources dealing
   with the Great Depression in Canada and British Columbia and the
   Unemployment Relief Camps most
   useful are; Eayrs, Chap 7; Ormsby,
   Chap 15; Swettenham, 1968,
   Chap 8; Struthers, Chap 3 and 4.

2 The Canadian Encyclopedia,
   p. 933-34.

3 Ormsby, p. 442- 446, Struthers
   Chap 2 and 3.

4 Struthers, p.81.

5 Eayrs, p. 124-125,
   Struthers, p.80-81.

6 NAC MG 30 - E133, Series II, 304
   Vol. 2.

7 *idem*.

8 *idem*

9 Charles Taylor, p. 29.

10 *idem*.

11 NAC, MG 30 - E133 Series II E304,
    Vol. 2.

12 QUA/JSB SI B3 F45.

12 NDHQ 675-1, Vol. 1, p. 186-188.

14 *Victoria Daily Colonist* photograph
    and story, 31 May 1933.

15 Charles Taylor, p. 29.

16 QUA/JSB SI B3 F45

17 QUA/JSB SI B2 F31.

18 QUA/JSB SI B3 F43

19 QUA/JSB SI B1 F13.

20 QUA/JSB SI B2 F31

21 QUA/JSB SI B1 F13

22   Charles Taylor, p. 30.
23   NDHQ 675-1, p.209-10.
24   QUA/JSB SI B1 F16.
25   Eayrs, p. 145-48.
26   Struthers, p. 98-103.
27   Charles Taylor, p. 22.
28   Granatstein, Chap 3, p. 67-68 & 70.
29   *idem*, p.71.

11: *Old Sweats and Aide-de-Camp*
(pp. 173 – 189)

1   Charles Taylor, p. 30.
2   NDHQ 675-1 Vol. 2, 189-204.
3   Stark, p. 6-8.
4   Minutes of the Twentieth Dominion Convention, September 5th-7th 1950, Winnipeg. p.97.
5   Personal letter from Craig Campbell, September 2002.
6   NDHQ 675-1, Vol. 1, unnumbered, dated 4 Oct. 1940.
7   A. Sutherland Brown, history of 177 Squadron, RAF, *Silently into the Midst of Things.*
8   Victoria Daily Colonist and Victoria Daily Times, 14 & 15 May 1951.

Epilogue *(pp. 191 – 192)*

1   Brennan, 2002 p. 5-9.
2   Eayrs, p.70-84,
      Gimblett, p. 68-77.

Acknowledgments & Primary Sources

This biography has been made possible by help from many archives and by friends. Canada is as fortunate in its Archives as it is disadvantaged by its great distances. Research is very expensive for private individuals from the West Coast who need access to the Archives in the Eastern cities. Fortunately the National Library has had many newspapers, both important dailies and local weeklies, microfilmed or microfiched so that these can be borrowed and read at numerous libraries and archives throughout Canada. The Archives and their personnel are invariably helpful. For this study for the most useful was the Queen's University Archive that holds my father's papers. The BC Archives were particularly helpful to me in accommodating and sponsoring my reading the weeklies of Simcoe, Ontario and Sydney, Nova Scotia, as well as the Victoria dailies. The National Archives are crammed with information of encyclopedic nature but they hold so much that the really useful is so diluted by related paper that it is a slow and frustrating search. The finding aids are particularly opaque for the non-specialist to find the grain amongst the chaff. Department of National Defence Headquarters files were released under Access to Information and, although somewhat random and selective, were essential.

My brother, Malcolm, deposited my father's papers in the Queen's Archives and so he is primarily responsible that this biography is based on primary sources. When he gave the papers to Queen's I was only slightly interested in his foresight. He was a graduate of RMC and Queen's and there could hardly be a better repository. Unfortunately my dear mother did not have the same objectives or foresight. On my father's death she had his voluminous diaries burnt, partly from a point of view of storage as she moved to smaller accommodation but also probably because she was alarmed about the frank views they would contain. Peggy, Malcolm's wife contributed photographs and encouragement. Ian, Malcolm's and Peggy's elder son, was helpful in the earliest days of my interest in writing this work by getting the available papers from the Department of National Defence (DND) through Access to Information. This material shows evidence of selectivity, censorship, and is full of chaff but, nevertheless, contains much useful information and some gems. Charles Taylor awakened my interest in my father's life and, while

Malcolm and I were principle informants to him, I also received information from him of importance. Professor William Rodney, former Academic Dean of Royal Roads Military College, balanced his encouragement with appropriate criticism while reviewing my manuscript. Likewise, Dr. Stephen J. Harris, Chief Historian of DND, was encouraging and helpful in discussions and by guiding me to useful sources. His book, *Canadian Brass*, written long before I knew him, treated my father's work and history in a searching but generous manner and was particularly useful in regard to the defence of Canada. Also Stephen agreed to write the Foreword to this volume. Tim Cook and Andrew Iarocci lead a tour in June 2002 of the battlefields of the World War I organized by Wilfrid Laurier University Centre for Strategic Studies which greatly added to my knowledge of the terrain and history of the Canadian Expeditionary Force. Tim also reviewed my manuscript particularly those chapters on WWI and suggested additional sources. Professor Desmond Morton also reviewed the completed manuscript. John Armitage skillfully prepared the maps and enhanced many of the photographs. Ruth, my second wife, contributed in more than understanding and tolerance by critical reviewing the text and contributed many useful suggestions. Brian Grant produced the formatted text and helped in many additional ways. I am indebted to Terry Copp for his support of the publication.

Bibliography

Anonymous (2000): *The Canadian National Vimy Memorial*, Veterans Affairs Canada.

Ashworth, Tony (1980): *Trench Warfare, 1914-1918, The Live Let Live System*, Macmillian Press.

Bell, Ken and C.P. Stacey (1983): *100 Years, The Royal Canadian Regiment, 1883-1983*, Collier MacMillan Canada Inc., Don Mills.

Bond, Brian (1972): *The Victorian Army and the Staff College, 1854 -1914, Eyre Methuen, London*.

Brennan, Patrick H. (2002): *Byng's and Currie's Commanders: A Still Untold Story of the Canadian Corps*, Canadian Military History, Vol. 11, No.2, p. 5-16.

Christie, N.M (1997): , *Letters of Agar Adamson 1914 to 1919, Lieutenant Colonel, Princess Patricia's Canadian Light Infantry*, CEF Books, Nepean, ON.

Cook, Tim (1999): *No Place to Run: The Canadian Corps and Gas Warfare in the First World War*, UBC Press, Vancouver.

Corns, Cathryn and Hughes-Wilson, John (2001): *Blindfold and Alone*, Cassel & Co., London.

Craig, J.D. (1919): *The First Canadian Division in the Battles of 1918*, Barrs & Co., London.

Daily Colonist (1929-1951): Microfilm in the BC Archives.

Department of National Defence: James Sutherland Brown papers, Central Registry file HQ 675-1, through Access to Information.

Douglas, John (1985): *The Attack of the Killer Mouse*, CBC Radio docudrama in a Series, Canadian Cranks.

Duguid, A.F. (1938): *Official History of the Canadian Forces in the Great War, 1914-1919 General Series, Vol. 1*, Kings Printer, Ottawa.

Eayrs, James (1964): *In the Defence of Canada, From the Great War to the Great Depression*, University of Toronto Press, Toronto.

Eyre, Kenneth C. (1967): *Staff and Command in the Canadian Corps, The Canadian Militia 1896-1914 as a Source of Senior Officers*, MA Thesis, Duke University.

Edmonds, J.E. (1948): *Military Operations France and Belgium: Official History*, HMSO, London.

Faulks, Sebastian (1994): *Birdsong*, Vintage, London

Featherstonehaugh, R.C. (1936): *The Royal Canadian Regiment, 1883-1933*, Gazette Print Co., Montreal.

Fraser, Donald (1985): *The Journal of Private Fraser, Canadian Expeditionary Force 1914-1918,* Edited with an Introduction by Reginald H. Roy, Sono Nis Press, Victoria.

Gardam, John and Greisler, Patricia (1982): *The National War Memorial,* Ministry of Supply and Services, Canada.

Gimblett, Richard H (1979): *"Buster" Brown: The Man and His Clash with "Andy" McNaughton,* Unpublished BA Thesis, Royal Military College.

Granatstein, J. L. (1993): *The Generals, the Canadian Army's Senior Commanders in the Second World War,* Stoddart, Toronto.

Griesbach, W. A. (1946): *I Remember,* Ryerson Press, Toronto

Haycock, Ronald G. (1986): *Sam Hughes, The Public Career of a Controversial Canadian, 1985-1916,* Wilfrid Laurier University Press, London, ON.

Harris, Stephen J, (1988): *Canadian Brass, The Making of a Professional Army 1860-1939,* University of Toronto Press, Toronto.

Hattersly, Roy (2000): *When 'honour thy father isn't an empty phrase',* a review of Alan Bullock's book *Building Jerusalem,* in *The Times* (London), 20 January.

Hillmer, Norman and McAndrew, William (1979): *The Cunning of Restraint: General J.H. McBrien and the Problems of Peacetime Soldiering,* Canadian Defence Quarterly, Vol.8 p. 40-47.

Hyatt, A.M.J. (1987): *General Sir Arthur Currie: A Military Biography,* University of Toronto Press, Toronto.

Keegan, John (1998): *The First World War,* Key Porter Books, Toronto.

King, James (2002): *Farley, the life of Farley Mowat,* Harper Collins, Toronto.

Joubert de la Ferte, Philip B.(1952) *The Fated Sky,* Hutchison & Co., London.

Livesay, J.F.B. (1919): *Canada's Hundred Days, With the Canadian Corps from Amiens to Mons,* Thomas Allen, Toronto.

Loomis, George (1998): *Heroes,* Notes to accompany a Decca CD record of Andreas Scholl.

Macdonell, Archibald C. (1918): Diary, National Archives of Canada, 3U Series G6.

MacKenzie, Lewis (1993): *Peacekeeper, The Road to Sarajevo,* Douglas and McIntrye, Toronto.

Masters, D.C. (1950): *The Winnipeg General Strike,* Toronto.

McCulloch, Ian (1998): "Batty Mac", Portrait of a Brigade Commander of the Great War, 1915-1917, *Canadian Military History,* Volume 7, Number 4.

Mills, Stephen (1997): *A Task of Gratitude, Canadian Battlefields of the Great War,* Vimy Ventures, Calgary.

Morton, Desmond (1992): *A Military History of Canada,* McLelland and Stewart Inc., Toronto.

Morton, Desmond and J.L. Granatstein (1989): *Marching to Armageddon, Canadians and the Great War 1914-1919,* Lester and Orpen Dennys, Toronto.

Norfolk (Simcoe) Reformer (1887-1917): Microfilm of the newspaper in the National Library.

Nicholson, G.W.L., Col. (1962): Canadian Expeditionary Force, 1914-1919, Queen's Printer, Ottawa.

O'Connor (2002): *Airfields and Airmen*, Somme, Leo Cooper, Barnsley, York-shire.

Ormsby, Margaret A. (1959): *British Columbia: A History*, MacMillan Co. of Canada, Ltd, Vancouver.

Preston, Richard A. (1974): *Buster Brown Was Not Alone: American Plans for the Invasion of Canada, 1919-1939*, Canadian Defence Quarterly, Vol. 5, No.4.

Pulsifer, Cameron (2001): *Canada's First Armoured Unit, Raymond Brutinel and the Canadian Motor Machine Gun Brigades of the First World War*, Canadian Military History, Volume 10, Number 1.

Queen's University Archives: The James Sutherland Brown Papers.

Ralph, Wayne(1997): Barker VC, Doubleday Canada Ltd., Toronto.

Render, Shirley (1999): *The Inside Story of the Double Cross, James Richardson and Canadian Airways*, Douglas & McIntrye, Vancouver.

Rodney, W. (1968): *Soldiers of the International. A History of the Communist Party of Canada, 1919 - 1929*, University of Toronto Press.

Roy, Reginald (1997): *For Most Conspicuous Bravery, A Biography of Major-General R. Pearkes, V.C. through Two World Wars*, University of British Columbia Press, Vancouver.

Ruckett, William (1983): *The Great Unfinished Task of Colonel J. Sutherland Brown*, a CBC Radio commentary and docudrama in the series, Ideas.

Simcoe (Norfolk) Reformer (!887-1917): Microfilm from the National Library of Canada.

Stacey, C.P. (1955): *The Old Red Patch*, Current Affairs, Ottawa.

Stark, Stuart (1986): *Oak Bay's Heritage Buildings: More than just Bricks and Boards*, The Corporation of the District of Oak Bay.

Struthers, James (1983): *No Fault of Their Own: Unemployment and the Welfare State*, University of Toronto Press, Toronto.

Sutherland Brown, Atholl (1997): *Silently into the Midst of Things: 177 Squadron RAF in Burma, 1943-1945, History and Personal Narratives*, The Book Guild, Lewes, Sussex, England, and Trafford, Victoria.

Swettenham, John (1965): *To Sieze the Victory, The Canadian Corps in World War I*, Ryerson Press, Toronto.

Swettenham, John (1968): *McNaughton*, Volume 1, Ryerson Press, Toronto.

Sydney Record (July 1009 - April 1910): Microfilm from the National Library of Canada.

Taylor, A.J.P. (1963): *The First World War, An Illustrated History*, Hamish Hamilton, London.

Taylor, Charles (1977): *Six Journeys, A Canadian Pattern; Brigadier James Sutherland Brown*, Anansi, Toronto.

Travers, Tim (1996): *Currie and the 1st Canadian Division at Second Ypres, April 1915: controversy, Criticism and Official History*, Canadian Military History, Volume 5, Number 2.

Warner, Philip (1995): *World War One, A Chronological Narrative,*Arms and Armour Press, London.

Watt, D.C. (1975): *Too Serious a Business, European Armed Forces and the Approach of the Second World War*, Temple Smith, London.

Wilson, Barbara (2001): *The Road to the Cobourg Court Room*, Canadian Military History, Volume 10, Number 3, p.67-73.

Winter, Denis (1992): *Haig's Command, A Reassessment*, Penguin Books, London.

Wise, S.F. (1980): *Canadian Airmen and the First World War*, University of Toronto Press, Toronto.

Glossary

AA - Anti-aircraft gun or fire

AAG - Assistant Adjutant General

AA&QMG - Assistant Adjutant and Quartermaster General

ADC - Aide-de-Camp

AG - Adjutant General

AN(&AF)VA - Army, Navy (and Air Force) Veterans Association

ANZAC - Australian and New Zealand Army Corps

BEF - British Expeditionary Force

Brig. Gen. - Brigadier General

CAF - Canadian Air Force

Capt. - Captain

CCC - Civilian Conservation Corps

CEF - Canadian Expeditionary Force

CGS - Chief of the General Staff

CinC - Commander in Chief

CIGS - Chief of the Imperial General Staff

CMG - Companion of St. Michael and St. George

CO - Commanding Officer

CNS - Chief of Naval Staff

CPO - Chief Petty Officer

Cmdr. - Commander

Cpl. - Corporal

Col. - Colonel

CRA - Commanding Royal Artillery

CRE - Commanding Royal Engineers

DA&QMG - Deputy Adjutant and Quartermaster General

DAO - District Artillery Officer

DCC - Dominion Coal Company

DEO - District Engineering Officer

Div. - Division

DM - Deputy Minister

DMO&I - Director of Military Operations and Intelligence

DMT&SD - Director of Military Training and Staff Duties

DND - Department of National Defence

DOC - District Officer Commanding

DSO - Distinguished Service Order

DS No. 1 - Defence Scheme No. 1

GSO 1 - General Staff Officer, First Class

GOC - General Officer Commanding

HBC - Hudson's Bay Company

HQ - Head Quarters

IDC - Imperial Defence College

IO - Intelligence Officer

KCMG - Knight Companion of St. Michael and St. George

KR&O - King's Regulations and Orders

Lt. - Lieutenant

Lt. Col. - Lieutenant Colonel

PF - Permanent Force

PoW - Prisoner of War

MC - Military Cross

MM - Military Medal

MD - Military District

Mk. - Mark

NCO - Non-Commissioned Officer

NDHQ - National Defence Headquarters

NPAM - Non-Permanent Active Militia

OC - Officer Commanding

OTC - Officers Training Corps

PPCLI - Princess Patricia's Canadian Light Infantry

Pte. - Private

PWA - Provincial Workman's Association

QM - Quartermaster

QMG - Quartermaster General

Q-Staff - Quartermaster General's Staff

RAF - Royal Air Force

RCA -Royal Canadian Artillery

RCAF - Royal Canadian Air Force

RCN - Royal Canadian Navy

RCR - Royal Canadian Regiment

RFC - Royal Flying Corps

RMC - Royal Military College

RN - Royal Navy

RNAS - Royal Naval Air Service

CFTS - Service Flying Training School

Sgt. - Sergeant

UEL - United Empire Loyalist

UNMA - United Mine Workers of America

URC - Unemployment Relief Camps

VC - Victoria Cross

WWI - World War I = Great War

WWII - World War II

Appendix A - Staff Positions of a Canadian Division, 1914-1918

The Division Staff normally consisted of eleven officers including G or General Staff, A or Adjutant General Staff and Q or Quartermaster General Staff (*see* Photo 6-6)[1]. The positions were:

General Officer Commanding, GOC

The General Staff Officers who were responsible for operational planning, intelligence and training. There were three grades of general staff officers: **GSO 1, GSO 2, GSO 3**; usually one GSO 1, commonly two GSO 2s and GSO 3s

The **GSO 1** was the GOC's deputy and this officer's principal focus was strategy and tactics by operational planning and methods of action as well as the general efficiency of the troops.

The **GSO 2s** were responsible for intelligence and communication.

The **GSO 3s** who, in Wellington's day were called the gallopers, were responsible for information and intercommunication.

Quartermaster General Staff were responsible for the collective needs of the troops to enable the Division to operate: rations, ammunition, supply, quartering, etc.

Adjutant General staff was responsible for the individual needs of the troops; pay, discipline, promotion, etc.

At the Divisional level there were three on these staffs; the **AA&QMG** who was the senior administrative Officer in charge of organization including, security, supply and personnel, medical, burial and transport. Beneath him were two deputies, the **DA&QMG** basically in charge of supply and the **DAAG**, Deputy Assistant Adjutant General basically responsible for discipline and personnel.

In addition there were two important specialists:

The **CRA** Commanding Divisional Artillery,
The **CRE** Commanding Divisional Engineers.

Finally, there was the GOC's **Aide-de-Camp**.

---

[1] Eyre, p. 113-114,
   QUA/JSB S11 B3 F54

Appendix B - Rank, Appointments, Qualifications and Awards Held by James Sutherland Brown

Rank, confirmed by Gazette and Acting ranks

Private,
39th Regiment, Norfolk Rifles, Canadian Non-Active Militia
                                                    1895-11-01

Corporal, Norfolk Rifles   1900-01-31

Sergeant, Norfolk Rifles   1900-05-31

Provisional Lieutenant, Norfolk Rifles   1902-02-17

Lieutenant, Norfolk Rifles   1902-09-17

Captain, Norfolk Rifles   1903-09-01 to 1906-06-25

Lieutenant,
Royal Canadian Regiment, Permanent Force   1906-06-25

Captain, RCR   1911-02-11

Acting Major   1914-09-29

Major, RCR   1915-09-16

Temporary Lt. Col.   1916-05-14

Brevet Lieutenant Colonel, RCR   1919-09-01

Lieutenant Colonel, RCR   1924-10-15

Temporary Colonel on the Staff   1928-01-01

Temporary Brigadier, General List   1928-07-01

Honorary Brigadier, on Retirement   1933-06-10

Appointments

Director of Organization   1919-01-19

Director of Military Operations and Intelligence   1920-12-04

District Officer Commanding, Military District No. 11
                                                                      1929-01-01

Retires   1933-06-28

Qualifications

Teacher's Training Certificate, Simcoe Model School   1901

Articled Law Student,
Simcoe, affiliated with Univ of Toronto   1905-06

Graduate of Staff College, Camberley, psc   1914

Graduate of the Second Course of Imperial Defence College
                                                                      1928

Awards

Commander of St. Michael and St. George   1918-06-03

Distinguished Service Order   1916-01-14

Mentioned in Dispatches   1916-01-01

Mentioned in Dispatches   1917-12-28

Mentioned in Despatches   1918-05-28

Mentioned in Despatches   1918-12-31

Mentioned in Despatches   1919-07-11

Life Member and gold medalist of the ANAFVA 1950-05-07

Appendix C - Report to the Secretary of DND on Unemployment Relief, 24 May, 1933

by Brigadier James Sutherland Brown, CMG, DSO, 1933-05-24

1. Limit of Responsibility for Unemployment Relief

It is the intention that HQ MD No.11 will take over the administration of unemployment relief for homeless unemployed men from the Province of British Columbia only when they have been organized in camps. Unemployment projects will be opened progressively as approved, and it is hoped to gradually absorb all the homeless unemployed in the Province. Until this has been done it is recommended that the Province continue to administer all homeless men who are not on the strength of the camps.

2. Present Distribution of Homeless Unemployed

The following are approximate figures of homeless unemployed in British Columbia:

in camps	4335
in smaller municipalities	7000 to 8000
in Vancouver and larger municipalities	12 300

3. The Political Situation

The present political situation in the Province is very clouded, and it is impossible to foretell the result. At the present time, four political parties are angling for support, with the result that politics appear to be more than the work of dealing with public questions in a public spirited way.

4. Political Patronage

As a result of the above mentioned situation, politics have been allowed, under the Provincial administration to enter into the question of appointment of engineers, foremen, and other officials.

It is proposed, when camps are taken over from the Province, to appoint the necessary personnel only on the advice of the Engineering Institute of Canada, the employment Agencies, and the Deputy Minister, Public Works, Victoria.

5. Homeless Unemployed in Cities

At present there are considerable numbers of homeless unemployed men living in cities. No one has necessary authority to order these men out of the cities into unemployment camps.

It is suggested that the Unemployment Service of Canada be empowered to do so, and that a single man who has been offered and refused employment in a camp be struck off the relief list.

6. The present Situation in Camps

All unemployed in camps in this province have been fed on a very generous scale, and most of them have had little or no work to do this past year. Some of the camps staff are efficient, but in other cases they have been spineless and inefficient. In many cases a committee of the men has taken over the management of the camps, and the camp superintendent has not been allowed to function. This situation has been allowed to exist by the Provincial authorities and by the Fordam Commission, but cannot be condoned when camps are taken over by the Department of National Defence.

I have been ordered to take over a situation where a Provincial Government, with several competent ministers and a loyal and capable civil service, has failed. I am expected to do so under still more difficult conditions, namely:-

(a) To put men to work who have been trained for twelve months of idleness and allowed to do what they pleased.

(b) A lowed scale of rations.

7. Rations

The question of a generous scale of rations is most important from the standpoint of contentment and efficiency.

The Provincial authorities allow for a varied and ample diet. There is no ration scale, nor are there any restrictions. The foreman in charge is expected to keep costs as low as possible. The present cost, without tobacco, is from 27 to 28 cents per man per day, but the Provincial authorities state that the cost would rise if the men were working. I am of the opinion, and the Provincial authorities agree, any reduction of the Provincial scale would cause disappointment, probably resulting in a refusal to work.

8. Segregation of Malcontents

It is recommended that the *Order-in-Council* by the Provincial Government, a copy of which is attached as Appendix "A", be supported by Federal legal machinery to deal with malcontents. This, however, is only a partial solution of the problem, as men put out of one camp may try to get into another camp as transients, and so cause trouble.

It is therefore desirable that the Federal authorities pass a special *Order-in-Council* empowering [RCMP], Provincial and local Police to deal with such cases.

In any event, it is considered necessary, as a deterrent, to establish a central camp where malcontents may be segregated and dealt with in a different manner from the well-behaved unemployed.

9. Administration of Homeless Men in Urban Centres

It is recommended that the Provincial authorities continue to administer all homeless men who remain in Vancouver and other urban centres. I consider it most undesirable that the [DOC] and his staff should be brought into contact with the system of local ward politics at present prevailing.

10. Road Construction - Selection of Engineers and their Staff

The attached map (Appendix "B") shows that portion of [BC] for which this District is responsible divided into Group Areas. "A" and "C": will be the first groups in which work will be commenced. Other group areas will be opened progressively as camps and works are taken over from the Province.

In both "A" and "C" it is proposed to make subdivision into projects. *Pro formae* covering these are now in course of preparation.

With regard to the selection of engineers and staffs for the respective groups, it is considered that the necessary personnel can be obtained without difficulty through the Registered Professional Association of BC, the Engineering Institute of Canada, and the Employment Services of Canada, supplemented by ex-employees of the Provincial Department of Public Works.

The District Engineers of the Provincial Department of Public Works will co-operate in laying out of the work as approved by the Federal and Provincial authorities.

11. Present Disposition of the Administrative Staff of the Province and the expansion of the Staff of the Military District

The Provincial system of administration is complicated and involves several departments. No one department is responsible for carrying out the policy of the government [*see* Appendix "C"]. The Board of Administration for single men (Fordam Commission), through administrative machinery established at Hamilton Hall, Vancouver, is responsible for the administration of relief of single homeless unemployed men from approved centres to the number of approximately 16 664. The Board administers all camps and, in addition, is responsible for the administration of relief to single homeless unemployed men and other urban centres, and to a very limited number of men who have been placed on farms. The men are paid by script in Vancouver and other urban centre, but there are also a number of selected hostels, both in Vancouver and elsewhere, which provide board and lodging for homeless men at relief rates. These hostels are paid by the board.

Quite apart from the activities of the above mentioned board, the Provincial Government, through municipalities other than urban centres, Government Agents, the Provincial Department of Public Works, and the Provincial Police, administer relief to approximately 7146 single unemployed men. The provincial authorities are unable to say, without consulting each municipality, what proportion of this last class are "homeless".

All medical and hospital arrangements are under the jurisdiction of the Provincial Board of Health, and part-time medical officers throughout the Province are in receipt of from $50 to $100 monthly.

It is impossible to arrive at an accurate estimate of the numbers employed by the Province in administration of homeless unemployed men.

Appendix D - Memorandum Re Retirement of Brigadier J. Sutherland Brown, CMG, DSO

Personal and Confidential

Returning from the Imperial Defence College in January, 1929, I reported in Ottawa to Major General McNaughton, lately appointed Chief of the General Staff. I saw at once that his former attitude of more or less friendliness toward me had changed to one of severe coldness. Having assumed the office over the heads of better qualified men he at once became a cold-blooded administrator. He objected to me having a private interview with the Hon. J.L. Ralston, Minister of National Defence. This interview was not my seeking, but requested by the Minister himself. ... I proceeded to Victoria, BC, and actually took over the command of Military District No.11 on January 23rd, 1929.

General McNaughton sniped at me for four and one-half years. Some four years ago he took advantage of a personal and confidential letter I sent him. This is unforgivable and nobody but a cad would do such a trick. I have administered this Military District to the full satisfaction of the [NPAM in BC], and to the admiration of the public generally. I have been loyally and energetically supported by the Permanent Forces, by the Church, by the Veterans organizations and all other organizations which stand for the public good.

Early in May, 1933, General McNaughton, in a light-hearted way without previous consultation of the [DOCs MD No. 11 and 13], offered to take over the unemployed situation in [BC]. He did not have the slightest conception of the problem from the local or political colour.

The buck was passed to the [DOCs] in question, who with their staffs entered into a very difficult problem and were meeting with a large measure of success when [NDHQ] entered upon a campaign of "plum and apple Jam", which drove the [DOCs], and their staffs to distraction. The main torrent of abuse and impractical orders were levied at me. As I had the confidence of most everyone in [BC] I can only take it that the [CGS] was trying to drive me into a corner where I should resign. This he accomplished.

I am no time server. Ever since I was able to form reasonable opinions I have acted upon certain principals. I have stood up for my subordinates when it was necessary for me to do so. I have expressed my opinions as a Commander should be allowed to do. These opinions were, of course, derived from local knowledge and from the recommendations of the [NPAM], with whom I was in the very closest touch. In order to save my self respect and to preserve my health, both mental and physical, I tendered my resignation on my birthday, June 28th, which was accepted on July 5th and immediately announced to the Canadian Press. I did not take this action in a moment of hot-headedness. I had considered it for a couple of weeks and before I sent my telegram of resignation I consulted my wife, who was always level-headed, and she agreed with me that I was in an impossible position for any self respecting man.

I reiterate that I had the full confidence of the [NAPM], loyal support of the [PF] and the confidence of the public generally. I make the following quotations from the many letters and telegrams I have received in sympathy with my action. I select these to indicate the various personalities.

1st. From Brigadier General Edward Panet, an old [PF] Officer and now head of the CPR Protective Service.

July 9th, 1933.

"Very sorry to learn of your retirement. The country cannot afford to let you go, there are too few [PF] Officers left."

2nd. From Captain James Robinson, DCM, late Regimental Sergeant Major of the 7th Bn. CEF.

Vancouver , BC, July 7th, 1933.

"My Dear Sir:-

It is a very great shock to me to read in the paper of your retirement from the Service. Sorry I am beyond words. I hope you will see your way to stay here with us. All ranks love and respect you, civil population as well. Now is the time we want people like yourself, when the forces of disorder is against the forces of law and order. However, God knows best and I wish you and yours where ever you go the richest blessing and protection of the old Flag. Believe me when I say this is from your very humble servant."

<u>3rd.</u> Telegram sent by Brigadier General J.A. Clark, without my knowledge or consent, a copy subsequently sent to me:

> "General The Hon. Donald Sutherland,
> Minister of Defence,
> Ottawa.
>
> Have heard with deep regret resignation of Brigadier Brown, who is especially well qualified to handle delicate unemployment situation and his retirement will be regretted by the public generally Stop He has been responsible for splendid spirit and high standard of defence forces here. His training schemes have been most diversified and instructive and I strongly urge you against permitting him to retire."

General Clark is an old pre war militia man and a CEF Officer of distinction and for several years a member of Parliament.

<u>4th.</u> This is from Sgt. Major (WO) E.J. Read. [He] is the supervising clerk at MD No. 11, efficient, painstaking, reasonable and loyal. This is written in his own hand.

> Victoria, BC, 7th July, 1933.
>
> "The attached is improper and this is equally so. I know that you will accept both communications in the spirit in which they are intended and I think you will derive satisfaction there from.
>
> The spontaneous expressions of regret voiced by the Warrant Officers, Non-Commissioned Officers and men in your case are unique in my experience.
>
> You have my own best wishes. May good fortune attend you. This is written, not to a superior from a subordinate, but to James Sutherland Brown, who is regarded very highly by Ernest John Read."

Some of my friends have moved to stop my resignation. The whole of the services in [BC] I know are terribly sorry and if I were a rotter enough to encourage it, the bulk of the officers of the [NPAM] in this Military District would tender their resignation.

I put my hand to the plow and it is undesirable that there should be change, but I submit this memorandum as a statement of facts as I see them in order to help you to help me get the one thing I ask for. Two senior officers have recently been retired from the Permanent Force. I speak of Brigadier General F. Lister and Major General C.J. Armstrong. Both these officers were appointed, respectively, to the rank of Brigadier General and Major General, some considerable time before they were retired. I ask that I be promoted to Major General from the 1st January, 1933. This will not in any way hinder the few of my brother officers who are senior to me in the Permanent Force.

Index

!

133rd Regiment · · · · · · · · · · · ·18
16th Canadian Scottish · 140, 163, 182
   Regimental Mess 177
   Second Battalion. 163
1st and 2nd Divisions · · · · · · · · ·77
1st and 4th Divisions · · · · · · · · · ·84
1st Division · · · · · · · · 61, 81-86, 91
2nd and 3rd Divisions · · · · 65, 84-85
2nd Canadian Mounted Rifles · · ·54
2nd Division · · · · · · · · · · · ·61, 81
39th Norfolk Rifles · · · · 10-11, 13-18, 21-23
3rd and 4th Divisions · · · · · · · ·77
4th Division · · · · · · · · · · ·83, 86-87

A

AA&QMG duties 63, 78, 83, 85-86, 91
adequate military facilities for the West Coast · · · · · · · · · · · ·133-136
Advance Party to France · · · · · · ·56
Advance to Mons · · · · · · · · · · ·85
Aerial Experimental Assoc. A. Graham Bell & others · · · · · · · · · ·102
aerial photography & mapping program · · · · · · · · · · · · · · · · · · ·145
Agadir Crisis · · · · · · · · · · · · ·35
aid to civil powers 29-33, 97, 102, 160, 162
Alderson, Lt. Gen. E.A.H. ·50, 54-55, 58, 61, 126-127, 192
   Alderson's Force 59
   Photo 5-4. 58

Alexander, Lt. Col. R.O. · 27, 121, 148
Allenby, Lt. General · · · · · · · · ·74
Allied campaign of movement · 82-86
American
   imperialistic policy 111
   Manifest Destiny. . . . . . . viii, 105, 112
Anderson, Gen. T.V. · · · · · ·148, 166
Anti-Americanism vii, 9, 37, 112, 134
ANZAC Divisions · · · · · · · · · · · ·81
   and Canadian Corps. 82-83
Ardennes · · · · · · · · · · · · · · · ·86
Arleau-en-Gohelle · · · · · · · · · · ·73
Army
   morale 138, 169-170
   pay and rank 29, 73, 116, 120-121, 126, 151-153, 167, 173-174
Army Service Corps · · · · · · · ·133
Army, Navy and Air Force Vets
· · · · · · · · · · · · · · ·177-179, 187
Artois · · · · · · · · · · · · · · · ·74, 84
Ashton, General E.C. · ·91, 117, 141, 167, 181
   Adjutant General 116
   Photo 11-3. 182
Ashworth, Tony
   Trench Warfare 3
Avonmouth · · · · · · · · · · · · · ·56

B

Bessboroug, Vicount · · · · · · · ·147
Badger, Pte. · · · · · · · · · · · · ·133
Balkan War · · · · · · · · · · · · ·35, 45
Banks, Col. Charles · · · · · · · · ·181

Battles of CEF
    advance to Mons. 85
    Amiens 83
    Cambrai. 84
    Courcellete 65
    Drocourt to Canal du Nord 84
    German Spring Offensive 81
    Hill 70 76
    March to the Rhine. 86
    Passchendaele. 77
    Second Ypres. 57
    St. Eloi 61
    the Scarpe 84
    Vimy Ridge. 71
Batty Mac (*see also* MacDonell) · · · 88
Bay Street Armoury · · · · · · · · · · 177
BC Archives · · · · · · · · · · · · · · 199
BC Dragoons · · · · · · · · · · 133, 143
Bee, QM Sgt. Thomas · · · · · · · 121
Beeman, Brigadier W.G. 123, 148, 169
Bell, Brig. A.H. · · · 145, 149, 163, 168
Bennett, Prime Minister R.B. · · · 151, 156-157, 170
Binyon, Lawrence
    poem, *For the Fallen* 67
Black Watch · · · · · · · · · · · · · 101
Blackwell, Baba · · 93-94, 98, 116, 123, 130, 133
Boak, Lt. Col. Harry · · · · · · · · · 74
Boer War · · · · · · · · · · · 15, 49, 107
Borden, A.H. · · · · · · · · · · · · · 39
Borden, Sir Fredrick · · · · · · · · · 22
Borden, Sir Robert · 46, 66-67, 70, 82, 95
Boulogne · · · · · · · · · · · · · · · 56
Bowker, John S. · · · · · · · · · · · 174
Brig. Generals Griesbach, Loomis and Tuxford · · · · · · · · · · · · · · 83
Brigadiers Farmar, Tuxford, Griesbach, Hayter and Thacker · · 88
British military establishment in Canada · · · · · · · · · · · · · · · · 107
British military support for Canada
· 111

British Norfolk Regiment · · · 23, 129
Brooke, Field Marshal Sir Alan · · 170
Brown family
    Chauncey 6
    Frank & Annie 8, 13
    Frank Augustus. 6-7, 9, 39
    John H. (Jack). 8, 13, 17-18
    Julia 13, 17, 23
    Margaret L. (Maggie) 8, 13, 17
        tragic death 8
    McArthur 6
Bruce, Randolph · · · · · · · · · · · 137
Bruhn, Chief Engineer, BC Public Works · · · · · · · · · · · · · · · · · 166
budget constraint of USA recce · 111
Bugle Band of 39th Rifles · · · · · · · 14
bugler · · · · · · · · · · · · · · · · · · 13
Bundy, Edgar, artist · · · · · · · · · 56
Burleigh, Col. W.W. · · · · · · · 41, 109
Bustard Camp · · · · · · · · · · · · · 54
Buster and Clare's wedding · · 62-63
Byng, Gen. Sir Julian · · 61, 69, 77, 84, 88, 114, 147

C

Cabeldu, Fred · · · · · · · · · · · · · 137
Caldwell, AG, Col. Clyde · · 142, 149, 163
Calling, as important social activity
· 137
Camberley (staff college) · · 36, 39-43, 91, 109
    syllabus 40
Campbell, Craig · · · · · · · · · · · 182
Camps (military)
    at Niagara-on-the-lake 13-14, 16
    Borden 100, 104
    Petawawa 26, 34-35, 42, 49, 116
    Valcartier 49-50
Canadian
    imperialism. 113
    independence from Whitehall. . . 117
    patriotism and nationalism37, 47, 56, 112, 126

sovereignty 68
spies 106, 110
sports for troops 82
topographic surveys 117

Canadian Air Force (CAF) · · · · · 100, 102-104
birth of 102
demobilized after WWI 104

Canadian Army
of 15 Divisions 97, 101-107

Canadian Corps · · · · · · · · · · · 71, 91

Canadian Defence Quarterly · · · 118

Canadian equipment,
deficiencies of 55

Canadian Expeditionary Force 35, 55, 93-94, 96, 99, 101
demobilization 93, 95-97
First Canadian Contingent 50
lack of history of senior staff 192

Canal du Nord · · · · · · · · · · · · · 84

Canon Scott, Lt. Col., the Reverend
· · · · · · · · · · · · · · · · · · 78, 80

Cape Breton miner's strike 29-33, 113

Carruthers, Dr. W.A. · · · · · · · · 157

Causes of WWI · · · · · · · · · · 45-46

cavalry and infantry camp at Vernon
· · · · · · · · · · · · · · · · · · 142-143

CBC docudramas
The Attack of the Killer Mouse . . . 2, 113
The Great Unfinished Task of Colonel J. Sutherland Brown 2, 114

Chambers, Major E.C.G. · · · 138, 143, 160-162, 169

Chanak (Canakkale) affair · · · · · 116

chlorine gas attact at Ypres · · · · · 57

Churchill, PM Winston · · · · · · · 187

Chysler, G.G. · · · · · · · · · · · · · 27

Clare in Court dress · · · · · · · · · 128

CMG · · · · · · · · · · · · · · · · · · 91

Coast Artillery · · · · · · · · · · · · 133

Coghill, Lt. Col. H.J. · · · · · · 101, 127

Colonels Greer, Pope and Major
Chambers · · · · · · · · · · · · · · · 160

Colonels Parsons, MacPhail, Mathews, Palmer, Harris and Dunlop · · · · · · · · · · · · · · · · 88

Colquhoun, Lt. Col. W.G. · · 138, 188

Combined Operations
training for 136, 145, 147

Comintern · · · · · · · · · · · · · · · 97

command & control
problems of, western terrain 131

Commodore Hose · · · · · · · · · · 117

communication, lack of between government and NDHQ · · · 94, 104, 108, 112, 118

Communism · · · · · · · · · · · 157, 159
Communist International 97
riots stimulated by 102

Corsan, Clare · 27, 31, 35, 62, 86, 123, 128, 136, 173-174, 188-189
death in 1973 189
presentation at June Court 130

Corsan, Sgt. Edward · · · · · · · · · 62

Corsan, Thomas · · · · · · · · · · · · 27

Courcelette · · · · · · · · · · · · · · 65

CPR · · · · · · · · · · · · · · · 11, 134

Crerar, General H.D.G. · 111, 171, 185

Currie, General Sir Arthur 50, 52, 61, 69, 74, 77, 81, 84-85, 87-91, 95, 99, 104, 119, 129, 152
2nd Brigade 57
and Macdonell 67
Principal of McGill 95
wins slander suit 119

D

Defence Committee, 1923
proceedings of 117

defence of Canada · 47, 102, 105-114, 192

Defence Scheme No. 1 · · · vii, 41, 93, 108-114
defending the long border 109
fallback centres 110
fallout 113-114
secrecy 111

staff opinions 111
time to mobilize National Guard 110
treated with ridicule. 108
US targets 110

Defence Scheme No. 2 · · · · · · · · 108
defence against Japanese invasion
. . . . 108, 117

Defence Scheme No. 3 · · · · · 108, 117

deficiencies in military supplies,
1930s · · · · · · · · · · · · · · · · · · 117-119

demobilization · · · · · · · · · · · · 94-97

Denison, Lt. Col. Septimus Julius Augustus · · · · · · · · · · · · · · · · · · · 34

Dept National Defence
files and information 199
policy & supply needs 1930s 117-119

Desbarats, G.J. · · · · · · · · · 147, 163

Devonport · · · · · · · · · · · · · · · · · 51

Dickens, Captain Gerald, RN · · · 127

Dill, Maj. Gen. Jack · 39, 123-124, 127, 147

Director of Military Operations & Intelligence · · · · · · · · · · · 93, 105-122

Director of Military Training & Staff duties · · · · · · · · · · · · · · · · · · 99

Director of Organization · · · · 93-105

Director of the Canadian Air Force
. . . . 117

District Officer Commanding · · 131, 138-169

District Staff · · · · · · · · · · 137-138

DOC's social duties · · · · · · · · · 136

Dominion Coal Company · · · · 30, 33

Donly family · · · · · · · · · · · · 10, 23

Douai to Mons · · · · · · · · · · · · · 85

Drocourt-Queant Line · · · · · · · · 84

Drocourt-Queant Switch · · · · · · 74

Drum, Major · · · · · · · · · · · · · 138

Drury, General · · · · · · · · · · · · 33

Duguid, Col. A.F. · · · · · · · · 59, 101

Duke of Connaught · · · 37, 45, 77, 82

E

Eayrs, James · · · · vii, 3, 108, 110, 113

Edmonds · · · · · · · · · · · · · · · · · 59

effective ways to retreat · · · · · · · 42

Eifel region, Germany · · · · · · · · 86

emerging Canadian nationalism · · 56

Esquimalt · · · · · · · · · 117, 134, 176
exercise to seize 147

expeditious Canadian mobilization
. . . . 41

F

Ferte, Air Cmdre Joubert de la · · 124, 127

Fages, Lt. Col. A.O. · · · · · · · · 34, 51

Farbus Wood · · · · · · · · · · · · · · 71

Farmar, Brig. General G. Jasper 78, 91

Faulk, Sebasian
Birdsong 3

Federal election of 1940 · · · · · · · 175

Federally supported work camps
. . . . 157-171

Fenian Raids · · · · · · · · · · · · 9, 105

Festubert · · · · · · · · · · · · · · · · · 59

First Division Staff, Photo 1915 · · 58

Fiset, Col. · · · · · · · · · · · · · · · · 33

Flanders · · · · · · · · · · · · · 73, 76-77

Foch, Marshal · · · · · · · · · · · · · 82

folk hero of Anti-Americanism · · 114

Fordham Commission · · · · · 157, 169

Fordham, Major J.G. · · · · · · · · · 157

Foster, Col. W.W. · · · · · · · · 137, 147

Fourth Battalion, CEF · · · · · · 96-97

Fraser Canyon · · · · · · · 134, 136, 192

French army mutinies · · · · · · · · 73

French, Sir John · · · · · · · · · · · · 66

Fresnoy · · · · · · · · · · · · · · · 71, 73

Fuller, General J.F.C. · · · · · · 39, 192

G

garrison commanders of Halifax and Quebec · · · · · · · · · · · · · · · 107

garrison in Victoria · · · · · · · · · 138

garrison, RCR to Bermuda 1914 · · 50

Generals Currie & Macdonell · · · 86, 89-90

Generals Griesbach, Hertzberg and Schmidlin · · · · · · · · · · · · · · · 185

Generals, Macdonell, Farmar, Hodgins, and Radcliffe · · · · · · · 78

German Army's Black Day · · · · · 83

German offensives, 1918 · · · · · · 81

Gibsone, Col. W.W.W. · · · 27, 94, 101

Gimblett, Richard H. · · · · · · · · · · 3

Givinchy · · · · · · · · · · · · · · · · 59

Glace Bay · · · · · · · · · · · · · · · 30

Glenn, Major J.A. · · · · · · · 100, 105

Gloucestershire Regiment · · · 36, 127

GOC of Canadian Corps (Currie) · 74

Gordon, W.A.
    Minister of Labour 157, 166

Government House, Victoria · · · 116, 176, 180-181

Granatstein, Jack · · · · · · · · · 3, 171

Great Depression · · · · · 153, 155-157, 159-170

Great War · · · · · · · · · · 2-3, 45-91

Green, J.M. · · · · · · · · · · · · · · 137

Greene, Lt. Col. Murray K. · · · · · 27

Greer, Lt. Col. Horace · · 138, 160-162

Griesbach, General · · · · · · 177, 185

Groos, Harold · · · · · · · · · · · · 182

Gwatkin, Gen. Willoughby · · 51, 97, 107

H

Haig, Field Marshal · · 40, 65, 73, 76, 81-82

Halifax · · · · · · · · · · · · · 95, 107, 117
    the Regimental HQ 29

Hamber, Hon. Eric W. · · · · · 180-181

harbour defences
    at Halifax 117
    base at Esquimalt 117, 134, 176

Harris, Dr. Stephen J. · · vii, 108, 200

Hart, Liddell · · · · · · · · · · · · · 129

Hazenbrouck · · · · · · · · · · · · · · 56

Hennessy, Lt. Col. Pat · · · · · · · 138

Hertzberg, Brig. H.F.H. · · 79-80, 188

Hill 70 · · · · · · · · · · · · 74, 76, 79

HMCS Fraser · · · · · · · · · · · · · 182

HMCS Naden · · · · · · · · · · · · · 182

HMCS Vancouver · · · · · · · · · 147

HMS Dauntless · · · · · · · · 144, 147

HMS Dragon · · · · · · · · · · · · · 147

Hoad, O.A., Australian Forces · · · 27

Hon Mr. Lemaire · · · · · · · · · · 150

Honorary Colonels · · · · 134, 137, 181

Hope, BC · · · · · · · · · · · · · · · 162

Horne, General Sir H.S. · · · · · · 76-77

Horne, Mary Ann · · · · · · · · · · · · 7

HQ 1st Division, War Diaries · · · · 73

HRH Prince and Princess Svasti · 147

HRH Prince Svasti · · · · · · · · · · 150

Hughes, Garnet · · · · · · · · 50, 55, 76

Hughes, Sam · · 48-51, 55, 86, 95, 101, 119, 191
    1st Canadian Expeditionary Contingent 50
    abhorrence of the PF 50
    bias for Ross rifle 35
    confused mobilization 46, 49, 101
    delusions in 1916 173
    firing of 65
    his baleful effects 50
    his personality 61-66
    MacAdam trenching tool 55
    Minister of Militia & Defence . . 18, 46
    political supporters 50, 54

Hundred Days · · · · · · · · · · · 82-91

I

IDC studies · · · · · · · · · · · · · · 127

Ideas program, CBC · · · · · · · · · 114

Imperial Defence College · · · 88, 108, 119, 121, 123-130

    class of 1928 124

Imperial Economic Conference · · 157

Imperialism · · · · · · · · · · · · · 2, 47

Infantry Corps · · · · · · · · · · · · 101

Infantry Depot No. 2 in Toronto · · 35

inter-service cooperation · · · · · 145

Ironsides, Gen. W.E. 'Tiny' · · · · · 39

J

Jellicoe, Admiral Lord · · · · · · · 111

K

Keegan, John · · · · · · · · · · · 3, 113

Kemp, Sir Edward · · · · · · · · 94, 97

Ker, Col. Russell · · · · · · · · · · 137

Kiggell, Brig. General L. · · · · · 40, 77

Kilfinan · · · · · · · · · · · · · · · · · 5

King and Queen of Siam · · · · · · 147

King George the Fifth · · · · · · · · 29

Kingham, Col. Reg · · · · · · · · · 137

L

Lake, General Sir Percy · · · · · · · 26

Lavarrack, Maj. General · · · · · · 148

Leach, Maj. Gen. E.P. · · · · · · · · 107

Leacock, Stephen · · · · · · · · · · 112

League of Nations · · · · · · · · · · 95

Lee Enfield · · · · · · · · · · · · 35, 61

    shortage of. 55

    troops discard Ross rifle for 59

Lee, Capt. Arthur, RA · · · · · · · 107

Letson, Lt. Col. Harry · · · · · · · 137

levee en masse · · · · · · · · · · · · 47

Lewis, T.L. · · · · · · · · · · · · · · 30

Liaison Officer, to the Canadian High Commissioner · · · 121, 123, 127

Liberal Government 1921 · · · · · 118

Loch Fyne · · · · · · · · · · · · · · 3, 5

Lord Strathcona's Horse · 50, 101, 191

Ludendorff, General Eric · · · · 81, 83

M

MacAdam trenching tool · · · · · · · 55

MacBrien, Maj. Gen. J.H. · 39, 52, 97, 101, 105, 119, 141, 148-149, 152, 166, 191

MacDonald, Sir John A. · · · · 11, 107

Macdonell, Maj. Gen. A.C. · · · 58, 76, 79-80, 86, 88-90, 127, 141, 191

Macdonell, Major A.H. · 27-28, 30, 32

Mackenzie King · · 116, 151, 175, 185

MacKenzie, Gen. Lewis · · · · · · · 24

Maclure, Samuel · · · · · · · · · · 174

Maguire, Mickey · · · · · · · · · · 137

Malkin, Col. Richard · · · · · · · · 137

Manifest Destiny · · · · · · · · 105, 112

Maple Bay · · · · · · · · · · · · · · 147

March to the Rhine · · · · 85-86, 89-90

Martyn, Col. D.B. · · · · · · · · 147, 182

Matthews, Brig. H.H. · 108, 117, 122, 151, 162, 167

    deficiencies of report 170

    report of VR Camps, 1933 169

Mayhew, Robert · · · · · · · · · · 175

McCarter, Brig. G.A. · · · · · · · · 189

McNaughton, Gen. A.G.L. · · viii, 3, 108, 118, 121, 126-127, 129, 138-139, 142-143, 148-153, 157-164, 166-167, 170-171

    as Deputy CGS 111

    Bell and Caldwell trio 149

    criticism of by Taylor 170

    delusions in 1943 173

    failings 151, 171

    family 5

    ingratiating himself with Minister or PM 153

Mabel, wife. 98
made Brigadier. 99
portrait 158
relieved of his command. 151
vindictiveness towards James Sutherland Brown 150-151, 167-168, 174
see also: Sutherland Brown, James, rivalry with...

mechanized infantry · · · · · · · · 110

Mewburn, Maj. General S.C. · · · · 83, 94-95, 104

Military
   aviation 102-105
   policy 118-119
   responsible for work camps. 155, 159-170
   supply deficiencies . . . 49, 55, 117-119
   training facilities 98, 137, 143-145

Military Intelligence105-106, 110, 117
   Canadian Army reconnaissance (spies) 110
   Intelligence Officers & staff 108

Militia · · · · ·46, 93-94, 107, 133, 160
   Buster appraises officer recruits . . 137
   mobilization of. 46
   myth. 47-48
   NPAM in BC 133
   schemes for organization 118
   Sedentary Militia 47
   state of preparedness for WWII . . 145

Millan, Col. J.K., US Army · · · · · ·78

Milne, General · · · · · · · · · · · ·129

miners strike, Cape Breton coalfields · · · · · · · · · · · · · · · · · 29-33, 112

mobilization
   Mobilization Committee 117
   of the First Canadian Contingent. . 49
   plan for the PF and Militia 117

Monroe Doctrine · · · · · · · · · · ·105

Morrison, General F.S. · · · · ·39, 191

Morton and Granatstein
   Marching to Armageddon 3

Morton, Geoffrey · · · · · · · · · ·148

motorized machine gun brigade · 50

Mt. Sorrel · · · · · · · · · · · · · · · ·62

Mullins, Col. J.H., BC Police · · · ·162

Murray, Commander L.W. · 145, 150

N

National Archives · · · · · · · · · ·199

National Defence Headquarters (NDHQ) · · · · · · · · ·93, 121, 129, 153
   attitude towards Buster. 142
   conscription planning 102
   impractical orders 163
   perceived deficiencies in 1930s. . . 148

National map index system · · · ·117

Neale, W.J. · · · · · · · · · · · · · ·120

nepotism & political-based favouritism in BC · · · · · · · · · · · · · · · ·157

Neuve Chapelle · · · · · · · · · · · ·56

Nicholas, Cpl. · · · · · · · · · · · ·133

Nicholson, G.W.L. · · · · · · · · · · ·4

Nisconlith Forest Reserve · · · · ·143

Niven, Lt. Col. Hugh · · · · · · · ·138

Norfolk County · · · · · · · · · · ·9, 20

Norfolk Reformer · · · · · · · · · · ·10

Norfolk Regiment · · · · · · · ·23, 129

Norfolk Rifles (*see* 39th regiment) 13, 16

Nova Scotia Regiment · · · · · · · ·36

O

objectives of 'flying columns' · · ·110

Old Red Patch · · · · · · · · · · · ·78

One Big Union (OBU) · · · · · · · ·97

Ormond, Brig. D.M. · · · · · · · · ·163

Otter Committee · · ·99, 101-102, 108

Otter, Gen. W.D. · ·22, 29, 37, 49, 97, 102

Overseas Defence Committee · · ·127

Overseas Minister, Kemp · · · · · ·102

P

Paardeberg Day · · · · · · · · · · ·119

Pacific Great Eastern Railway ·· 134, 136

Palmer, Col. A.Z. ········· 66, 73

Panet, Maj. General H.A. ··· 121, 130

Parsons, Col. J.L.R. ·· 80, 88, 137-138, 141

Passchendaele ··········· 40, 77

'passed staff college' p.s.c. · 39, 66, 73
    casualties..................... 43

Patullo, Thomas D., BC Premier · 137

Pax Britannica ············· 3

Peace Conference in Paris ····· 95

Pearkes, Maj. Gen. G.R. ·· 4, 24, 111, 133, 137-138

Permanent Force ···· 93-94, 97, 101, 118-119

Pershing, General, US Army ···· 82

Petawawa ·26, 34-35, 42, 49, 115-116

Petit Thier ············· 86, 89

Petite Douve ············· 61

Pinsent, Gordon ··········· 113

planning
    for Canadian Military Establishment
    .... 94, 101
    for defence of Canada...... 105-112

Plumer, General Herbert ······ 86

policy for Canadian Militia · 118-119

Pooley, BC Attorney General R.H.33, 162, 175

Pope, E.W. ··············· 27

Port Hope Guide ··········· 119

Port Rowan ·········· 18, 21, 27

possible USA aggression ······ 97

Post-Bellum Conference on Imperial Defence ················· 97

PPCLI ········· 65, 101, 133, 191

Premier S.F. Tolmie ····· 137, 175

Preston, Brig. J.F. ·········· 189

Preston, Brig. W.T.R. ········ 119

Preston, Richard A. (Duke Univ.) ·3, 108, 112-113

Prime Minister Bennett 151, 156-157, 170

Prince of Wales (Edward VIII) · 86-87

Prince of Wales (George V) ····· 29

Princeton, BC ··········· 160-161

Princeton, NJ ············· 187

provocateurs (UMWA) ········ 30

Q

Quebec Garrison Commander ·· 107

Quebec Tercentenary ········· 29

Queen Charlotte Sound and Johnstone Strait ··········· 134, 192

Queen's Own Rifles of Canada ·· 101

Queen's University Archives ·· 3, 93, 108, 110, 168, 199

Quick, Pte. ············· 34, 36

R

Ralston, Col. J.L., Minister of Defence 147, 171

rapid deployment force ······· 109

Rawlinson, General ··········· 84

RCA ··················· 31

Render, Shirley ········ 3, 151, 170

Reynolds, Major H.M. ········ 138

Richardson, James
    desire to create a national airline 151

Richmond, Admiral Sir Herbert · 124, 127, 130

Rideau Hall ··········· 116, 136

Riel Rebellion ············· 22

riots in UK ··············· 96

riots in Winnipeg ··········· 97

Roberts, Field Marshal Lord ···· 29

Robertson, Gen. W.R. ······· 39, 67

Robertson, Gideon ··········· 156

Rockliffe ··············· 26

Rodney, Professor William ···· 200

Ross rifle · 25, 27, 46, 49, 55, 59, 61-62

Mk. 1, defects 25
Mk. 2. 35
Royal Air Force · · · · · · · · · · 82, 102
Royal Canadian Air Force · · · · · 136, 144-145, 147, 163, 185, 187-188
Royal Canadian Artillery · · · · · · · 30
Royal Canadian Dragoons 25, 39, 50, 54, 191
Royal Canadian Engineers 30, 84, 185
Royal Canadian Mounted Police · 97, 152, 170
Royal Canadian Navy · 134, 136, 145, 147, 150
Royal Canadian Regiment (RCR) · 23, 26-32, 34, 37, 39, 50, 65, 101, 112, 127
   'shino boys'. 191
   at Halifax. 28-29
   JSB joins Royal Canadian Regiment 25
   officers in Sidney 32
   posting to Bermuda 35, 51
   Prince of Wales enquires about . . . 29
Royal Flying Corps · · · · · · · 78, 102
Royal Military College of Canada 21, 34, 185
Royal Naval Air Service · · · · · · · 102
Royal Navy · · · · · · 107, 109, 144-145
Rycroft, Major · · · · · · · · · 108, 138

S

Sailly-Sur-Lys · · · · · · · · · · · · · 56
Salisbury Plain · · · · · · · · 42, 51-54
Sarajevo · · · · · · · · · · · · · · · · · 45
Sarcee, near Calgary · · · · · 134, 143
Schlieffen Plan · · · · · · · · · · · · 46
Seaforths · · · · · · · · · 101, 133, 143
Second Battle of Arras · · · · · · · · 84
Second Battle of Ypres · · · · · · · · 57
Second Contingent mobilization · 50
security of the Commonwealth · · 123
Shepard, Brig. Gen. G.S., RFC · · · 78
Shornecliffe · · · · · · · · · · · · 55, 60
Simcoe · · · · · · · · · · · 3, 6-11, 27, 39

and Norfolk County 7
Armories. 11
Simcoe Reformer · · · · · 3, 5, 7-8, 18, 23
skewed staffing of NDHQ · · 148-149
Smith, Lt. Col. Seely · · · · · · · · · 36
Smith-Dorien, Gen. Sir Horace · · · 56
Somme · · · · · · · · · · · · · · · 76, 83
soup kitchens · · · · · · · · · · · · · 155
Special Constables · · · · · · · · 33, 162
Spry, Col. D.W.B. · · · · · · · · 157, 169
St. Nazaire · · · · · · · · · · · · · · · 56
Staff College, Camberley · · 37, 39-43, 91, 109
staff duties · · · · · · · · · · 69, 76, 85-86
staff of the 1st Division · · · · · 56, 58
stalemate on the Western Front 56, 79
Stanley Barracks · · · · · · · · 25-26, 33
status of MD No.11, 1933 · · · · · · 153
Stevenson, Lt. Col. Brooke · · · · · 182
Stockwell, Brigadier C.V. · · · · · · 184
Stonehenge · · · · · · · · · · · · 53-54
strike, Cape Breton coal miners 30-36
Stuart, Major Ken · · · · · · · · 138-139
Sub-Militia Council · · · · · · · · · · 66
substandard Canadian equipment 55
Sutherland Brown, family
   Atholl. 115-116, 132, 187-188
   Coat of Arms. 5, 19-20
   family & social life . . 98, 114-116, 123, 130, 133, 174, 176-177, 181, 183
   family life in London. 125
   Ian Macdonell . . . 76, 98, 115, 132, 187
   Ian James 199
   Malcolm . . . 77, 93, 115, 120, 132, 168, 174, 185, 199
   Malcolm and Ian 123
   sept of Clan Lamont 5
Sutherland Brown, James vii-viii, 1-2, 11, 17, 26, 179, 188
   Anti-American ?. 37, 112
   association with veterans 177-181
   awards. 59, 66, 91, 178, 209
   Buster Brown Day 113
   capabilities 121-122, 137, 183

Cape Breton miner's strike 29-33
Col. J. Sutherland Brown Volunteer Brigade 114
Commissioning of the 'Brigadier Sutherland Brown'. 185-186
confidential report. 141-142
death and funeral 188
diaries 3, 199
Director of Military Operations & Intelligence 105-122
Director of Organization. . 88, 94-105
family connections to USA 8-9
family origins 5
gazetted Lieutenant, Norfolk Rifles 21
harassment by McNaughton 163, 168
Honorary Life Membership, AN&AFV. 178
icon of Anti-Americanism 2, 114
Imperialism. 37
invalided out of the Line 65
letter to Secretary DND requesting to serve out his career in MD11. . . . 167
marriage. 62-63
mentioned in 'Canadian Brass' vii-viii
Mentioned in Dispatches 91, 209
mentioned in 'Six Journeys' vii
patriotism 2, 112, 126
pay & pension 173-174, 187, 217
personal papers, discovery of . . . 108
personality. 88, 121
philosophy. 67, 120, 153
political candidacies. 175
promotion to Captain, Norfolk Rifles 29, 208
ranks confirmed by Gazette. 208
recruiting prospective officers. . . 133
relations with RN, RCN, RCAF . 136, 145
religious beliefs. 183
resignation. 168, 173
rivalry with McNaughton 99, 117-118, 121, 130, 138-142, 148-149, 153, 155, 159, 166, 168, 214
Scottish heritage 15
Senior Aide-de-Camp. 176, 181
Teacher Training Certificate 13
technical support for Canadian War Memorial. 129
visits the USA 187
waiting for the Call 184

War service 66
wartime malady returns. . . . 105, 187
Sutherland, James, MP · · · · · · · · 20
Sutherland, Lt. Col. D.M. (Minister) · 147, 149
Swettenham, John · · · · · · · · · 3, 151
    Andy McNaughton. 3
    To Seize the Victory 3
Sydney Record · · · · · · · · · · · · · · · 3

T

tank support · · · · · · · · · · · · 64-65
Taylor, A.J.P. · · · · · · · · · · · · · · · 4
Taylor, Austin · · · · · · · · · · · · · 137
Taylor, Charles · vii-viii, 1-4, 24, 120, 137, 162-163, 168, 199
    criticism of McNaughton. 170
Tedder, Wing Commander A.W. 124, 127
Temperance Groups, opposition to wet canteens · · · · · · · · · · · · · · · 54
Thacker, Ashton...and Panet · · · · 150
Thacker, Maj. Gen. H.C. 83, 114, 121, 130, 141
Thacker, Major P.E. · · · · · · · · · · 27
Thackery, Major W.C. · · · · · 138, 189
The Great Depression · · 151, 155-159
The Great Unfinished Task of Col Sutherland Brown · · · · · · · · · 2, 114
The Journal of Private Fraser · · · · · · 3
the Pimple · · · · · · · · · · · · · · · · 71
the Royal Twenty Centers · · · · · 160
Third Battle of Ypres · · · · · · · · · 77
Tireachadh · · · · · · · · · · · · · · 19-20
Tolmie, Simon Fraser · · · · · 137, 175
topographic mapping · · · · · · · 145
Toronto Regiment
    3rd Battalion CEF 97
Treaty of Brest-Litovsk · · · · · · · · · 81
Tremaine, Major Victor · · · · · · · 138
Turner, Maj. Gen. R.E.W. 57, 61, 102, 104

U

U-boat bases in Belgium · · · · · · ·74
Unemployment Relief Act · · · · · · ·157
Unemployment Relief Camps33, 153, 155-170
    Col. H.H. Matthews appraisal . . . 168
    contrast between systems 159
    deficiencies of Matthew's report. . 169
    DND camps. 159-170
    Sutherland Brown's appraisal of . 160, 164, **210**
    troubles after Buster resigned. . . . 170
Union **Army**, large and unemployed
· ·105
United Empire Loyalist · · · · · · · ·8
United **Mine** Workers of America
· · · · · · · · · · · · · · ·29-30, 33, 112
US Army · · · · · · · · · · · · ·81, 109
USA · · · · · · · · · · · · · · · · · ·93
    plans **to** attack Canada . 108, 112-113, 192
    US War Plans Division 112

V

Valcartier · · · · · · · · · · · · · · ·49
Vanier, Lt. Col. G.P. · · · · · · · · ·148
Venezuelan Incident of 1898 · · ·105
Vernon · · · · · · · · · · · · ·142-143
Vickers Vedettes · · · · · · · ·144, 147
Victoria Daily Colonist · · · · · · ·3, 163
Victoria's VIP visitors · · · · ·136, 147
Vimy **Ridge** · · · · · · · · · · ·70-71, 79
vulnerability, highway and railways in Fraser Canyon · · · · ·134, 136, 192

W

Wadmore, Lt. Col. R.L. · · ·30, 32-33
War **Diary** of 1st Division HQ · · ·69
War of 1812 · · · · · · · · · · · ·9, 105
war of movement · · · · · · ·79, 81-91
War Office staff · · · · · · · · · · ·107

Warner, Philip
    World War One 3
Watson, Maj. General David · ·86-87
Westminster Regiment · · · ·133, 143
wet canteens · · · · · · · · · · · · · ·54
Whitton, Charlotte · · · · · · · · ·157
Willerval · · · · · · · · · · · · · · ·73
Willington, Lord & Lady · · ·139, 147
Willoughby, Capt. A.E. ·27, 62-63, 77
Wilson, Sir Henry, CIGS · · · · · ·111
Winnipeg riot · · · · · · · · · · · ·97
Winter, Denis
    Haig's Command 3
Wolsley Barracks · · · · · · · · · ·26
Woodward, Lt. Col. W.C. · ·137, 181
Work Point Barracks88, 131-132, 143, 148
World War I
    assassination of Arch Duke Ferdinand 42
    attrition as viable tactic 65
    battle honours. 99, 101
    Canadian preparedness. 46
    Canadian troops' capabilities. . 67, 78, 84-85
    Canadian troops' health and cleanliness 54, 61, 74, 78
    Canadian troops' individuality. . . . 67
    causes 45
    expectations 47
    post-war reserve strength 101
    training Canadian troops 54
World War II · · · · · · · ·45, 151, 153

Y

Ypres, Second Battle · · · · · · · · ·57
    salient 77

ISBN 141202522-2

Atholl Sutherland Brown was a decorated Beaufighter pilot in the Burma air war, then a distinguished geologist in British Columbia and recently a writer of three well reviewed histories.

Buster, the latest book, is a biography of his father, Brigadier James Sutherland Brown, a controversial senior Canadian Army officer in the 1930s. He was the author of a scheme to defend Canada from possible attack by the USA in the 1920s. Later, he w also the loser in a confrontation with his superior, General A.G.L. McNaughton.

"The history is bang on... the personalities shine through... [and] the complexity of the situation of the final break [with McNaughton explained]"

Stephen J. Harris

"A significant addition of knowledge ... This bool makes us rethink some old beliefs about Canada between the world wars."

Desmond Morto

TRAFFORD

ISBN 141202522-2